D0734574

Developmental
MANAGEMENT

INTUITION

Developmental Management

General Editor: Ronnie Lessem

Charting the Corporate Mind
*Charles Hampden-Turner**

Managing in the Information Society
Yoneji Masuda

Developmental Management
Ronnie Lessem

Foundations of Business
Ivan Alexander

Greening Business
John Davis

Ford on Management
*Henry Ford**

Managing Your Self
Jagdish Parikh

Managing the Developing Organization
Bernard Lievegoed

Conceptual Toolmaking
Jerry Rhodes

Integrative Management
Pauline Graham

Total Quality Learning
Ronnie Lessem

Executive Leadership
Elliott Jaques and Stephen D. Clement

Transcultural Management
Albert Koopman

The Great European Illusion
Alain Minc

The Rise of NEC
Koji Kobayashi

Organizing Genius
Paul Thorne

European Strategic Alliances
Sabine Urban and Serge Vendemini

Intuition
Jagdish Parikh, Fred Neubauer and Alden G. Lank

*For copyright reasons this edition is not available in the USA

Developmental MANAGEMENT

Intuition

THE NEW FRONTIER OF MANAGEMENT

JAGDISH PARIKH

in collaboration with
Fred Neubauer and Alden G. Lank

First published 1994

Blackwell Publishers
108 Cowley Road, Oxford OX4 1JF, UK

238 Main Street
Cambridge, Massachusetts 01242, USA

British Library Cataloguing in Publication Data

A CIP catalogue record for this book is available from the British Library.

Library of Congress Cataloging in Publication Data

Parikh, Jagdish.
Intuition: the new frontier of management / Jagdish Parikh; in collaboration with Fred Neubauer and Alden G. Lank.
p. cm. — (Developmental management)
Includes index.
ISBN 0-631-19225-5 (alk. paper)
1. Management. 2. Intuition (Psychology) I. Neubauer, Franz-Friedrich.
II. Lank, Alden G. III. Title. IV. Series.
HD38.P314 1994 93-25066
658'.001'9—dc20 CIP

Typeset in 11 on 13 pt Ehrhardt
at The Spartan Press Ltd, Lymington, Hants
Printed in Great Britain by T. J. Press (Padstow) Ltd, Padstow, Cornwall

This book is printed on acid-free paper

Dedicated to everyone who seeks deeper understanding of the accelerating uncertainties and complexities in the world of business. This book offers a powerful tool to increase comprehension, namely, the process of direct knowing: intuition.

Contents

Figures

Tables

Foreword

If there is one thing that successful leaders seem to possess it is that capacity to foresee future events, what I call the 'Gretzky Factor'. This world-famous hockey player once said that what is important is not where the puck is, but where it is going to be. It seems to me that that is what the responsibility of leaders is. It's not companies that fail; it's their leaders who fail. If I can generalize from my 15 years of observing leaders, I would say that the most successful ones are those who have recognized that we are moving to a stage of idea-intensive production and away from material-intensive production. They realize that if a leader is going to be successful, it is going to be through intellectual capital. That is what creates wealth; that it is people with ideas who are going to make the difference.

A vivid and recent example of that is the number of front page stories about Jose Ignacio Lopez, this Basque engineer whom nobody had heard of a year ago. But General Motors (GM) and Volkswagen (VW) realized that he had the brains to reduce costs by transforming the automobile companies' relationships with vendors, at a rate nobody up to then had thought possible. Wasn't this strange? Two of the world's largest companies competing for the service of a Basque engineer?

It isn't strange if you consider that what Lopez and others like him offer is intellectual capital, ideas, expertise, know-how. If I were to express in one phrase everything I've learned about leadership and organizations over the past 30 years, it would go like this: the key to competitive advantage in the 1990s and beyond will be the capacity of top leadership to create a learning environment, an adaptive, agile, athletic social architecture capable of generating intellectual capital. Now, that is fairly abstract, but the key to it all is intellectual capital.

All the great leaders I know are concerned with only three things, and they all pertain to resource allocation: people, dollars and ideas. If they pick the right people, and they allocate the right number of dollars to particular divisions, and if they break down the smokestack bureaucratic roles so the best practices get transferred immediately from one division to the next – well, then I think we are going to see success.

In this book, Parikh and his colleagues creatively demonstrate that the key to intellectual capital is intuition, that obscure and evasive word to which they give new meaning. I suppose beneath that they show conclusively that without organizations that can release the potential creativity, we'll be observing organizations headed for failure. And quickly, at that.

Most of us, whether European, Asian or American, grew up in bureaucratic organizations that were dominated by a command- and-control orientation. It was memorialized by the prose of German writer and sociologist Max Weber, who was the first to bring to the world's attention that this bureaucratic machine model is a genius of social invention, designed to harness the manpower and resources of the nineteenth century. Most organizations still have that kind of command-and-control macho mentality.

If there are three words that best describe the mind set of that paradigm, these would be: control–order–predict. It has an interesting acronym: COP. Bureaucracies are characterized by strong divisions of labour, specialization, hierarchies and multiple levels.

As Parikh and his colleagues point out, the organizations of the future will resemble networks or modules. The successful ones will have flattened hierarchies and more cross–functional linkages. I would use three words to describe the mindset: acknowledge–create –empower – also an interesting acronym: ACE. Given the speed and complexity of the business environment – what the authors refer to as 'raplexity' – I don't think we have any alternative but to move away from COP toward ACE.

Leadership is all about innovating, initiating, creating and envisioning. Walt Disney once said that if you can dream it, you can do it. Leaders take people to a new place, not always provable but doable, they enrol people in their vision. Unless leaders and managers can deploy and develop their intuitive skills and create an environment where intuition is cherished and rewarded, make no mistake, they will not be effective.

What Parikh and his colleagues have shown in this important and seminal book is how leaders and their organizations can move forwards intelligently into the twenty-first century, not back in to it. It is the only book I know that not only articulates the need for intuition but, in so doing, demystifies it and shows that it is in the grasp of each of us, if only we tried. The alternative is disastrous.

Warren Bennis
Chairman, USC Leadership Institute

Editor's Comment

Background: Intuition in Context

It is not surprising that a book on intuition in management should be appearing at this stage of the development of our series, for the two economies that have been the most successful over the course of the last decade – those of Japan and the former West Germany – are both well endowed with intuition. Whereas Japan is blessed with the contemplative outlook of the orient, Germany, at least within an occidental context, is famed for its deeply intuitive philosophers, Hegel and Marx being perhaps the most well known. It is perhaps also not surprising, then, that Jagdish Parikh hails from the East – from India – while Fred Neubauer is German, and Alden Lank is originally from Canada, the one part of the world which has consciously set out to establish a cultural mosaic within it.

Moreover, our three authors are based in Switzerland, which, while on the one hand being the home of clockwork rationality, is also the birthplace of Carl Gustav Jung. In fact at the time of this particular book's coming, Jung is himself re-emerging within management circles. For, more than anybody, he has positioned intuition at the frontiers of corporate life, albeit indirectly, through his American disciple Isobel Myers Briggs.[1]

The Inner Businessphere

The Advent of Organizational Psychology

Until comparatively recently, that is within the last thirty years or so, culture and psychology were considered to be entirely peripheral to business activity. Economics and politics, coupled with technology, ruled the commercial roost. I can well remember, as a young aspiring businessman in the late 1950s, being told by the then minister of finance in colonial Rhodesia that psychology was for 'backroom boys'. Still to this day, business in its raw and primal context is much more about buying and selling than it is about personal development and cultural evolution. Similarly economics, as a rationally based science underpinning business activity, is concerned with culture-free notions of 'monetarism' or 'scientific socialism'. In fact, whereas at least since the 1960s industrial and organizational psychology, if not also anthropology, has entered into mainstream MBA curricula, economic policy at large has remained dominated by the capitalism–socialism polarity. To that extent such evolved European philosophies as French rationalism, Italian humanism and Germanic holism have remained on the periphery of the businessphere, eclipsed by empiricist Adam Smith and dogmatist Karl Marx. This oppressive duopoly was apparently first broken by the Japanese and their overtly successful brand of collectivism,[2] which seemed to bypass the conventionally polarized economic wisdom.

In fact, the most viable alternative to the ideological duopoly was probably the one developed by that globally minded European, the psychoanalyst Carl Jung, as early as the 1930s, and was adopted by management psychologists in the 1970s. However, while Jung in the thirties was seen to be totally disconnected from the world of business, the Myers Briggs inventory developed in the seventies has become all too often disconnected from Jung.

Jung's Psychological Types

From the vantage point of Developmental Management, and for reasons which will soon become apparent, Carl Jung[3] is likely to play the role within the global businessphere of the twenty-first century that Smith and Marx played in the previous three centuries.

Jung's role, in fact, will be to break down the duopoly in political and economic thought, and to replace it with a quaternity (see figure F.1), in psychological and cultural as well as managerial and ultimately commercial terms. Carl Jung, while of Swiss nationality, was particularly international in his perspective. A student of the literature and mythologies of cultures all around the world, he took a particular interest in China and also spent a considerable amount of time in Africa. Most of his work was conducted in Europe and he made frequent lecture tours to the United States. As a psychoanalyst, as a philosopher and as a human being, Jung was truly a cosmopolitan of the twentieth century.

Thinking

Sensing *Intuiting*

Feeling

Figure F.1 Psychological types

Basic personality differences, for Jung, arise out of the way people prefer to use their minds, that is the way they perceive and the way they make judgements. *Perceiving* involves processes of becoming aware of things, people, occurrences and ideas. *Judging* includes the processes of coming to conclusions about what has been perceived. Whereas perception determines what people see in a situation, judgement determines what they decide to do about it. Humankind, then, for Jung, is equipped with two distinct and sharply contrasting ways of perceiving. One means is the familiar process of *sensing*, whereby we become aware of things directly through the five senses. The other is the process of *intuition*, which is indirect perception by way of the unconscious, incorporating ideas and associations that the unconscious tacks onto perceptions coming from the outside. These range from the merest masculine 'hunch' or 'woman's intuition' to the crowning examples of creative art or scientific discovery. When people prefer sensing, they are so interested in the actuality around them that they have little attention to spare for ideas coming faintly out of nowhere. Those people who prefer intuition are so engrossed in pursuing the possibilities it presents that they seldom look very intently at the actualities.

With the advantage of constant practice, the preferred process grows more controlled and trustworthy. Children become more adult in their use of the preferred process than in their less frequent use of the neglected one. Their enjoyment extends from the process itself to activities requiring the process, and they tend to develop the surface traits that result from looking at life a particular way. Each group becomes relatively adult in an area where the other remains childlike. Both channel their interests and energy in activities that give them a chance to use their minds in the way they prefer.

Such a quaternity of psychological types, of management domains and of evolutionary stages will be mutually interdependent rather than mutually exclusive, in both space and time. In other words, as a manager or organization develops over a life span or spreads across the globe, each will need to migrate across the quaternity. For unlike capitalism and communism, which shut each other out, the inner worlds of sensing, intuiting, thinking and feeling will welcome each other in, if growth takes place.

Let us now purposefully proceed towards what I have termed the 'inner businessphere'.[4] In his theory of psychological types Jung conceives of four personality attributes within each human being. These types emerge out of two distinct ways of perceiving combined with two equally distinct ways of judging. *Thinking* is a predominant characteristic of the structured organizations of the North. It can also be seen in Britain as more Scottish than English, and in Italy as more Piedmontese than Neapolitan. Thoughtful analytical management, then, adopts an objective approach to decision-making. *Feeling*, conversely, is a predominant characteristic of the personalized organizations of the South. It is more Irish than Scottish, more African than European, more humanist than rationalist. Managerial judgement is generally exercised on a subjective basis.

The Outer Businessphere

The global manager's inner space has its mirror image in the global business's so-called outer space. The West is endowed with lots of common sense; the North with a level head; the East with feminine intuition; and the South with intensity of feeling. The truly global corporation, having reached maturity, spans the whole of the businessphere not only geographically, but also psychologically. While it retains its indigenous bias, it becomes whole through its interactions with other psychological and geographical domains. It thereby creates an action-centred enterprise, a rationally structured organization, a quality product and an inspired culture. To the extent that it succeeds in such a global endeavour, such a corporation embraces a cast of eight characters, representing the hard and soft sides of each of Jung's four psychological types. The character with which this book is most concerned is the intuitive, so often left out of the cold in our Western managerial tradition, focusing as it does on action-centred leadership. Jung referred to this active mode as a 'sensing' one.

Sensing v. Intuiting

Anyone, according to Jung's disciple Myers Briggs, preferring sensing to intuition is interested primarily in actualities, while anyone preferring intuition to sensing is mainly interested in possibilities. The sensing types, by definition, depend on their five senses for perception. What comes directly from the senses is part of the sensing types' own experience, and therefore trustworthy. They tend to define intelligence as 'soundness of understanding', a sure and solid agreement of conclusions with facts.

Intuitives are comparatively uninterested in sensory reports of things as they are. Instead, they listen for the intuitions that came up from their unconscious with enticing visions of possibilities – a soaring take-off from the known and established, ending in a swooping arrival at an advanced point, with the intervening steps apparently left out.

Sensing	*Intuitive*
Face life observantly, craving enjoyment.	Face life expectantly, craving inspiration.
Reluctant to sacrifice present enjoyment for future gain.	As they live in the future, it is little sacrifice to forgo present satisfaction.
Desire chiefly to possess and enjoy, wanting to have what other people have.	Desire opportunities and possibilities, oblivious to what others have and do.
In danger of being frivolous, unless balance is attained through judgement.	In danger of being fickle, unless balance is attained through judgement.

Myers Briggs, in fact, identifies four different kinds of manager, each of whom has a strongly intuitive side:

- *troubleshooters.* These managers tend to be independent and impersonal in their relations with people. They are more apt to consider how others may affect their projects than vice versa. They may be inventors, troubleshooters or promoters, stronger in initiating projects than in completing them. They feel charged with a mission to realize a possibility.
- *facilitators.* Such individuals are more enthusiastic than their thinking counterparts, and more skilful at handling people. They are drawn to counselling, and are extremely perceptive of the views of others. At their best, their gift of insight is combined with an ability to inspire people.
- *creators.* These are the most independent of all the managerial types. Whatever their field, they are likely to be innovators. In business they are born reorganizers. Intuition gives them an iconoclastic imagination and an unhampered view of possibilities; extraverted thinking supplies a keenly critical organizing faculty.
- *harmonizers.* These managerial types naturally concern themselves with people, caring enough about harmony to want to win acceptance for their purposes. Their visions are likely to concern human welfare. They are stimulated by difficulties and ingenious in solving them.

Sensing v. Intuiting Organizations

Another contemporary interpreter of Jung working in a managerial context is the American organizational psychologist William Bridges.[5] Having broadly compared and contrasted sensing and intuitive organizations, he goes on to identify a variety of such intuitively based organizations.

Sensing organizations	*Intuitive organizations*
At their best with detail.	At their best with the big picture.
Can handle masses of data.	Can spot emerging trends.
Prefer solid routines.	Are carefree about routines.
Prefer incremental change.	Prefer transformational change.
Make improvements.	Change paradigms.

Sensing organizations	*Intuitive organizations*
See future as extension of the present.	Believe the future can be created.
Emphasize targets and plans.	Emphasize purpose and vision.
Trust experience and authority.	Trust insight and creativity.
Organize functionally.	Organize cross-functionally.

Each type of organization hereafter represents a basically intuitive approach, combined with a different blend of introversion (I) and extraversion (E), thinking (T) and feeling (F), judgement (J) and perception (P). I have added my own suggestions as to their representative organization, in a global context.

The ETJ Organization – Technocratic (ALCATEL/ ALSTHOM)

The heart of this type of organization is strategy. It evolves policies that are subordinated to such a strategy, expecting people to fit in, without necessarily explaining their importance. The strategy is set based on an intuitive grasp of a situation, and the organization goes after its objectives singlemindedly, often being careless about the human side of what it is trying to do. As it goes about its business in an impersonal way, personal issues are swept under the rug. At its best the organization is straightforward and unequivocal; at its worst it is prescriptive and dogmatic. It particularly wants to be in charge of its own destiny, and whenever that control is threatened the organization will be troubled.

There is always a model of reality behind the plan of such an organization, and the model often explains how things should work. The organization, as a result, is better at the grand strategy than at the tactics of implementation. For both its customers and employees, moreover, it has a tendency to approach situations from an engineering perspective, looking for mechanistic solutions, and weighing variables carefully. The leaders of such organizations, who in fact tend to be individualistic, may endorse self-development – that is, their own rather than that of others. All in all, their approach to handling people is simplistic. People are supposed to get the idea behind the plan, and that is supposed to be enough. They are expected to be able to engage in heavy verbal give-and-take.

The ITJ Organization – Informatic (CPG, Bull)

This type of organization is independent, innovative, iconoclastic and likely to regard itself as unique. It is often based on intellectual or scientific ventures, and the voice of authority means little if they see what they believe to be the truth or the reality.

Everything demands proof, and is up for discussion. There are no sacred cows. This organization often discovers possibilities, particularly of a practical or technological nature, where others do not.

The organization's forte is strategy, not tactics. Often the creative solution is more interesting than the detailed plan of turning the idea into a viable product. There is more interest in understanding than in making things, and a tendency to want to conform to an intellectual model rather than accepting things as they are. It is also liable to be insensitive to the human aspects of whatever it is doing. It mutes criticism by hiding what is going on. The organization likes to deal with information and is impatient with the softer, relational side of communication, which it dismisses as small talk. So it does not handle its human relations well, forgetting that people need appreciation and that there is a wisdom of the heart as well as the head. Internally, this mode of operation may befit the information technology function within an organization.

The ETP Organization – Adaptable (Lego, Novo, Norsk)

This type of organization's love of conceptualizing and problem-solving can turn work into a game. It is at its best, therefore, designing and inventing an answer to a difficult problem. To say that something cannot be done is a great intellectual challenge. On the other hand, once the problem is solved, even if the solution is still on paper, the excitement may disappear. Hence it may move on to a new problem before benefiting materially from the insight and creativity it has exercised on the old one. At its best it may make important discoveries; at its worst, these may never materialize into profitable ventures.

This approach capitalizes on improvisation, both internally and externally. As a result it is good at adapting to changing situations, though it may become too enamoured of change. These organizations are seldom hierarchical, and leadership is a matter of intelligence and creativity rather than position. Such leaders have colleagues and associates rather than followers. They act quickly and are prepared to take risks. People are supposed to hold their own with criticism and challenge, to get the picture quickly and start developing and refining it. To be slow and deliberate is not to fit in. Formal procedures and regulations are therefore not treated seriously, so that the organization's practical affairs may be in a mess. Internally this may reflect a research and development function within a business.

The ITP Organization – Egalitarian (IKEA, Eriksson)

This type of organization is best at dealing with systems and designs, but its focus is on understanding or creating them and not on implementing them or building them into replicable products. It does not engage in activities that require it to do things over and over again in a routine way. The organization is attuned to whatever is emerging in the world, often finding itself at the cutting edge of its field. Its efforts are most stimulated by complexity.

Such organizations tend to be loners in the business world, going their own way, and not joining in with associations or joint ventures. They do not even communicate very well with their clients, and are relatively unaware of their employees' feelings. Leadership makes heavy demands on its people, expecting the excitement of the work process to be its own reward. Interpersonal relations are distant, though egalitarian. Good ideas are respected, no matter who produces them. Overall, there is a strong 'the-way-things-ought-to-be-done' quality about their view of the world. Such an orientation befits a design group within an existing organization.

The IFJ Organization – Harmonic (Mitsubishi, Toyota)

This type of organization operates quietly, but behind the scenes there is a powerful commitment to the goals and values that it espouses. Whatever field the organization is in, its beliefs are what define its purpose and strategy. Moreover, one can easily underestimate the organization's power, imagination and passion because of the aura of responsibility it conveys. In fact some of its decisions are made and ventures initiated with a kind of sixth sense for the possibilities of the situation.

The leadership is likely to be adaptable and responsive to changing situations – that is, until one of its basic values is threatened. Then the whole organization will dig in with inordinate stubbornness. At the same time conflict is avoided as much as possible, and staff harmony is sought and expected. While there is sensitivity to criticism, internally, an awareness of the real needs of the client and organization is manifest. Personnel policies tend to emphasize using people's individual capabilities, assuming heavy commitments from them in return. Developmental activities of all kinds fit the organization's style – training, mentoring, coaching and career planning. With their emphasis on bringing everyone on board, moreover, these organizations an weather severe storms.

The IFP Organization – Innovative (Apple, Honda, Sony)

This type of organization is liable to be on a crusade of some kind, either a social crusade or a quest for a better product or service. There is a basic dream of improving the world. Its values are powerful, though they may not be clearly articulated. It has a quality of optimism and hopefulness, whatever its degree of maturity. This can make the organization somewhat naive, and it is likely to resist formal structures and systems.

The organization operates on the assumption that people mean well. For that reason it has difficulty with individuals who do not have the best interests of the organization at heart. It can run into difficulty when competing with an organization which feeds off more basic human instincts. In handling change, the organization is best at sensing the potential of situations, especially human situations. This gives it an early cue as to trends and makes it possible to launch changes effectively. Its weakness lies in follow-through. At the same time, with its tendency to do things in an aesthetically pleasing way, the organization is able to flow from one thing to another in a way which would pull other organizations apart.

The EFP Organization – Communal (Cashbuild, Olivetti)

This type of organization tends to fall into two categories – the creative ones that develop new ideas or products for people, such as Olivetti in Italy, and the idealistic ones that develop, serve or enlighten people, such as Cashbuild in South Africa.[6] In either case they see the possibilities in and for people. Leaders in such organizations try to resist issuing orders and mandates. They try to persuade, often by appeal to common values.

These organizations have some difficulty with detail and follow-through. They see the vision, and then expect that things will unfold according to some natural pattern. They prefer oral to written communication. They tend to be egalitarian – everyone has a voice, and even a vote. No one feels left out, though consensus may be achieved at the expense of production. They are subtly responsive to environmental trends, though trend spotting may degenerate into trendiness. Internally, there is an expectation of harmony, but within a context of individuality. They are good places for people who value freedom but less so for those who value supervision. They run the danger of becoming so fluid that they are always on the verge of dissolving.

The EFJ Organization – Charismatic (Benetton)

This type of organization is dynamic, and has a positive, energetic style. It handles change better than many other organizations, emphasizing the envisioned goal and ensuring everyone shares it. In fact it is more comfortable talking about its vision than most. As a result it is characterized by a high degree of human interaction. Cooperation is expected and human issues are espoused, although the action of the organization may often fall short of its ideals. Because, moreover, human needs are taken so seriously, this kind of organization frequently has an undercurrent of conflict behind the cooperative surface. Cooperation and conflict are two sides of the 'people-are-important' coin.

These organizations take values and cultures seriously, so that ideas and principles may take a back seat. Communications will tend to be less rationalistic and more symbolic. People are expected to be proactive once their roles have been spelt out. They have high goals, and they manage to live up to them surprisingly often. Depending on people – not on their roles but on their talents and integrity – means that these organizations tend to underestimate the importance of rules and standards. Leadership is often focused on a charismatic individual, or diffused among a tightly knit team. There is much talk of teamwork and a distrust of fixed hierarchies. Leaders in such organizations are likely to operate somewhat intuitively. The organization, in fact, handles unstructured situations better than most.

Conclusion: The New Frontier of Management

The unique contribution that Parikh and his colleagues at IMD have made to Developmental Management is manifold. First, they have taken the time and trouble to take intuition in management seriously. Second, as professors in the complementary areas of self-development (Parikh), organization development (Lank) and business development (Neubauer), they have adopted a depth and breadth of approach which is unprecedented in the management literature. Third, as respectively Western (Lank), Northern (Neubauer) and Eastern (Parikh), their work is much more cosmopolitan than anything that has appeared in the management literature hitherto. Fourth, they have combined a holistic appreciation of intuition in its conceptual management with a rigorous empiricism, through their extensive survey work across the globe. Finally, and for the first time to my knowledge, they have combined intuition as a personal phenomenon and vision building as a managerial and organizational one.

Ronnie Lessem

Notes

1 I. Myers Briggs, *Gifts Differing* (Consulting Psychologists Press, 1980).
2 M. Albert, *Capitalisme contre Capitalisme* (Editions du Seuil, 1991).
3 C. Jung, *A Dictionary of Analytical Psychology* (Ark Paperbacks, 1987).
4 R. Lessem and F. Neubauer, *European Management Systems* (McGraw-Hill, 1993).
5 W. Bridges, *The Character of Organizations* (Consulting Press, 1992).
6 A. Koopman, *Transcultural Management* (Blackwell, 1991).

Preface

> There are more things in heaven and earth, Horatio, than are dreamt of in your philosophy.
>
> *Hamlet, Act I, Sc. V*

> It is fashionable stupidity to regard everything one cannot explain as a fraud.
>
> *Carl Gustav Jung (1875–1961)*

During the last decade, our approaches to management – in teaching and practice alike – have come under forceful attack. Scholars raise the alarming question: 'Management and management education in the West: what's right and what's wrong?'.[1] Practitioners complain that our business schools produce hordes of managers who may be brilliant analysts, but would not know how to create and build a business.

Why this disenchantment with our approaches to management? One of the hypotheses is that we may be teaching solutions suited to solve the problems of yesterday and applying them to the problems of today. There would not be anything wrong with that if our problems had not changed profoundly. In the period up to the 1980s (when we faced long stretches predominantly characterized by growth) the overriding problem was to select from a vast pool of opportunities those which were particularly lucrative. A host of analytical tools – many of them developed in response to the key issues of that period – assisted us admirably in that process.

Since then, we have had to learn painfully that our main management task has changed: one of the major management issues of today is the need to revitalize companies whose profits (and often sales) are sagging and to do so in a business environment characterized by fast and complex change. Equally painfully, we have had the experience of discovering that our shining tool kit, heavily influenced by the long admired (and copied) Anglo-Saxon business schools, is no longer so well suited to handle these new issues. In fact, countries that have followed these prescriptions particularly faithfully seem to be having the greatest difficulty in climbing out of the current recession. To make matters worse, some observers seem to provide evidence that teaching and applying these analytical tools virtually drives out exactly those qualities – creativity, entrepreneurship – which are generally considered prerequisites for a successful revitalization of stagnant companies.

It is this constellation which has encouraged a number of scholars and practitioners in management to search for unconventional avenues in order to find a way out of the difficulties we are facing. One of these avenues is the effort to understand better the role of intuition in management.[2] There is no need to go overboard: at this point, nobody is suggesting burning at the stake our time-honoured analytical tools. There is widespread consensus that we should keep using them – in those situations where they are suitable. All that proponents of a non-rational way of thinking are asking for is that we give a similar amount of attention and air time to the intuitive way of managing and to the analytical approaches.

It is in this spirit that this book has been written. It is only realistic to realize that good managers walk on two legs in their managerial lives: in a decision situation they certainly analyse every bit of information they can lay hands on; but at the same time, whenever a decision point arrives, they regularly also consult their guts. How does it feel to decide in favour of this or that alternative? When asked what criteria played the main role in the choice of his successor, Hermann Strenger, the outgoing CEO (chief executive officer) of the German chemicals multinational Bayer, answered that to be a good executive, it is important 'to be able to think strategically, to motivate others and *to have a feel for people, trends and tendencies*, whether in business, technology or politics' (emphasis added).[3]

Managers are not alone in this approach. A collector of old manuals for seafaring captains in the British Royal Navy told us that in the guidelines for preparing a ship for an approaching storm every captain was instructed to carry out a number of routines – systematic, logical steps – to safeguard the ship and its crew against a possible disaster. But after having carried out all these prescribed measures, he also was requested to ask himself how he actually felt about the situation and the preparations.

While in some cases it may only be a case of paying lip-service to it, we now have evidence that intuition does indeed seem to play a key role in the professional lives of managers. Our International Survey on Intuition ('Survey' for short), described below, shows that 53.6 per cent of the sample state they use Intuition and Logic/Reasoning in equal measure on the job. Some 7.5 per cent declare that they use more of Intuition while the remainder (38.9 per cent) claim that they use more of Logic/Reasoning at work. What they are telling us is that there is more to management than that which can be counted, weighed and measured.

This book is intended primarily for managers and management educators, although there is much to intrigue anyone who is interested in intuition and its application more broadly. Chapter 1 explains why intuition has attracted increasing attention, and classifies the reasons as being at global, organizational and individual levels. Chapter 2, while giving credit to the quantitative/analytical approaches to management, argues that they are no longer sufficient to cope with today's and the future's challenges. It answers the question, 'Why do we need intuition in management?', and makes clear the role of an intuitive management style in creating a vision, choosing a direction and making a decision.

Chapter 3 takes an eclectic approach to trying to define this elusive phenomenon. It is characterized as being multidimensional (as a skill, as a trait, as being), multicontextual (instant response, short-term, ongoing) and at multilevels of consciousness (logical consciousness, subconsciousness, unconsciousness, supraconsciousness). Intuition is then illustrated through its manifestations as noun, verb and adjective. The chapter ends by stating what intuition is not and listing the attributes of authentic intuition. This is probably the most thorough treatment of the definitional issue to be found anywhere in the literature on intuition.

To access intuition requires the ability to relax and receive, while to enhance it requires facilitating the creation of an insight and the capacity to apply it. Chapter 4 introduces the reader to the processes and techniques for doing both.

Chapters 5 and 6 focus on the overall results of the Survey. Arguably the most ambitious survey of its kind, it reports on the findings derived from a questionnaire completed by 1312 top and senior managers coming from relatively large industrial and service organizations representing a population estimated at 1 463 000 in nine countries. The geographic spread is broad: Europe (Austria, France, the Netherlands, Sweden, the United Kingdom), the United States of America, Japan, Brazil and India. Thus, the sample reflects viewpoints from industrial market economies, middle-income developing countries (Brazil) and low-income developing countries (India). The subjects covered include:

- an objective rating of Intuition as a self-rating, and an analysis of the association between the two ratings;
- descriptions given of Intuition;
- extent of agreement with three given descriptions of Intuition;
- perceived relevance of Intuition in business management and other fields;
- stated means of identification of Intuition and the extent to which Intuition is perceived to be accompanied by different phenomena;
- the extent of use of Intuition (as opposed to Logic/Reasoning) in professional and personal life;
- opinions on certain notions about and aspects of Intuition.

For readers interested in the more technical dimensions of the Survey, the individual country reports and the actual questionnaire used are contained in the appendices.

Chapters 7 and 8 are closely interlinked. The former presents the overall concept of vision and visioning. It addresses the characteristics of a good vision and the importance of working from rather than to a vision in the corporate planning process. With this background, chapter 8 presents in considerable detail the nine-step Parikh–Neubauer model of creating a corporate vision. Starting with reflective (logical) visioning, the authors move to intuitive visioning; this leads to an integrative vision which, when compared to current reality, can lead to implementable action plans.

As exciting as we, the authors, have found these efforts to set out to discover fresh horizons in management thought, we are as conscious as anybody else of the limitations of the effort. One of the reasons for these is that one finds only very few mileposts on the way to fresh horizons. We nevertheless embarked on the effort, as we felt there was a dire need for it. We put the result before the reader in the spirit of a sentence by the Roman poet Horace: 'If you know it better let me immediately know; if not, accept this, I beg you.'

Notes

1 Harold J. Leavitt, 'Management and management education in the West: what's right and what's wrong?', *London Business School Journal*, Summer 1983, pp. 18–23.
2 The word 'intuition' is capitalized whenever a specific reference is made to our International Survey on Intuition. Otherwise the 'i' is in lower case.
3 'New chairman inheriting Bayer tradition', *Wall Street Journal*, 24 April 1992.

NOTES

[illegible]

Acknowledgements

A considerable number of people helped to make this book possible. Of these, only a few can be cited here by name. In the first place Dr Juan F. Rada must be mentioned. As Director General of the International Management Institute (IMI) in Geneva, Switzerland, and subsequently when at the helm of the International Institute for Management Development (IMD-International) – the 1990 result of a merger between IMI and IMEDE in Lausanne), he encouraged and backed the research which led to this book. Following him, IMD, under the leadership of the interim Director General Dr Xavier Gilbert, continued its support. Without IMI's and IMD's help, this book simply would not have seen the light of day.

A significant proportion of this book is devoted to the results of our International Survey on Intuition. This survey was conducted by a special research committee comprising the three authors under the chairmanship of Jagdish Parikh. Successful implementation thereof was dependent on the nine country coordinators, whose main task was to enlist respondents – a huge undertaking. In Austria, this role was filled by the Hernstein Institute. The other coordinators were Luiz Villares (Brazil), Jean-Louis Servan-Schreiber (France), Peter Idenberg (the Netherlands), Jagdish Parikh (India), Nobumitsu Doi (Japan), Marika Marklund and Jan Bakelin (Sweden), John Pontin (the United Kingdom) and Herman Maynard (the USA). To them, we extend our grateful appreciation, as we do to the 1312 top and senior managers who gave significantly of their valuable time to complete the lengthy questionnaire. Their insights and contributions on intuition and its use as a non-rational tool in management enriched this publication enormously. We are also indebted to C. Parthasarathy, statistician, who managed the mass of numbers coming out of the Survey.

During the long gestation period of this book, the authors were particularly influenced by a group of seminal thinkers on intuition. We would like to state our special appreciation to Karl Pribram, Mike Aron, Willis Harman, Michael Ray, Frances Vaugham, William Millar, Karen Buckley and Larry McKenny. We hope they see in this book the proof that their time with us has resulted in the enhancement of the literature of the field to which they have devoted so much intelligence and energy.

Our thanks also go to IMD Professor Ahmet Aykaç, who throughout the project has been available for advice. The intuition project was only one of the endeavours at IMD which benefited from the piercing mind of this ideal discussion partner. In this context also, Professor Ronnie Lessem from the City University, London, has to be mentioned. As the editor of the Blackwell series on Developmental Management, he made important and very much appreciated comments on the manuscript.

Lastly, there are three other important persons whose back-up support was vital to the authors. First of all there is Victoria Fernandes of Bombay, whose patience and secretarial skills turned a seemingly endless number of drafts into a presentable manuscript. At IMD, secretaries Sandra Bodmer and Juliet Greco assisted in many ways, including keeping the international communications flowing between the three of us.

Despite our indebtedness to all those acknowledged above, the responsibility for any shortcomings this book may have is, of course, exclusively ours.

Jagdish Parikh
Fred Neubauer
Alden G. Lank
Bombay/Lausanne

I

Intuition in Context

I turned my chair to the fire and dozed . . . Again the atoms were gamboling before my eyes. This time the smaller groups kept modestly in the background. My mental eye, rendered more accurate by repeated visions of this kind, could now distinguish larger structures, of manifold conformation; long rows, sometimes more closely fitted together; all training and twisting in snakelike motion. But look! What was that? One of the snakes had seized hold of its own tail, and the form whirled mockingly before my eyes. As if by a flash of lightning, I awoke . . . Let us learn to dream, gentlemen.

Friedrich August von Kekulé (1829–96), German organic chemist, describing his revolutionary discovery of the closed-ring structure of the molecules of certain organic compounds

In recent years, intuition as a concept has attracted a growing degree of attention and interest. There are several reasons for this phenomenon, particularly in the business world. These can be grouped as being on global, organizational and individual levels.

Global Level

Change, Complexity, Uncertainty, Conflict

One of the most outstanding features of the last few years has been the experience of change – quantitative as well as qualitative. In all dimensions of life – techno-economic and psycho-social as well as political – the pace of change has accelerated. As a result we face increasing complexity, uncertainty and conflict. The new buzz word is 'raplexity' (rapid complexity). The conventional, analytical, logical patterns of thinking are no longer sufficient either to understand or to cope with the current and emerging scenarios. Therefore one has to rely, consciously or unconsciously, on intuition, which is generally described as a way of 'knowing' spontaneously without the conscious use of logic or analytical reasoning.

To cope with such accelerating change, one requires a sense of inner stability; to cope with complexity, one needs an anchor of simplicity; to cope with uncertainty, one has to develop a deeper level of internal support system; and to cope with conflict, one needs a special ability of synthesis, a deeper level of perception. Intuition seems to facilitate the cultivation of these qualities (see figure 1.1).

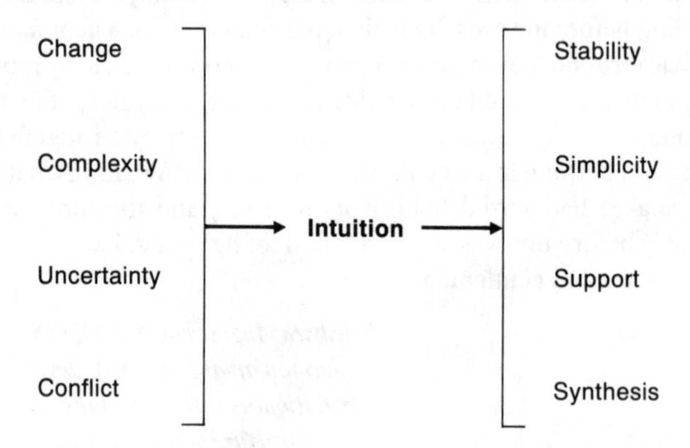

Figure 1.1 Role of intuition in coping with change

Human Consciousness

One can also view the phenomenon of change around us from a human evolutionary standpoint. We have been evolving through geological, biological and ideological revolutions and now it has been suggested that we are transiting towards what is described as a 'consciousness' revolution. This implies that we are collectively moving towards a greater awareness about, and access to, our inner dynamics, our 'inner space', or consciousness. Intuition from this standpoint is viewed as a higher or deeper level of consciousness in which a different kind of 'knowing' takes place: supposedly by accessing other arenas of information not normally accessible in the ordinary, sense-related consciousness.

All this emphasizes that the conventional/analytical ways of thinking are no longer adequate to enable one to function effectively in the emerging scenario. Intuition has to be relied upon. Intuition is useful generally, but when the road ahead is foggy, it is essential. One could, in this sense, say that 'Necessity is the mother of intuition'.

We are therefore noticing a growing amount of literature on intuition, an increasing amount of attention to it from the media, and recently even conferences, seminars and workshops on it proliferating in several countries. Interestingly, this is happening not only in the context of business but also in other domains of scientific inquiry.

No Anchors Left

One of the most interesting and distinctive features of our contemporary scenario is that almost all the conventional psycho-social givens are being seriously questioned. For several decades various 'isms' or ideologies provided a sense of belonging to many people across the world. However, recent happenings have exploded the basic fabric of most of the prevailing ideologies, whether communism, capitalism or different brands of socialism. None of these has been able to fulfil the promises enshrined in its manifesto in terms of either standard of living or quality of life. Something similar has happened with regard to value systems, whether materialistic or spiritualistic or any combination of the two (see figure 1.2). Pursuit of only materialistic values in life has

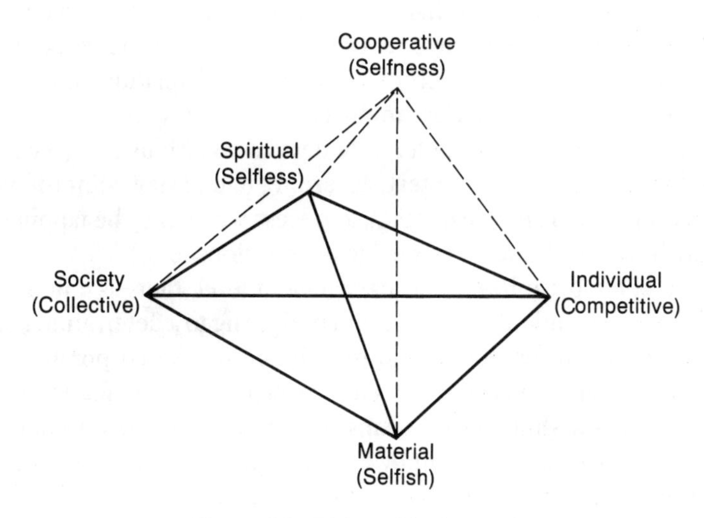

Figure 1.2 Values–ideology axis

not really enriched anyone's life in terms of real happiness, nor have any existing communities claiming pursuit of spiritual values been able really to achieve a spiritual quality of life or a significant material standard of living. What is therefore necessary is to evolve a synergistic synthesis of (and not a compromise between) all the parameters of both the axes; beyond selfishness and selflessness, beyond collectiveness and competitiveness, to a cooperativeness based on selfness. Intuition can facilitate this process.

There is hardly any institution left in the various spheres of human endeavour (social, educational or even religious) which continues to provide the kind of anchor that most people are seeking. Even the basic institutions of marriage and the family are rapidly disintegrating. It is quite disturbing to realize that there are hardly any relevant role models available among people living today that are worth emulating in any profession. In such a situation, perhaps only one's own intuition can provide the anchor within – a basic human need.

Paradigm Shift

At a deeper level, the phenomenon of accelerating change and the disappearance of conventional anchors can be viewed as a shift in fundamental world views about reality. There is a paradigm shift from the conventional, classical physics based upon the Cartesian–Newtonian model of reality to the new physics based on the quantum relativistic model – a shift from a positivistic, deterministic, reductionist, materialistic and mechanistic view of reality to that which views ultimate reality as subjective, approximate, holistic, networking and thought-like, a complex web of interconnected relationships. It is a shift from an atomistic view towards that which considers ultimate reality to be some kind of order or pattern or consciousness (see figure 1.3). Intuition is, in this context, according to one viewpoint (of which the Eastern mystic is an example), a process which may be tapping and tuning into this ultimate knowledge or consciousness.

Even at the organization or management level, there is a noticeable shift from conventional planning and budgeting to a determining of the overall direction for the organization based on the corporate vision. Also, the main emphasis is not on 'organizing' but on alignment and networking – a shift from systems and styles focusing on control to those which mobilize and empower. While profits naturally continue to be of principal interest, the core value of the organization is to fulfil a purpose and to develop ongoing learning, treating profit more as an

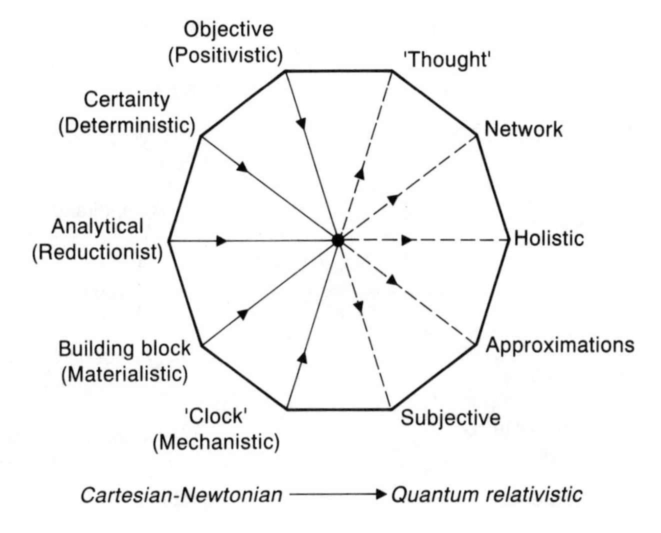

Figure 1.3 Paradigm shift: changing world views

essential resource than as an ultimate objective or purpose of business (see figure 1.4).

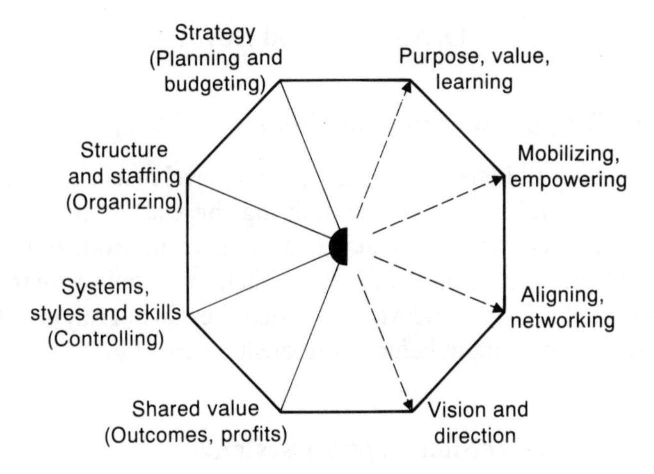

Figure 1.4 Transformative management

The implication of all this for individual managers is shown in figure 1.5 – a shift from self-consciousness ('me in the world') to consciousness of self ('the world in me'). It implies the use not only of logic, words and numbers but also of intuition, pictures, music, and all the other dimensions shown.

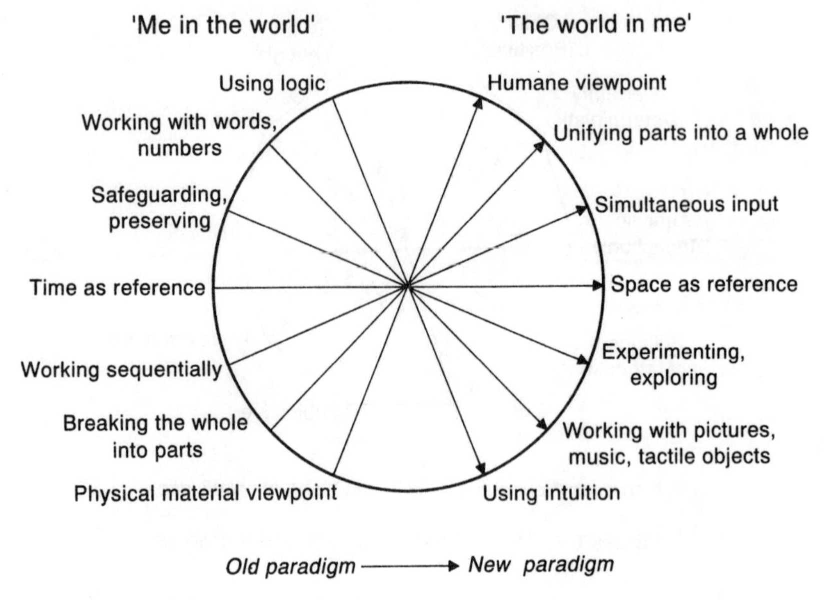

Figure 1.5 Implications for the individual manager

Organizational Level

Growing Respectability/Recognition

We are finding an increasing number of top-level managers, including CEOs, more and more openly admitting the use of 'gut feeling' or intuition in their decision-making, as is evident from our various Survey chapters and appendices. In fact, it is being increasingly emphasized that even those who claim that they do not rely on intuition are, and have to, without being consciously aware of it.

Computerized Decision-Support Systems

In management education and practice, the major thrust and dependence have been towards and on analytical problem-solving. With the advent of computers as well as the expert and knowledge-based systems, the problem-solving roles of managers, on the basis of available data and information, are being increasingly taken over by computerized decision-support systems. However, computers can only (so far) compute, and an exclusive reliance on analytical problem-solving frequently leads to what is known as analysis paralysis. The managers in the changing scenarios are being increasingly called upon to contribute in areas which cannot be automated or computerized. This is where the use of intuition becomes significant. In earlier days, intuition was being resorted to because there was too little data or information available. Now computers are churning out so much information and data that, even to sift out the relevant information, the use of intuition becomes essential.

Unpredictable Variables

Earlier, many decisions were made on the basis of analysing variables which were reasonably predictable. Now, in the context of what is stated above, there are so many forces and factors operating and changing all the time that there remain hardly any variables which can be predicted with a reasonable amount of certainty. This is accentuated by the technological revolution. The 'long' range for several industries has shortened to about three years. In such a climate of uncertainty, one has to do some inner guesswork or gut feeling – in other words, use intuition.

Lack of Precedents and Ill-Structured Problems

One of the guidelines in conventional decision-making was the reliance on precedents. Many of the situations that are now emerging have hardly any precedents or parallels! Intuition must be used. Likewise, ill-structured problems which do not lend themselves to conventional analytical treatment, such as recruiting executives, acquisitions/merger decisions, etc., require intuition.

Choosing from Balanced Alternatives

With technological and economic advances almost everywhere, the number of opportunities visible and not so visible is growing at an accelerating pace. The implication of this is that frequently managers find themselves surrounded by almost equally balanced alternatives from which to choose. In such situations, again, one has ultimately to rely on one's intuition.

Individual Level

Human Information-Processing/Mental Abilities

Another reason for the increasing focus on intuition is that it can also be looked upon as one of the exceptional mental abilities of a human being which has so far not been sufficiently understood or developed. The mental abilities which have been generally pursued are absorption (observing and recording), retention (memory and recall), and reasoning (analysis and judgement). It is only in recent years that interest has been growing rapidly in the field of creativity, and it is in the search for creativity that the process of intuition has assumed special significance. This is echoed in our Survey.

Integration

With the growing attraction of the field of human consciousness, interest has been expanding in understanding inner dynamics as well as in integrating these with the external environment. Intuition is supposed to provide the link which could help resolve the apparent conflicts and contradictions, both inner and outer. Intuition is understood as helping develop the vision of unity and wholeness in apparent separateness and conflict.

Muscle, Head, Heart

The development of intuitive ability could be seen as the logical next step in human problem-solving on a global basis. When we were primitive, our power was in our hands, and muscles made the difference. Civilization has brought us to the point where ideas are as powerful as armies, and a good strategy is more valuable than a strong arm.

Although we can make ourselves muscular with exercise and work, there is still no exercise to make ideas. In fact we do not make ideas; we get ideas, and we therefore have to learn to be open and receptive to them. We catch ideas at the right time because we are ready for them.

As we evolve to the next stage of more sophisticated consciousness, we will be seeing increasingly a tendency to go beyond analytical intelligence when dealing with our world. We will need more than stronger muscles; we will need advances in consciousness. We will need wisdom. We will need to act with our hearts as well as our heads, to cooperate and synthesize between ourselves, between our nations, our continents and our hemispheres. We only recently became better than the other animals; now we can learn to become better humans.

Surviving to Thriving

This is the challenge we face: up to now, we have been tormented with the pressures of survival, with mind-sets forged in that ancient mould of necessity. Most of us are beyond that stage now. We have abundant technology and a world population that contains billions of fellow humans who want to share in the world, which is no longer as dangerous a challenge as it used to be, but is becoming our common home and perhaps our future fulfilment.

The time has now come to think about how to understand and discover more fully human nature. We must go beyond survival. Even in the developing regions of the world, significant progress is being made to supersede daily maintenance as an underlying cultural and personal imperative. Our mind-set itself is capable of higher development, so it can support us in developing our world in ways more wonderful than our ancestors could have imagined. We can do much more than survive – we can learn to thrive. Humanity got this far by its wits, but now we must learn about wisdom for the next stage in human development. If we are to go further, we have to refine consciousness itself so that it can accept a thriving, coexistent, even occasionally illogical, multicultural world.

The old maintenance mind-set made us fearful and worried. We saw everything from diplomatic troubles to global warming as dangers threatening us from all directions. It is time to leave our mental caves of fear and doubt and learn to thrive in a shared vision of a world that can nurture us all and provide for us and our children. Attention to intuition will help us trust, and train, our insight as well as our analysis. With better hearts and minds, our daily work can be experienced as part of a greater vision for the world for which we all hope. It is possible now to address these possibilities – which is why it is so important to examine the requisite tools.

Existential Issues

The enterprise of philosophical thought is aimed at unravelling four major questions. We all seem to want to understand the need for freedom, the causes of isolation, the meaning of life, and the nature of death. Despite the fact that nobody has been able to come up with a universally accepted understanding of any of these major topics, they still lie at the base of the great majority of human mental endeavour. Intuition seems to be the only anchor for this.

Conclusion

In other words, at all the different levels discussed above, intuition seems to be the instrument which can: help us to achieve constancy and stability to manage change; provide consistency and simplicity to manage complexity; develop courage and inner support to cope with uncertainty; and generate the clear criteria and synthesizing ability necessary to manage conflict.

2

The Role of Intuition in Management

> The term [intuition] does not denote something contrary to reason, but something outside the province of reason.
>
> *Carl Gustav Jung (1875–1961)*

Business management, and within it the field of corporate strategy, has been typified by enormous progress during the last three decades. One major characteristic of this progress has been the development of highly analytical managerial tools and concepts. These range from extensively quantified procedures, such as discounted cash flow analysis for investment decisions, to the multiple regressions and statistical methodologies found in broader areas of strategic planning and problem-solving.

This development of a reliance on hard facts and tough analysis was necessary and timely. It helped to solve the problems which were typically faced by businesses in the 1960s and the early 1970s. This was the time of high growth rates in many of the economies of industrialized and developing nations, which offered a wealth of business opportunities. The overriding managerial priority was to analyse multiple options, and to select skilfully from among them.

Two additional developments were both fundamental and catalytic to this rapid growth in the use of analytic technique. The first was the advent and availability of electronic data processing to array and analyse vast amounts of information, and the second was the increasing inflow of econometricians, computer scientists and operations researchers into the field of business management. Soon, managers without these tools, or lacking staff skilled in these techniques, were considered hopelessly archaic. The hard edge of quantitative, technically elegant techniques appeared to provide a new and powerful approach to management decision-making.

All of these tendencies, grouped together, added up to a rather remarkable result: an impressive edifice of systematic knowledge in the area of business management characterized by a Cartesian, highly analytical approach exemplified and promoted by the growing number of MBA programmes offered by academic institutions in almost every developed, and developing, country of the world. During the last decade, however, there has been a growing perception that there was something incomplete about this modern paradigm, heretofore considered a major driving force in the admirable upswing of modern business management. In articles and at symposia, an increasing number of academicians, as well as experienced practitioners, began to suggest that there might be inherent flaws in the tendency to treat the economy like a huge machine, working like clockwork, with definable inputs and outputs, clear causes and logical effects.

Faced with new pressures related to population control, resource management and other interacting constraints on otherwise free market philosophies, unlimited growth has been exposed as a false and unrealistic goal. Adam Smith's innocence has been modified all the way to propositions such as the 'zero sum' society. In the light of stagnating markets, enormous restructuring efforts, and growing unemployment problems in many countries, it now seems questionable whether the problems faced by tomorrow's managers will be solved quite so readily by the powers of shrewd analysis alone, as suggested in chapter 1. Central to this new, and more flexible, understanding of the multiple elements of a more comprehensive philosophy of modern management is the notion of creative solution finding.

'Insight' and 'creativity' are words which seem to crop up these days with increasing regularity. Radically new technologies and techniques vie with the accepted rote of complete analysis and well-managed growth. In fact, statistics themselves indicate that the majority of new jobs created in the United States (and presumably elsewhere too) during the last decade or two have not come out of the planned expansion of large established corporations. In more cases than not, the older firms have watched their numbers of employees drop, while the new jobs have been generated by a new generation of young, highly entrepreneurial firms built on the creative ideas of individual owners and managers. It is the innovative, largely intuitive, grasp of the evolving global marketplace which has made modern giants from minor firms such as the pocket radio manufacturer Sony or the motor cycle builders of BMW and Honda.

Creativity of this nature is not the typical result of convergent, analytical thinking. It is more the outgrowth of divergent thinking, of highly intuitive approaches – knowing what is right without being able to prove it at the outset, to paraphrase Schumpeter. The concept of an intuitive process leading to creative business ideas, subsequently supported by *ex post facto* analysis, has been an underlying theme behind a large number of the wealth- and employment-creating enterprises which have caught so much of our attention today.

The recognition of intuition as a major component of good management has not been restricted to smaller companies. In larger corporations as well, many successful business executives and professionals now openly admit that they have learned to trust their intuition and, moreover, that this intuition has become more reliable and accurate through the very process of trusting. References to the role of intuition in decision-making are turning up ever more frequently in the most reputable business journals. Its importance is emphasized at the individual, the organizational and even the global level, as noted in chapter 1.

Some people just seem to have a gift for making the right decision at the right time, almost as if they had a wizard with predictive powers on the payroll. Everyone has heard of the intuitive artist or healer, and each of us has met at least one manager who seemed almost psychic at times. He buys, and the market goes up; or she is prescient when it comes to bidding on important contracts. It seems that some people are just tuned into another source – some non-ordinary or even cosmic phenomenon that feeds them the answers. Recently, this sort of observation has begun to translate as a next frontier for the philosophers of management science.

This is so much the case, in fact, that managers around the world are paying considerable sums of money to attend a variety of seminars and symposia purporting to stimulate this type of creative decision-making. We will put aside until the next chapter the question of just what 'intuition' may be all about. The great majority of popular programmes and even more of the philosophical essays and articles generally neglect to ask an even more primary question.

Why Do We Need Intuition in Management?

We have done quite well – from the caves to the stars – with the standard, analytical thought process. Is there any reason why we ought to study the phenomenon of intuition as anything more than an oddity exhibited by a lucky small minority of otherwise reasonable professionals? We have all had our intuitive insights, but they usually flash and disappear like shooting stars, leaving us none the wiser as to their origin, or their purpose. If we are to spend some time learning about intuition and how to use it, we should at least have some work for it to do. It is nice to be sensitive, but is there any reason to develop this skill if it is not as valuable as some real professional training, or a new supercomputer? Is intuition really necessary in management?

The first answer is that intuition is not simply knowing the future state of things. It has to do with the way some people manage the present state of things. It requires no intuition at all to understand why it is becoming important to learn more about intuition, and how to use it. In fact, it may be the essential skill by which effective managers may some day be judged, and well before the dawn of the next century. The reason for this is found in a general appreciation of what the most important assets are for managers in situations where a clear decision is required among alternative solutions.

Managing Change

Well-reputed business schools are known to have advocated the view that the greatest advantage accrues to the player with the best information. The state of perfect information leads to the state of endless wealth, and has occasionally been referred to in class as the 'phone line to God'. This phone line has, typically, been seen as worth an infinite amount of money, since anyone with perfect information would always make the right decision. Any information less perfect than that one line has been seen as worth commensurately less money.

However, we now know that professional managers in the late twentieth century face the problem of information overload. Most of us have, by now, read dire accounts of the sheer build-up of information as ever more networked communciations and media shrink the globe into a mass of unread articles and missed citations. Learning from the well of wisdom once required serious effort. Now it more resembles taking a drink from a fire hydrant. Nobody has any way of keeping track

Then

Now

of all the new and useful information being generated in the world these days. If the business of locating the right information comes down to sorting through it, we are facing a losing battle against an ocean of fresh facts washing at our consciousness every day.

Fortunately, the various parts of society function somewhat independently of each other; and nobody has to know everything. On the other hand, this information explosion is driving a number of social engines faster than ever before. The most obvious of these is the rapidity with which change itself is becoming nearly a constant. Philosophically speaking, this is a contradiction in terms, since a change suggests a transformation from one state of affairs to another. It is generally assumed that there will be a rest state before the next discrete change. In actual practice, however, the impact of constant improvements in both physical and analytical tools is now creating a nearly steady state of change, as new developments rapidly supersede each other.

This rapidity of change, accelerated by a growing information overload, has left today's managers unable to assess carefully all the implications of progress both within and without their specific areas of business. If one were able to give careful attention only to the more important articles in one's own area of expertise, it would take several hours every morning just analysing whether, or how much, each day's new changes could eventually affect one's own enterprise.

Keeping up with change is nearly impossible already, and it becomes more difficult all the time as even more people using more innovative techniques seek to adapt and improve their methods, their materials, and their management styles and systems. Like Alice's Red Queen, well-informed managers have to run as fast as they can just to stay in the same place; to get ahead would mean running even faster.

This, then, is a major area in which intuitive guidance may play an increasingly important part in the daily operations of the twenty-first-century professional. Intuition is neither a conscious rational process nor a linear exercise in sorting out the parts and making consecutive decisions. The ability to scan large amounts of information without a predetermined agenda, and yet be able to tap that subconscious trove of possibly pertinent data, may become the only way that the managers of the next century will be able to keep ahead of the competition.

An intuitive framework of thought becomes necessary even to keep abreast of change in a world which changes more, and faster, every day. Just as jugglers are more concerned with rhythm than with keeping their eyes on each of the balls in the air, so intuitive managers keep to their own rhythm, and to the rhythm of the information coursing around them. The sharp eye for detail which aided the cost accountants of the last fifty years may be yielding to a softer focus as the static management environment yields to more fluid and chaotic scenarios, which characterize interactions of multiple events occurring much too quickly for a classic analytical approach.

With change becoming the new constant, we will be needing new methods to define and maintain any constancy in our goals, our strategies and our daily tasks. Intuitive ability may be the only skill which will keep the modern professional both up to date and on course. The gyroscope stays upright not despite its whirling centre, but because of it: as change tries to whirl us out of control, we can keep constant only by finding the axis of our mind and moving forward in dynamic balance.

Managing Complexity

As intuition can provide managers with a certain constancy amid the rising instabilities of a changing environment, it can also help make sense when too much complexity begins to reduce the problem to nonsense. When it is just too much, we may need that intuitive guidance within to help us place our priorities for management action.

This is not the same as simply wading through the onslaught of information overload. It has to do with the way we prioritize our attention at any given moment. In the previous centuries of human existence, we could be aware of the details only to the extent of our own eyesight and our own mental images, which nearly duplicated the physical world around us. Those who were aware of the more complex interactions between the forces of nature, or the forces of society, often used this gift. A healer with extraordinary empathy could become the local shaman; a strong leader with a gift for intrigue could become the local ruler. However, the complexities of natural as well as social order were hidden from the vast majority.

But this is no longer the case. The impact of ever more capable analytic tools, combined with a growing sophistication in the science of information transfer, has made us all aware that things are a lot more complex than they seem to be. Each step forward in human civilization has resulted in another stage in our understanding that things will not be figured out completely this evening, or even by tomorrow afternoon.

In fact, it usually happens that the more we investigate a subject to get better information, the more likely it is that new complexities will make themselves known to us. Levels of detail grow by the very work we do trying to find a simple answer.

This trend seems to have reached an end point, at least in the generation of the complex by the simple, in the mathematical work of Benoit Mandelbrot. Here, a mathematical manipulation of any value through a formula known as the Mandelbrot Set can lead to levels of complexity which simply grow by the number of manipulations. When these manipulations are used to drive a video display, the detailed patterns which emerge exactly mimic the shapes of clouds, of cliffs, and of other strangely beautiful organic shapes. The more these images are magnified, the more complexity they exhibit, as if the programme were a microscope enlarging detail without limit and complexity without end.

The complexity of our life and work continues to grow at an increasingly rapid rate. This has problematical aspects for the manager, who is now left midway between two propositions. On the one hand, it is important to examine each problem thoroughly; on the other, it is equally important to keep the project on schedule. Deciding what level of detail is necessary is a matter of judgement every time.

Intuition seems to be an excellent tool for cutting through needless complexity. In individuals who exhibit an intuitive management style, this skill can prove to be very practical on a day-to-day basis. In an environment which is by nature fluid and changing, there is a premium on knowing the appropriate level of attention to any detail. Without an internal consistency of vision and direction, attention can be too easily diverted, or absorbed when it should be available. When the job is to spray the forest, we cannot get too involved with every single tree.

Moving along in a project, it is helpful to develop some intuitive direction and rhythm. Intuitive overview helps to identify simple underlying patterns, defusing the broad demands of too much complexity. Paying attention to all and everything can lead to wasted energy and efforts; one can learn when to zero in and when to back off for a better perspective. Without using the term 'transcend', most would agree that the ability to disengage mentally and get above the situation can be a very valuable asset for any manager.

Only by exercising this ability on a regular basis can one move forward in a consistent manner. When asked the secret of his financial success, the great financier Bernard Baruch once said, 'I have never gambled. I am a speculator. It comes from the Latin "speculo", "I look over." I look over each situation, and then I make my decisions.' Getting too close to the details is like flying too close to the ground; we need to keep an inner perspective to keep us moving forward with consistency. The use of intuition helps many keep their agendas simple when the complexities of the situation make gamblers out of wise people.

Managing Conflict

In a world environment characterized by increasing change and increasing complexity, conflicts will also increase. In most instances, this increase in conflict has little, if anything, to do with the sort of motivations which we customarily assign to the term. In a fluid and changing scenario, no person or group has to be identified directly in any way with anyone or anything to be in conflict with others. The simple desire to do one's best in a situation leads inevitably to conflict unless all parts and personnel move from point to point in an identical framework of goals and timing. Leadership can eventually become subsidiary to a strategy based on coordination, rather than cooperation.

The problem faced when orchestrating this sort of total control over a multifaceted operation, which consists of different individuals with differing amounts of information of varying complexity, is that we begin inevitably to sacrifice the flexibility which is so necessary in such a scenario. Like the ropes that the climbers tie together on a mountainside, the lines of command provide a common safety against individual mishap, but at the same time they can inhibit and diminish both the forward motion of the project and the creativity often required on an *ad hoc* basis, and practised by individuals as they perform their tasks as part of a team.

Dealing with conflicts, which will naturally arise as these pressures continue to mount, requires more than patience and good humour. Those qualities will suffice for the individual, so that he or she does not develop ulcers or other manifestations of stress in the work environment. However, it does not help in the day-to-day activities of a complex enterprise if the manager stays cool while the project goes out of control due to conflicting ideas as to priorities, planning or project supervision. The successful manager must be able to discern those modes and methods which are inherently the most likely to win support and agreement in an environment which is a challenging mixture of old plans and new developments. Otherwise, the management style will begin to slow down into a series of multiple, overlapping, corrective moves and jury-rigged adaptations designed to smooth down the lively, if somewhat confusing, day-to-day progress towards the major goals. If an overly organized leadership style leads to the progressive diminution of creative problem-solving by the members of the management team, an overly conciliatory style can lead to a lack of clear objectives and deadlines.

Once again, the ability to tap into an intuitive frame of mind can allow busy managers to select clear criteria among the conflicts inherent in multiple and evolving responses to a dynamic and unstable situation. Creating synthesis from conflict without confusion or stress requires the detached talent of a jazz musician, who leads and creates simultaneously without losing the beat or the direction of the overall composition, and without slighting or unfairly showcasing any particular instrument. Intuitive managers, like talented athletic coaches, earn the respect of their colleagues and subordinates alike by the ability to build on the past and prepare for the future on a moment-to-moment basis. There simply is no time to take a new opinion poll every few days, or hold a strategy session every time a change impacts on the plan. Ongoing conflicts must be met, and synthesized into ongoing modifications in a manner characterized by constant reframing of criteria in a clear and well-communicated manner. If the team is to work together, they must know that the manager is firm in his or her goals, and yet flexible at the same time; sensitive to situational imperatives while keeping to the overall objectives of the work.

Direct Effects of Intuitive Management Style

The combined pressures of change, complexity and conflict are a global phenomenon, as mentioned in chapter 1. They have an impact on us all daily in both obvious and subtle ways and contribute to a growing sense of confusion and chaos. The rise of religious demagogues and popular gurus illustrates the common and sometimes dangerous tendency for people to seek and promote any person or system which purports to provide stable and reassuring philosophies and structures in this time of rapid reassessment of our purpose and place in life.

In a world of constant metamorphosis, management cannot act as a restraining factor. This leads only to a build-up of pressure and an eventual breakdown of any system trying to impose its own authority on the disparate parts of the global network which characterizes modern business. Managers must provide a form of guidance which is appropriate for our times – a focusing of energy and resources rather than the restraints of an unnecessarily mechanical system. As the poet Robert Frost once noted, 'Freedom is moving easily in harness'. A harness is not rigid, but quite flexible; and in the hands of a driver who knows the path and the direction, it can link and yoke together the power of a number of individual horses. When we recall that the same Sanskrit word is at the root of both 'yoke' and 'yoga', we are again faced with the image of bringing powers together under a system which can combine and guide. As a yoke links the oxen, so a yogi attempts to link the personal with the universal, to tap the powers beyond his or her own accepted limitations.

In the same manner, intuition can help managers by allowing them to link the internal and external, so that the organization is, in fact, organic and whole rather than confused and complex. To delineate this more precisely, one can reduce the direct effects of intuitive management style into three clear categories.

Creating a Vision

First, such a style allows managers to tap into an ongoing vision of the purposes and ultimate ends of any enterprise, even as it is moving forward. 'Lifting off' for an intuitive look is almost like the captain climbing up to the crow's-nest to scan the sea before him. Goals can be seen in a consecutive rather than a static fashion, and the enterprise can continue its progress without having to stop and reassess the situation whenever change or conflict begin to mount. It is almost an axiom today in the business world that unless you innovate you cannot survive. Moreover, even if one is successful so far, to maintain success one has to innovate continually. How does one do it? Innovation does not just happen. Besides having a desire for and a positive attitude towards innovation, one needs to develop a capacity, a skill for formulating a vision and for understanding and reading reality in a different way, and the insight to identify the leverage points for adopting and implementing the appropriate strategy.

Even if one is aware of this at a personal, group or corporate level, one encounters much resistance towards innovation at a psychological level. People may talk favourably about innovation, but deep down, generally, people feel uncomfortable and insecure about it because it implies change, which creates uncertainty and therefore anxiety, which lead to resistance.

One of the most positive and effective ways of overcoming such resistance is to convert this negative, stressful feeling into a positive energy. This is possible if one can generate a sense of courage in those who experience anxiety about innovation and change and therefore resist. Over and over again it has been found that the creation of a shared vision within the organization results in the release of an incredible amount of positive energy towards the realization of a commonly experienced and owned dream. The process helps in creating an understanding of the innovative thrusts, an acceptance of them and finally a positive commitment to them (see figure 2.1). The process of vision building – the steps for developing a reflective, intuitive and integrative vision – are described in chapter 8, which focuses on the application of intuition.

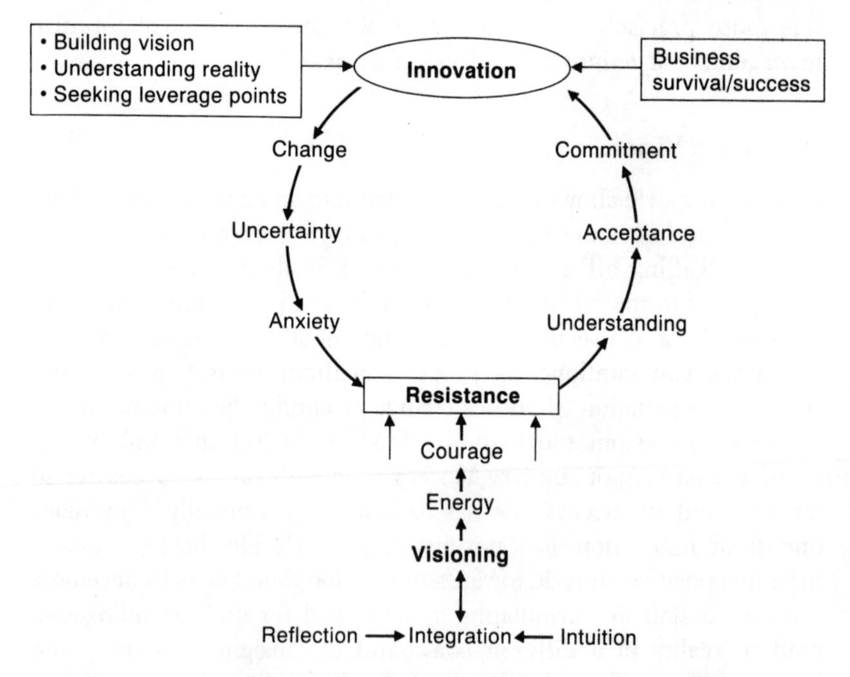

Figure 2.1 Creating a shared vision

Choosing a Direction

Second, once goals are visualized, this activity leads naturally to choosing the most direct path for the efficient attainment of these goals. By helping managers to choose and adopt a direction for the organization, intuition enables them to devise clear strategies to accomplish these goals.

Making a Decision

Finally, with directions defined and strategies delineated, managers are much more capable of reaching decisions as to which tasks should be performed, and in which order, so as to keep all the parts and personnel of the project moving together in harmony. From the ultimate overview to the daily assignment of tasks, an intuitive style can be one of the most useful management tools for accomplishing the desired results with a minimum of false starts, wasted efforts or frayed tempers.

A refined sense of intuition in management helps one to gain a better day-to-day grasp of unfolding situations, without constraining the steady motion towards projected and accepted goals. In the long run, the ability to maintain an internal intuitive 'compass' continually synthesizes new conflicts into shared challenges. In the medium term, this same ability allows one to identify those new directions that lend themselves to clear strategies. Only then can managers make the decisions as to which tasks should be addressed from one moment to the next.

Conclusion

Creating a visual image of goals which can be shared, choosing the directions which lend themselves to strategic decision-making, and making those decisions which delineate specific objectives into definable tasks can be easily accomplished with a well-developed capacity for intuitive judgement on a moment-to-moment basis. Only in this manner can modern managers ever hope to escape being overcome by the problems of change, complexity and conflict characteristic of the modern business environment.

To develop the ability to maintain a wise outlook – one which is constant, consistent, and communicated through clear criteria throughout the organization – one must go beyond the calculations of conscious, quantitative decision-making. One can gain a significant advantage by putting some time into learning the meaning, and the usefulness, of intuitive insight as a management tool.

Intuition helps to strengthen our common sense in action, keeps us unchanged in the midst of the change and simple in the face of complexity, and helps to provide clear criteria when surrounded by conflicting pressures and opportunities. With the development of one's intuitive abilities, the creation of a wise outlook from intuitive insights ultimately serves managers far better than another management training programme or a faster computer.

We seem to be moving, in an evolutionary sense, from muscle power as the early major vehicle for progress, through brain power, and now towards consciousness/intuition power, or, metaphorically speaking, from hand through head towards heart. To quote Blaise Pascal, 'Le coeur a ses raisons que la raison ne connaît point: on le sait en mille choses' ('The heart has its reasons which reason does not know at all: one experiences this in a thousand things').

Intuition is more than a toy for the psychic or the inspiration for the artist. It is a method for our mental and physical development for a new age of humane and responsive stewardship over the resources of our world. It is one of the most important abilities we can cultivate. It can do more than make us financially successful as managers. It can help us fulfil ourselves as individuals, strengthen our enterprise, and ultimately give us the creative and questing openness of vision which is becoming necessary for a comprehensive personal and global perspective.

From the global to the personal, relying on intuition is already helping some managers cut through the build-up of information, the complexity of life, and the conflicts of existence in our new global society. Standing between the needs of the person and the needs of the project, twenty-first-century managers must more than ever gently harness the mental and physical energies of the many to the goals of the organization. For this, managers will need something going beyond calculation and analysis. They will need to be intuitive people who can interpret their feelings and their hunches into a clear and appropriate management style.

3

Defining Intuition

> At any given moment one is conscious of only a small section of what one knows. Intuition allows one to draw on that vast storehouse of unconscious knowledge that includes not only everything that one has experienced or learned either consciously or subliminally, but also the infinite reservoir of the collective or universal unconscious, in which individual separateness and ego boundaries are transcended.
>
> *Frances E. Vaughan,*
> *American psychologist*

Professional managers are aware of the need to define problems before they can be solved, and solutions before they can be effectively implemented. A lack of a shared definition of the purpose of any project can lead not only to confusion but to a serious waste of energy; without a focus, efforts can easily go astray. Definition seems crucial to understanding, no matter what the ultimate purpose may be.

But how do we define a phenomenon which occurs only when it is needed; or a talent which appeared without a teacher? In athletics and the performing arts, we can appreciate skill and we can applaud talent, but no two people can really define either of them in a way that explains the manner of a fast triple play on the baseball diamond or the emotional impact of a gifted musician. When it comes to the topic of intuition, this problem of definition acts as a barrier both to investigation of the phenomenon and to the process of learning techniques which are reported to improve an individual's ability to make use of it.

One of the reasons that intuition continues to resist definition is that it seems so often to be completely idiosyncratic. It is used by people in all areas of their lives, as if it were a universal skill, but remains intensely personal to each. This results in definitions which tend to resemble the definer more than the phenomenon itself.

To illustrate the wide variations in the perception of the term 'intuition', we sought out the help of experts in a number of areas who would be willing to provide a definition from the point of view of their own specialities. The following tabulation attempts to articulate a somewhat simplistic summary and points out the different standpoints from which different areas perceive and treat the concept of intuition.

Area	*Intuition as*
Philosophy	Insight (knowledge)
Epistemology	Process (skills)
Psychology	Trait (attitude)
Arts	Creative expressions
Neuroscience	Chemical processes
Mysticism	Altered states of consciousness

Comparing these varying points of view, it becomes obvious that intuition is hardly a myth. Furthermore, beyond being simply a multidisciplinary phenomenon, intuition lends itself to a multilevel approach as well. It is not a concept without description, but neither is it a phenomenon that lends itself easily to detailed examination.

Intuition as a Multidimensional Phenomenon

Intuition as a Skill

At the most practical and somewhat mechanical level, intuition is often defined as if it were a skill that one can develop, much as one can develop or improve musical or artistic skills by practice under the guidance of an expert. It is this dimension which is most often discussed and explored in articles, essays and symposia directed at modern management professionals. This is not unusual, since managers are usually looking for techniques which can be acquired by any individual willing to spend some time in the study and practice usually required to master a new skill.

Once again, the elusive nature of a phenomenon which apparently cannot be studied in the absence of a personal context results in a number of differing theories, many of which are highly personal in nature. Buddhist and Hindu philosophies seem to aim at those practices which use one-pointed concentration to develop a mind both open and attentive to greater possibilities, rather than previous presuppositions. Western practitioners of intuition 'training' typically are more likely to stress goal-oriented techniques, such as positive visualization, which concentrate on the attainment of defined goals and help to develop one's mental confidence and capabilities in the process. As goal-oriented or goalless exercises, these practices range from the disciplined meditative training typical of serious religious practitioners, to the weekend 'sensitivity training' seminars which have been, and personal growth workshops which are now, in vogue among Western managers.

Intuition as a Trait

Competing with those who define intuition as a skill which can be developed by any normal person, and improved through the practice of specific techniques, is another group of social psychologists, who perceive intuition not as a skill, but as a trait. In this instance, nature, rather than nurture, plays the predominant role in the ability to exhibit the phenomenon.

Intuition, to these investigators, could be an inherent trait more available to certain types, or available under certain conditions, rather than a technique available, on call, to all who practise a certain form of mental training. Among those in this second group are psychologist-philosophers such as Carl Gustav Jung, whose concept of the 'collective unconscious' is well known. Based on the Jungian analysis, the Myers Briggs Test classifies individuals into specific psychological types:

- perceptual/judgemental;
- extrovert/introvert;
- sensing/intuiting;
- thinking/feeling.

According to this view, certain individuals are more 'intuitive' than others. In other words, intuition is an innate personality trait and intuitive ability is somehow inherent in some types of people, and not in others. Other traits are often found combined with the intuitive sense, but the talent is provided by inherited genes rather than by any attempts to refine an ability found in all of us.

In fact, most people describe intuition as a sort of talent, a lucky twist in the DNA. After reviewing a very lengthy recommendation on an important general due a promotion in World War II, it is recorded that Winston Churchill placed himself squarely in this camp when he looked at the recommender and said, 'But you have not told me anything about the most important aspect of this man. Is he lucky?'

Intuition as Being

There is a third dimension to intuitive behaviour which has also been noted by several authors and authorities. It is when the intuitive skill, or trait, becomes the predominant mode of an individual's work and life.

This does not often lead to an easy interface with the multiple structures of civilization. The power of our technology over the organic world we came from is the power to repeat. Only with repetition come skill and mastery in the world around us. We mastered the earth because we could repeat our efforts until we achieved our ends.

Nothing in the natural world has ever repeated, excepting in a very general sense. Nothing in the world of technology works if things do not repeat in a very specific sense. This sets up a difficult role for the predominantly intuitive, who live in a daily synthesis of identity, a free-flowing but attentive manner which is guided by a conscious decision to follow not any specific goals, but a straight path in accordance with personal intuition.

This is frequently accompanied by great success in the various fields of endeavour in which these people have been found. They are usually regarded as original leaders, whether their aims are internal, external or eternal. We all know of Pope John XXIII, the Dalai Lama, or numerous other religious figures from either hemisphere, and have celebrated these great saints and intuitive spiritual guides.

On more earthly planes, there are the significantly intuitive who have illuminated one area or another: the Einsteins, the Henry Fords or the Jim Lears. How could Lear have invented the car radio, Motorola, the 8-track tape player, and the Lear Jet after having gone to school only until the age of 14? What talent allows a Mahatma Gandhi to intuit the psyche of an entire nation, or propels a Chuck Yeager past the speed of sound? Other original and catalytic masters of technology are Edwin Land of Polaroid, Robert Watson of IBM and Harold Edgerton of MIT, all of whom had to draw from their intuitive wells.

However brilliant their calculations, their mind-sets and personalities are often far from analytical when not caught up in the specific project at hand. The original theoretician of computer sciences,

Norbert Wiener, founder of the science of cybernetics, met Albert Einstein only once, by chance, on a train travelling along the side of Lake Geneva in Switzerland. Wiener recounted that during the entire hour that they travelled together, they never once spoke of either physics or mathematics, but were mainly enthralled by the poetry of the colours in the clouds and the lake – the arenas of imagination and intuition. The world was speaking; and they listened together in appreciation and delight – the receptive attitude conducive to intuition.

In moments such as these, we can observe that those giants of intuition who have shaped the patterns of our very lives are hardly lost in a spiritual trance. They are always acting within a real-world context. Nor does the mind-set of the intuitive being have anything to do with the emotional manipulations of some clever or popular leaders. These are merely charisma. Individuals totally guided by intuition are both open and giving, aware of the world, and sensitive to life. In them, the barriers between experience and reflection are nearly nonexistent.

For many of us, however, there at least seems to be a general agreement that intuition is something like a talent, which may be inherent in all of us, and capable of being developed. If it is a skill, it is most definitely available to all who learn the various methods to enhance it.

Intuition as a Multicontextual Phenomenon

Another reason that intuition has been hard to define is that it is a phenomenon with no specific time period for its effects to be seen or acted upon. A talent for dancing does not desert dancers if they have to dash out of the path of an automobile. Likewise, intuitive managers may discover that there are all sorts of contexts for intuitive abilities.

Instant Response

When everything seems to be going out of control, intuitive abilities come alive in the reactions and decisions of those capable of crisis management. The dollar is down, we buy Arabian oil at how much? Is this man telling us the truth about his financial backing? Is there something to that pattern in the print-out or the unexpected reaction in the beaker?

Short-Term

Short-term intuition is probably the area of most interest to managers. Although it is handy to be able to rely on an intuitive ability to get out of a difficult place, most of the time things are not so stressful, and intuition has a longer time frame. This is the process of 'feeling out' the problem, 'getting a feeling' for the project, or trusting one's 'gut feeling'. In all of these descriptions of intuition, the word 'feeling' appears, demonstrating a clear separation from the analytical or logical reasoning process by which we normally make our decisions.

In the work of the physician, this talent can lead to an uncanny ability for diagnosis. In the business professional, it is called an uncanny feel for the market. The word 'canny' comes from 'can' in the sense 'to know how'. The very term 'uncanny', once again, suggests a power that is beyond the logical – even beyond creativity, or cleverness.

The ability to diagnose problems created by rapid change, complexity and conflict may require an intuitive frame of mind to achieve the best results. As practices and exercises which can promote intuitive ability are usually followed on a regular basis, the ability to rely on our intuitive as well as our analytical judgement, then, is one which can increase over time. This sort of talent seems to require a relaxed frame of mind; it can almost be an excuse for taking a break to let things fall into place, and get a feel for the situation.

As they are not associated with emergencies, these short-term intuitions are characterized by the ability to step back mentally and emotionally and size things up. This short-term, soft-focus intuition is probably the sort most enhanced by the various techniques which will be discussed in the next chapter, and, as diagnostic enhancement, is probably the most valuable to the professional manager.

Ongoing

Finally, there is the intuition which, for some people, never turns off. This is the ongoing intuitive ability of individuals who have learned the value of intuition as a personal driving force, as well as a useful tool in an emergency, or to get a good feel for a situation.

The practice of an intuitive lifestyle is not the wilfulness of the self-indulgent dilettante who confuses instant gratification with confidence of being. One can be always in touch with one's feelings and still not be a slave to one's whims. To be open and childlike is the gift of the wise; to be self-centred and childish is the tendency of the individual who still wants to control a process totally, rather than be sensitive to it.

Long-term intuitive ability will always have an effect on individuals that reaches far beyond the workplace. Even personal areas such as clothing, diet and social activities fall within the scope of the ongoing practice of personal intuition.

It seems then that intuition is not restricted to any particular time frame. It can appear in the context of a snap decision, a gut feeling or even a lifestyle. It always appears in context, but the contextual expression can be as varied as the individual and as long, or as short, as necessary. Good intuition is, like energy, ultimately a conserved phenomenon. Whether in an instant, an hour or a lifetime, there is never too much.

Intuition as a Multilevel Phenomenon

The mind has many levels and only one of them is the conscious and rational. Since professional managers are usually skilled in the logical manipulation of acquired data, it would seem that the ability to call other levels into play would be an advantage if it could be done with any regularity and trust: 'Use it or lose it!' If intuition is a phenomenon generated at another level, we need another level of language to express or explain realizations that words cannot express. It would certainly help to explain the difficulty of definition if it were determined that intuition was inherently unexplainable. Intuition could well be a form of intelligence at a level we simply cannot access with rational thought. To aid in the examination of this possible aspect of intuition, 'consciousness' has been divided into four hierarchical levels: logical consciousness, subconsciousness, unconsciousness and supraconsciousness.

Logical Consciousness

At the most mechanical and analytical level is the logical consciousness with which we normally think and communicate. This is the part of our mind with which we are consciously in touch during most of our waking hours. It is a consciousness which is in direct contact with the sensory data input.

Normal thinking consciousness is characterized by a dependence on observable, and hopefully provable, phenomena. It holds the patterns of our perceptions, our knowledge and our beliefs. It tends to be selective, so that information not according to our current interest may not be perceived at all.

The information available in this form of consciousness requires ongoing contact with, and attention to, the specific source of whatever information is being reviewed. It cannot function, it seems, in and of itself. It needs a context which is not only conscious, but can be communicated as well. This is the supercalculator aspect of human mental activity, the Cartesian aspect of the mind. It cannot work without a subject, and its basic object is to keep us alert and alive in the here and now.

Subconsciousness

The subconscious level of the mind is always active as well, but it is usually not available to the conscious mind. However, it is similar to logical consciousness in the sense that information available to it was acquired at the same time as the information used in our waking, conscious perceptions.

For instance, if a manager is scanning the literature for a certain article, he or she cannot avoid reading the names of dozens of other articles with similar names. Once entered, that data is as much a part of the memory as any other – the difference is only in the number of re-entries. If we recognize the face of a friend in a crowd, we also see other faces on both sides, and these are retained in our visual memory even though we cannot access them consciously. The information is not organized for conscious retrieval; it is not strung on a line of thought.

Likewise, we hear things when we are not listening, we understand things we do not think about, and the mind knows where your left hand is when you are attending to the spoon in your right hand. Taken together, there is a vast amount of subconscious memory available to each of us. Most have read accounts of the ability of hypnosis to access these 'forgotten' areas. The existence of this subconscious has been accepted by even the most rational among us.

It is entirely likely that information from the subconscious is always interfacing with the conscious. It could add a subtle amount of data, and influence a decision, but would be defined as a gut feeling. There would be no conscious memory to review.

Many theories and techniques which attempt to stimulate 'creative problem-solving' are designed to help individuals bridge the gap between the selective conscious mind and the more unorganized, more holistic, subconscious mind. Being sensitive to the resonances which occur when a subconscious thought is useful to a conscious plan or strategy is one way to gain a subtle edge. Furthermore, since that vast trove of information is disorganized, it can at times deal with systems more complex than those which can be figured out in our conscious minds. We are consciously inhibited by what we consider real; the subconscious deals with possibility.

Once again, we should note that many of these techniques tend to emphasize a relaxed and reflective mental state as the most receptive to creativity and intuitive advantage. If we relax conscious language and organization, the subconscious can make itself known in all its richness of experience which we have just 'forgotten'. We all have more to work with than we know; and most managers would be glad to learn how to use that additional dimension with greater regularity. It costs no extra.

Unconsciousness

There is a level below the subconscious, however, more basic and more disorganized. This is the level of the true unconscious. This is where memories which are nearly biochemical interact with the world at a level completely outside contact. A mother feels when her child is in danger; a manager knows that a recession is coming. There has been no sensory contact, for either conscious or subconscious retrieval; but there is still a sense of something which can prompt action. This is the realm of ESP, where the uncanny ability to connect at some other level is not along any familiar lines. Does the body remember the heartbeats and count them down in some vastly unconscious way so that a parent's death is announced by a dream hundreds of miles away?

Intuition could originate here, as far from the subconscious as the subconscious is from the logical conscious. If consciousness is the sun that directs and illuminates our life, this unconsciousness would be outside the solar system. It would be like an Oort Cloud, the vastly distant place which gives birth to the comets which come into our solar system, and have their effects completely outside the rules that govern the power of the sun.

Still, these intuitive feelings are grounded in our perceptions about ourselves. We are in contact with another mind, perhaps, but it is a particular other mind. We have a sense of emergency about a child, or a project – but it is about that particular child or project. Where logical consciousness uses clearly remembered data, and subconsciousness uses all the other available data that happened to be there (inside one's skin), unconsciousness uses all the other available data that happened to be out there. Unconsciousness does not rely on having a previous sensory experience. It is an original mental event with its source in the connection to other minds and/or matter.

Supraconsciousness

There remains, then, one final level. Although the most difficult to define, this could, like computer source code, be a universe of pervasive intelligence subtly and nearly invisibly showing itself only when we lose sight of ourselves. It is like the combined light coming from a starry sky on a moonless night – infinite specks of intelligence, as meaningless to the mind as a million ones patterned among a universal nothingness of zero limitations.

To understand what is really going on you have to get completely outside your personal frame of reference. Staring at the night sky, Einstein had a hunch which led him finally to the theory of relativity. In the moments that we lose touch with the details, and open ourselves to the truly universal aspects of the mind, the very greatest and most universal ideas may suddenly appear.

The 'background intelligence', which goes beyond the biochemical intelligence that provides our sensory organs with their many powers, is so diffuse that specific attribution of the cause is impossible, even in the sense of the communications received by the unconscious. This pervasive mind communication has been recently studied in a series of Japanese experiments in which some monkeys on separated islands were taught to wash the food with which they had been supplied by the researchers. Unexpectedly, when a certain number of monkeys had learned to wash their raw yam slices, other monkeys in colonies on completely separated islands began doing the same. It was always a numerical phenomenon. The effect did not happen until a certain number had learned. It was referred to as the 'hundredth monkey phenomenon': one more monkey seemed to be enough, in some instances, to put the idea into a sort of monkey mind circulation. The well-known British scientist Rupert Sheldrake calls this 'morphic resonance'.

There are movements that seem to erupt spontaneously in different parts of a country, as if there were some common communication line available to all of us at the most basic, the most universal level. Here, at a level beyond any understanding, or even feeling, there can arise a sense of knowing. It is known to all the very wise people of any age. From this place comes the basis of the universal mind, since every other level requires greater and greater restriction and selection.

We are all in contact with this level all the time. We just cannot know it unless we notice that we seem to be in tune with the times, unsurprised and at ease with cultural and philosophical insights which affect individuals, groups and sometimes entire peoples.

This is the intuition we all tap into as a people, or as a person in the way we exhibit our own creative and original variation of the universal wisdom of our species. When it is time for the supraconscious to move, some will move with it, as energy travels through the water in a wave, until it washes onto the shore of consciousness. Just as the waves constantly rearrange a shoreline, so supraconsciousness constantly rearranges the basics of human life as humans constantly evolve and develop. If intuition results from the interactions between these other levels of consciousness, it is easy to understand why any specific definition would prove limiting. Definitions by themselves work only within the levels of mental activity, and not between them. If intuition is the spark that arcs between the subconscious and the logical conscious, or between the supraconscious and the unconscious, it must be the essence of communication and fundamentally hardly the sort of phenomenon which would stay around to be measured or examined.

Figure 3.1 illustrates these four levels of consciousness and the corresponding levels and kinds of mental processing. The arrows pointing inwards are indicative of the continuous flow of intuition available to us. Notice the dotted circumferences of all the circles except the innermost, indicating the general resistance of the logical mind.

Intuition as Noun, Verb, Adjective

Cutting across this variety of perceptions, multidimensional, multicontextual and multilevel, one notices that the phenomenon of intuition has aspects as a noun, a verb or even an adjective (see figure 3.2).

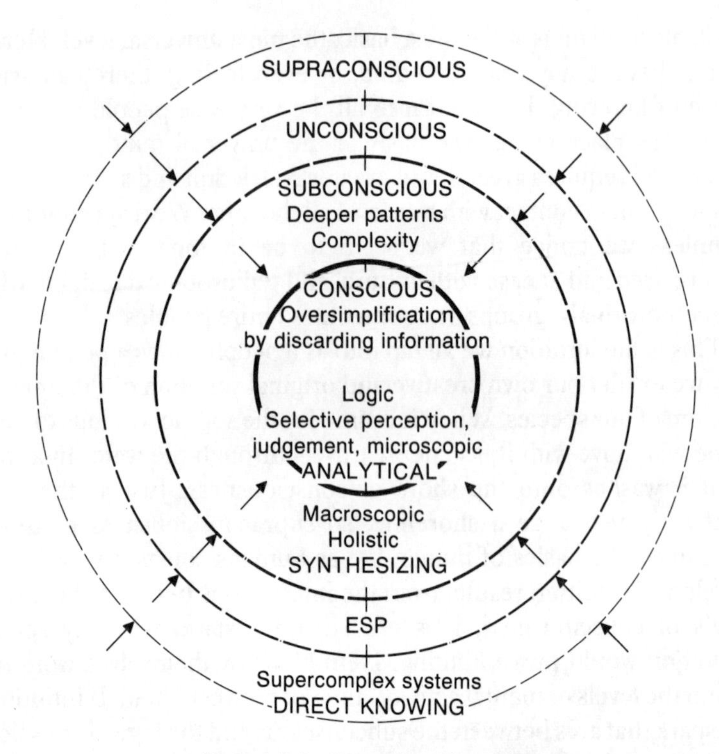

Figure 3.1 Structure of intuition

Noun

The process of intuition results in a certain kind of perception based on various levels of consciousness, ranging from the ordinary sensory consciousness to supraconsciousness. However, the next stage in our thinking after perception is judgement, as is very lucidly explained by Carl Jung. This judgement is also referred to as an intuition. It may be about fundamental reality or about a particular, immediate situation. There can be a whole range of people, events, things or ideas about which one can have an intuition or judgement.

Verb

Seen in the aspect of a verb, 'intuition' refers to the process of intuition. It is an internally experienced phenomenon, but it is also influenced by external elements. To understand this, we need to look at the structure of intuition.

Figure 3.1 illustrates the structure of intuition, showing the four

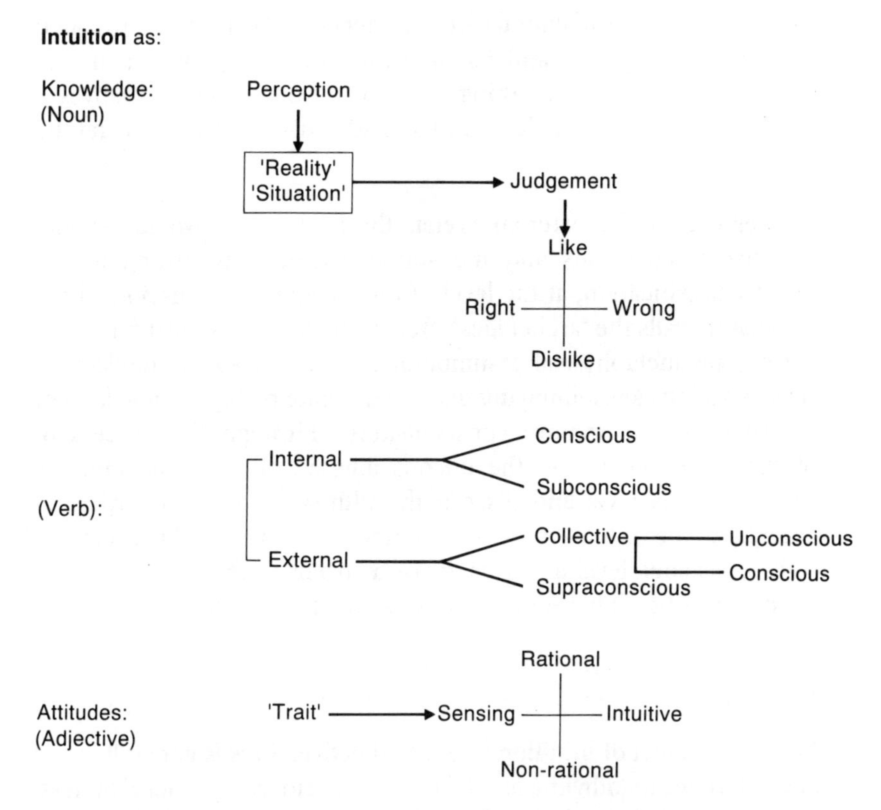

Figure 3.2 Intuition as noun, verb and adjective

levels of consciousness, namely the logical conscious, subconscious, collective unconscious (including the personal unconscious) and the supraconscious. In a sense, the logical conscious and the subconscious dimensions refer to one's internal process, whereas the collective unconscious and supraconscious refer to the external ('outside the skin') phenomena.

Referring to the internal experience at the logical conscious and subconscious levels, there are two components of intuition:

1 At the conscious level, it consists of recognition of a pattern, or what could be described as 'if . . . then' statements, and retrieving them rapidly without the conscious use of logic or analytical steps. This is also described as rapid inference.
2 At the subconscious level, the process consists of accessing the

internal reservoir of cumulative experience and expertise developed over a period of years, and distilling out of that a response, or an urge to do or not to do something, or choose from some alternatives – again, without being able to understand consciously how we get the 'answers'.

Referring to the external arena, there are also two levels: the collective unconscious and the supraconscious. According to the Jungian classification, at the level of the collective unconscious there are what he calls the 'archetypes'. According to the mystical traditions and certain metaphysical assumptions, there is also the (collective) supraconscious level, implying that the ultimate reality is some kind of pattern or order or pure consciousness. Through the process of intuition one can access the unconscious as well as tune into the supraconscious level and discern the ultimate pattern or order. In either case, the intuitive process generates a resonance which surfaces at the conscious level as an image or a strong feeling or a clear and compulsive urge. This entire process is an intuitive one.

Adjective

The third aspect of intuition is as an adjective. This is generally used with reference to individuals, who may be considered as 'more' or 'less' intuitive. In other words, it refers to intuition more as a skill or attitude. Here again, according to Jungian classification, one can base one's perception and judgement either on one's senses or on one's internal intuition.

To weave the above three aspects of intuition into one statement and thereby summarize the total concept: 'An intuitive (adjective) person can intuit (verb) and experience an intuition (noun).'

We can now turn to the arena of the application of intuition as a verb or a noun or even an adjective. The use and application of intuition are so widespread in practically all fields of human endeavour that it can be described as an all-pervading phenomenon. However, to select just a few dominant disciplines – namely philosophy, epistemology, psychology, arts and aesthetics, neuroscience and mysticism – one may identify the kinds of application of intuition in each (see figure 3.3).

Taking the arena of philosophy, there are two basic approaches: that of those who recognize intuition and that of those who do not – intuitionism and empiricism. Those philosophers who believe in intuition would describe it as a direct, non-inferential and immediate

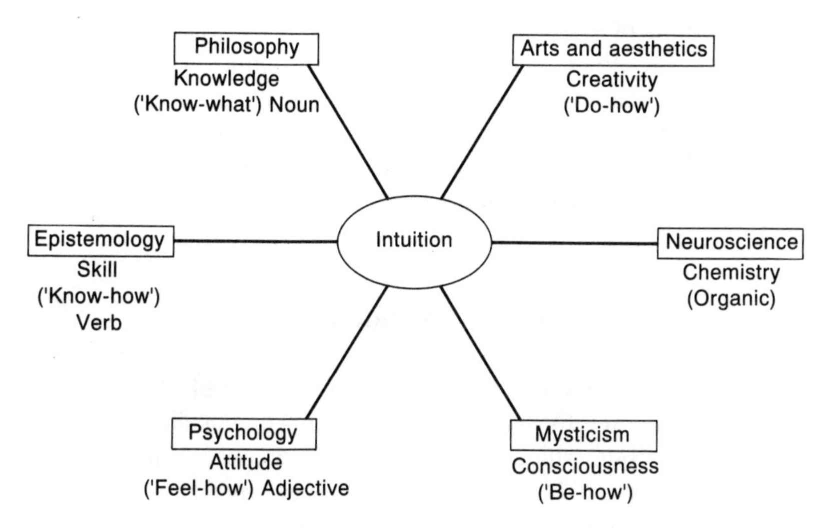

Figure 3.3 Multiple facets of intuition

knowing. This may be 'truth' about a priori or ultimate reality or about anything else. The second approach, namely empiricism, which does not recognize intuition, considers what may appear as intuition as still an inference. According to this view, all knowledge is inferential.

Under philosophy the concern is about knowledge. The main thrust is about what is to be known. Therefore intuition here is in the nature of a noun. In the second discipline, namely epistemology, the main thrust is about how we know what we know; this refers more to the process or skill and therefore seems to be treating intuition as a verb. In psychology, one of the major interests is in developing insights about human nature and traits. Here we have a very interesting classification given by Jung of various human styles of processing information. According to Jung, there are two basic aspects of information processing: perception and judgement. In terms of perception, people fall into two broad categories: those who perceive on the basis of their intuition and others who depend primarily upon their sensory experiences. In terms of judgement, too, people fall into two types: those who depend upon their rational thinking and others who depend more upon their feelings. In other words, there are persons who may be more intuitive than others as part of their personality traits. Here intuition is treated more as a trait of a person, or as an adjective. Taking the arena of arts, intuition is the source and substance of creative and artistic expression. Neuroscience is concerned with the chemistry of the brain at an organic level – in other words, a study of the configuration of the brain waves and their patterns or the neural networks and their behaviour when the intuitive processes are supposed to be operating. Finally, in the arena of the mystical traditions, the main interest is in various levels of consciousness or 'being'. The intuitive level is supposed to be that when one is in tune with pure consciousness: intuition as a way of life.

What Intuition is Not

It is clear that intuition is many things to many people. However, the common element is that intuition is something practically everyone has experienced, but which hardly anyone has been able to define precisely. In view of this, one may be tempted to say that people have an 'intuitive' understanding of what it is!

The most important thing in this context, therefore, is to ensure, as far as possible, an understanding of what intuition may not be. There are many experiences similar to that of intuition which we need to be clear about, so that they are not confused with the experience of authentic intuition.

Instinct

Instinct is supposed to be an inherent, organismic intelligence that serves the purpose of survival in both humans and non-humans. Its core characteristic is that it is outside the threshold of awareness. It is an inbuilt mechanism that automatically leads to activities for survival unless consciously interfered with. Such interference is observed only among human beings. Instinct thus appears to be almost the opposite of intuition, if the latter is characterized by heightened awareness.

Impulse

Impulse is a momentary kick-back to a stimulus. We may call it programmed reaction. It appears to be a way of behaving based on past habits, influences, training, preconceived notions, etc. In popular language we often call it impulsive, implying thoughtless action. It must of course be distinguished from spontaneous action, which, although immediate, is aware and without inhibition. Impulsive behaviour is programmed and has the quality of compulsiveness. A bull is programmed to attack the red cape of the matador; a human being can be programmed to react negatively to certain signs and symbols.

Ingenuity

Ingenuity works within the field of the known; intuition brings the unknown into play. Ingenuity can find new connections, new uses, new combinations, but within the perimeter of old materials, conceptual or physical. Its raw material is known knowledge – for example, it develops a new recipe using old ingredients.

Inspiration

Inspiration is an experiential phenomenon rather than a conceptual one. We speak of our spirits lifting, of opening a door to the cosmic world, of a heightened state of living which sometimes may lead to creative expressions, etc. We speak of the composer being 'inspired' to create a new symphony.

Intellect or Intelligence

Intellect is a function of the mind closely related to ingenuity – a high degree of intellect is necessary for a computer analyst's work, for example. Intelligence, on the other hand, is wisdom involving discretion, understanding, perceiving appropriateness, ability to see things in a total perspective, clarity and sharpness of perception, etc. Intelligence comes closest to intuition.

Inclination or Wishful Thinking

There is no clear way to distinguish between intuition and wishful thinking. There cannot be proof from any 'scientific' (public, quantitative) test since this is in the realm of personal experience. The only thing one can say is that in intuition there is a sense of certainty, a feeling leading to a decision or action, and, most important, an absence of self-motivation. Wishful thinking is a manifestation of the self in search of satisfaction. In wishful thinking one sees what one wishes to see; in intuition one sees what is available without interference from personal likes or dislikes – the personal ego.

Hence the question still remains: how can one distinguish between authentic intuition and wishful thinking? One of the ways in which one can approach this question is to observe certain symptoms supposed to be commonly experienced when one is experiencing authentic intuition.

Symptoms of Authentic Intuition

Body/Physical-Sensory Level

There seems to be a consensus that usually one experiences a kind of warmth, comfort or vibration of positive energy during the intuitive process. Some people even experience a kind of inner voice as a manifestation of intuition.

Mind

It is frequently stated that a different kind or quality of clarity or certainty is experienced in the mind during the intuitive process, which is also more intense.

Emotion

A compulsive urge or feeling of excitement is generally experienced as a consequence of intuition for doing or not doing something.

Neurosensory Level

This area has not been sufficiently researched yet to explore whether there is any particular brain-wave pattern or hemispheric synchrony that could be correlated with the experience of intuition. So far the hypothesis has been that there is a predominance of alpha/theta waves when there are flashes of intuition. It is also hypothesized that there may be a synchrony of these waves in both the left and right brain hemispheres, implying that the amplitude of the waves in both the hemispheres is similar.

Consciousness
It has also been suggested that experience of a different kind of heightened consciousness, luminosity or 'glow' is indicative of authentic intuition.

The above are only pieces of empirical evidence which differ with different individuals. If none of the above symptoms is experienced, it does not necessarily mean that authentic intuition cannot or does not happen. These are enumerated here only as additional information about the kind of symptomic evidence which is believed usually to accompany a genuine intuitive experience.

Conclusion

We seem to be able to agree that intuition has a utility in the work of managers; and we can even narrow down those areas where intuition can be specifically helpful. Finding a working definition, however, appears to be harder. We can ask the experts in many disciplines, and get many answers. We can investigate intuition as a skill, or train it like a talent, or just be sensitive to the management of crises – the diagnostic gut feeling which some can trust better than others – or see it as an ideal mental state.

We still lack the specific coordinates to define this phenomenon in the ways we like to define things. Perhaps in the context of communication between the wordy realm and the worldly realm, between the mind of the self and the mind of the species, between what is and what might be, we can gain some sort of understanding that understanding is not the mechanism which can ever illuminate intuition. If anything, understanding could very well inhibit intuition, just as a definition could limit it.

4

Refining Intuition: Accessing and Enhancing

When I am, as it were, completely myself, entirely alone, and of good cheer – say, travelling in a carriage, or walking after a good meal, or during the night when I cannot sleep; it is on such occasions that ideas flow best and most abundantly. Whence and how they come, I know not; nor can I force them.

Wolfgang Amadeus Mozart (1756–91)

As the title of this chapter implies, there are two elements as far as development of intuition is concerned. One is the stage of accessing intuition and the other is cultivating or enhancing this process of intuition. As has been observed earlier, intuition in a sense is always there, implying that information is everywhere. Take the metaphor of a radio: a radio can be switched on and tuned into a particular frequency, tap into any programme that is broadcast, receive the programme in the form of waves, and convert them into a frequency of sound which the human ear can experience. Much in the same manner, if we have developed a technology or process which we call the intuitive process, then we also can tap into sources of information internally – within us – as well as externally – outside of us – as figure 3.1 illustrated. From this standpoint, one can say that intuition is 'raining down' all the time, but most people, most of the time, have the habit of using an umbrella, thereby blocking the input of 'rain' or 'information' from intuitive sources.

There are several blocks within our own rational mind, so-called thinking, that prevent us from receiving useful information. Therefore, at the first stage of accessing intuition there are two things which must be done: develop receptivity (also called 'preparation'), and have a kind of awareness and attention which enables us to receive the information.

In other words, 'relax' and 'receive' are the two elements of the first stage of accessing intuition. There are many processes which we shall describe shortly which facilitate relaxation and receptivity. In the second stage of enhancing intuition there are again two aspects: creating an insight, and applying it. For this too there are some processes available, which can be described as deliberate intuition.

The first stage is also referred to as passive intuition and the second stage as active or deliberate intuition. The processes, however, which one can learn are common to both stages. Basically they imply, first, creating a relaxed and choiceless awareness for receiving information, and, second, that whenever there is a specific issue or a question, by using specific processes (after reaching the state of choiceless awareness), one can get specific responses.

Choosing a Direction

As shown in figure 4.1, broadly speaking there are two approaches: one is for choosing a direction and the other for making a specific choice or a decision between alternatives. As will be noted, there are five

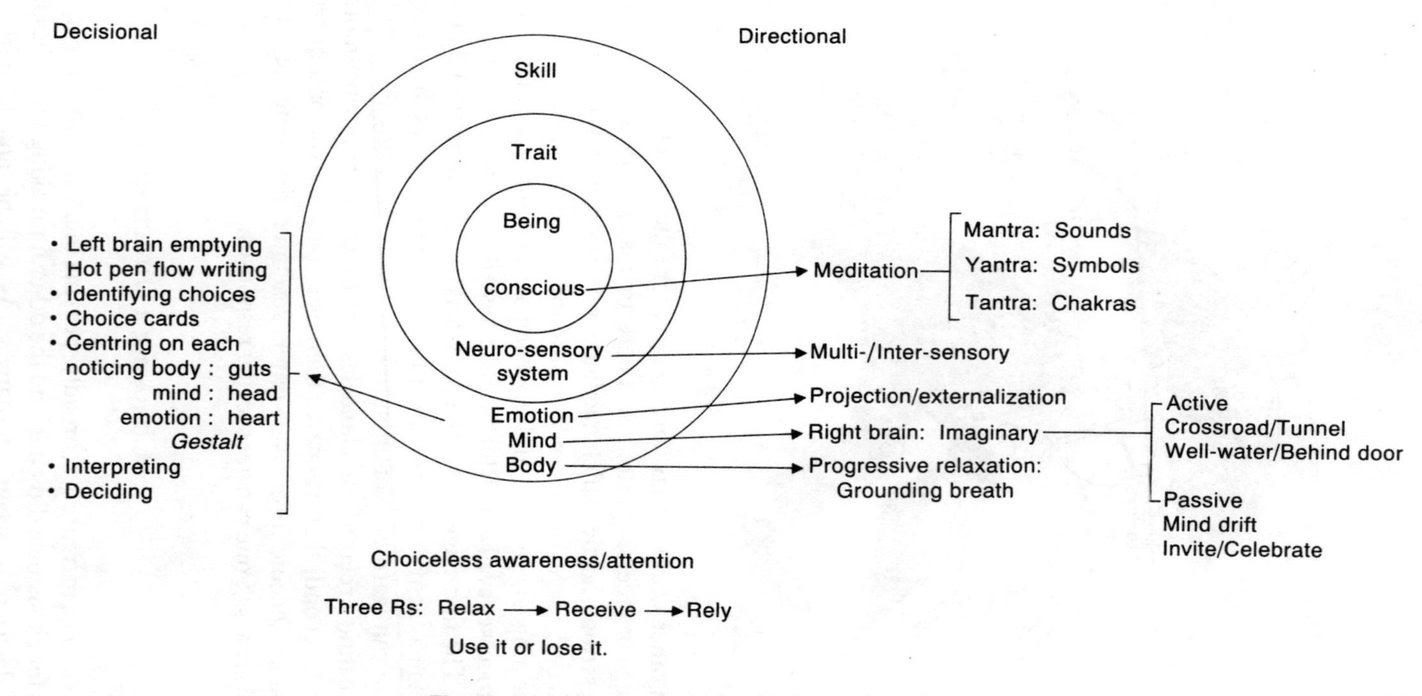

Figure 4.1 How to access and enhance intuition

dimensions of the self: body, mind, emotion, neurosensory system and consciousness.

1 Starting at the body, at the physical level there are several relaxation processes such as deep breathing, progressive relaxation, etc.
2 At the level of the mind, one has two kinds of process: (a) passive and (b) active.
   (a) At the passive level, one allows the mind to wander, the thoughts to become loose and drift, inviting images to flow in. Whatever images appear, they are welcomed and in a sense celebrated, thereby encouraging the images and thoughts, whatever they may be, to flow passively but with positive emotion at witnessing them.
   (b) At an active level, one goes through a guided series of images – either going up the hill, reaching the top and meeting a 'wise person', or going down the hill, into a tunnel, down to a deeper level and there reaching a retreat and meeting a 'wise person'. The dilemma or the question is posed to this person and a dialogue takes place in which some insights may emerge.
3 At the level of emotion, there are processes known as 'projection' or 'externalization'. Here one identifies oneself with any non-living or inanimate object, poses certain questions to one's own self and notices the responses that one receives. In these processes, because one's level of wishful thinking is eliminated by the detachment from oneself and the identification with an inanimate object, one's real subconscious condition – gut-level feelings and information – surfaces.
4 At the neurosensory level, there are processes for the cultivation of multisensory and intersensory perceptual abilities. By sensitizing and enhancing these we can receive more and different kinds of information.
5 And finally at the (pure) consciousness level, there are several processes of meditation which can help in accessing deeper, more intuitive levels of consciousness.

The above processes help in enabling one to 'choose' a direction intuitively.

Making a Decision

The other level of making a decision basically refers to a process of becoming sensitive or developing the ability to 'listen' to the body, the mind and the emotions in response to a specific question or choice to be made from alternatives. In simple terms, what one does in these processes is identify the alternatives from which one has to choose, such as alternatives (a), (b) and (c). Then one has to imagine that one has chosen alternative (a) and, remaining in touch (in imagination) with the situation of alternative (a), and truly believing one has chosen it, ask oneself how one feels about these three dimensions of one's own body, mind and emotion. This involves asking oneself (while remaining in touch with the experience of the chosen alternative) how it feels first in the gut (body), second in the head (mind), third in the heart (emotion), and fourth and finally as a totality (*Gestalt*).

It is really very surprising and quite impressive that one does receive different responses when one asks these questions to the gut, to the head, to the heart and to the totality of oneself. When the responses are positive in all four, then the chances are that one has tapped into an authentic intuition and is not in touch with what one may call one's wishful or ego-related thinking.

5

Global Report: International Survey on Intuition

Introduction to the Survey

The first four chapters have exposed the reader to the authors' views on the nature, importance and role of intuition in various contexts – especially in the decision-making process in purposive organizations. What is missing – a significant void in the relevant literature – is an account of how intuition is perceived by top and senior managers in various countries around the world. To fill this vacuum, we embarked on the International Survey on Intuition to determine how those on the front lines of coping with the world of business 'raplexity' understand and use intuition in their professional and personal lives. In one of the most ambitious projects* of its kind, 1312 managers from relatively large non-governmental industrial and service organizations responded, representing a population estimated at 1.463 million. The nine countries chosen are drawn from highly developed market economies (Austria, France, Japan, the Netherlands, Sweden, the United Kingdon, the United States), middle-income developing countries (Brazil) and low-income developing countries (India).

This chapter and the next report on the overall results of this International Survey on Intuition. The format of each is identical, sharing the following sub-headings:

- profile of the Survey population;
- intuition ratings;
- what is intuition;
- perceived relevance of intuition;

*The research project was sponsored by IMI (Geneva) and later supported by IMD, Lausanne, Switzerland under the chairmanship of Jagdish Parikh.

- how does one identify intuition;
- use of intuition;
- opinions on certain notions;
- views on certain aspects;
- interest in further participation.

By design, the chapters move from the most general synthesis – the global report here – to less broad synthesis – the inter-country report in chapter 6. For those interested in the individual, detailed country reports, these can be found in appendices 2–10, which also share the same structure and sub-headings. Appendix 1 describes the Survey design, while Appendix 11 reproduces the Survey questionnaire itself.

The Survey chapters and appendices provide a wealth of data which undoubtedly will lead to further research and refinement. As of now, this is the best empirical research available on the perceptions of managers around the globe about the role of intuition in their lives.

Profile of the Survey Population

The total number of managers in the nine selected countries conforming to the Survey specifications has been estimated at 1.463 million. A profile of the Survey population, together with a breakdown of the total sample of 1312, are shown in table 5.1. Here and throughout the book, the countries are dealt with in the following order: developed European countries in alphabetical sequence, USA, Japan, Brazil (middle-income developing country) and India (low-income developing country).

It will be seen that (correcting the proportions for NR):

- 12.1 per cent of the managers are females;
- the majority (57.3 per cent) of the managers are relatively advanced in age, being 45 years old or more;
- 39.4 per cent of the managers belong to the industry sector, the balance belonging to the services sector;
- 37.2 per cent of the managers belong to the top level;
- the USA and Japan alone account for as much as 64.0 per cent of the total Survey population, while France, the UK, Brazil and India together account for 30.9 per cent, and the three small countries – Austria, the Netherlands and Sweden – together contribute a mere 5.1 per cent of the total.

Table 5.1 Profile of the Survey population

Category	Sample count	Estimated population (000s)	%	% corrected for NR*
Sex				
Male	1197	1275.3	87.2	87.9
Female	99	175.2	12.0	12.1
NR*	16	12.8	0.9	
Age				
Below 35	112	111.6	7.6	7.7
35–44	497	505.9	34.6	35.0
45–59	614	713.3	48.7	49.3
Over 59	68	116.5	8.0	8.0
NR*	21	16.0	1.1	
Organization type				
Industry	660	557.5	38.1	39.4
Services	643	857.8	58.6	60.6
NR*	9	48.0	3.3	
Functional area				
General management	384	610.8	41.7	44.2
Finance	167	91.4	6.2	6.6
Marketing	179	136.4	9.3	9.9
Production/Operations	165	185.4	12.7	13.4
Human resources development	158	159.6	10.9	11.6
Other	206	197.1	13.5	14.3
NR*	53	82.6	5.6	
Management level				
Senior	538	846.5	57.8	62.8
Top	259	501.0	34.2	37.2
NR*	515	115.8	7.9	
Country				
Austria	114	17.2	1.2	1.2
France	118	106.2	7.3	7.3
Netherlands	89	31.7	2.2	2.2
Sweden	456	24.5	1.7	1.7
UK	52	145.4	9.9	9.9
USA	143	638.7	43.6	43.6
Japan	56	298.4	20.4	20.4
Brazil	204	80.4	5.4	5.4
India	80	120.8	8.3	8.3
Total	1312	1463.3	100.0	100.0

*NR = Not reported.

Intuition Ratings

Objective Rating

Paired alternatives

Responses to the query regarding choice between ten given pairs of alternatives (where one of the terms is taken to indicate orientation towards Intuition and the other towards Logic/Reasoning) yield the pattern shown in table 5.2.

Table 5.2 Choice between paired alternatives

Intuition-oriented		Logic/Reasoning-oriented		Extent of non-expression of preference (%)
Description	Extent of preference (%)	Description	Extent of preference (%)	
1 Invent	44.0	Build	53.8*	2.3
2 Vision	60.0*	Common sense	37.0	3.0
3 Abstract	31.7	Concrete	65.5*	2.8
4 Innovative	79.0*	Conventional	18.2	2.8
5 Creative	67.5*	Analytical	29.9	2.6
6 Ideas	70.8*	Facts	26.5	2.7
7 Imaginative	53.3*	Realistic	44.3	2.4
8 Ingenious	49.0	Practical	48.8	2.3
9 Fascinating	49.4	Sensible	48.4	2.2
10 Spontaneous	52.7*	Systematic	44.5	2.8

*The observed preference is statistically significant (at the 5 per cent level).
The two alternatives in each pair were presented to the respondent in a predetermined random sequence (see question 2 of the questionnaire in appendix 11).

It will be seen that of the eight cases where the observed differences are statistically significant, in as many as six instances the term associated with Intuition was preferred to its counterpart associated with Logic/Reasoning, while it is the other way about in the remaining two cases. This indicates *prima facie* that the Intuition orientation of the Survey population as a whole is of a reasonably high order. A more comprehensive rating of the managers on this dimension is attempted later in this section.

Overall Intuition score

By assigning 1 to the choice indicating orientation towards Intuition and 0 to the one towards Logic/Reasoning, an overall score has been computed for each responding manager. Where there was no indication of preference for one term over the other in a given pair (evidenced by the respondent ticking both the alternatives or leaving the section blank), a score of ½ has been awarded; however, where no clear preference was indicated in respect of even one of the ten given pairs, it has been treated as a case of 'Not reported' (NR). It is clear that the overall score ranges from 0 to 10 in steps of ½.

Classification

Based on the overall intuition score, a three-way classification of managers has been devised as follows:

Score	*Category*
0.0–3.5	L: Low orientation
4.0–6.0	M: Medium orientation
6.5–10.0	H: High orientation

It will be noted that this classification has been used as one of the standard backgrounds in tabulation of the Survey responses. This is referred to as 'objective rating', as distinct from the 'self-rating' carried out by the respondents, which is discussed later.

Distribution

The above classification has led to the distribution shown in table 5.3.

The proportion of female managers rated high, at 50.3 per cent, is significantly larger than the corresponding proportion of 38.4 per cent for male managers (correcting the proportion for 'Not reported' in both cases), indicating that the former may be considered more Intuitive.

By the same yardstick, Intuition orientation appears to peak in the age group 45–59, but the observed differences in the proportion are not statistically significant. The same is true of the differences observed between the industry and services sectors and the senior and top manager groups.

Among the countries, managers in Japan, the USA and the UK appear to be the most Intuitive, while those in Sweden turn out to be the least Intuitive. Considering that Sweden is as developed as these other countries, it is hard to see why it should deviate from the pattern to such a marked extent.

Table 5.3 Distribution based on objective rating on Intuition

Category*	Low (%)	Medium (%)	High (%)	NR (%)
Sex				
Male	21.9	39.2	38.1	0.8
Female	15.1	33.2	48.9	2.8
Age				
Below 35	22.0	41.0	37.0	–
35–44	22.9	36.9	37.7	2.6
45–59	18.7	39.1	41.9	0.2
Over 59	27.5	37.9	34.5	–
Organization type				
Industry	19.8	42.5	36.9	0.8
Services	22.9	35.0	40.9	1.2
Management level				
Senior	20.6	38.2	41.1	0.1
Top	23.8	37.2	36.4	2.6
Country				
Austria	22.7	40.1	37.1	–
France	41.6	29.5	27.1	1.7
Netherlands	30.0	39.9	30.1	–
Sweden	30.5	48.0	18.2	3.3
UK	13.9	43.3	40.6	2.2
USA	20.9	36.1	43.0	–
Japan	10.3	42.4	44.6	2.7
Brazil	20.2	45.7	33.2	0.9
India	33.9	37.1	29.0	–
Total	20.9	38.6	39.5	1.0
(% corrected for NR)	(21.1)	(39.0)	(39.9)	

*NR (= Not reported) omitted from all categories.

Self-Rating

Self-rating by the managers regarding Intuition on a given five-point scale (ranging from very high to very low) has yielded the distribution shown in table 5.4.

It will be seen that, on an overall basis, 65.9 per cent (corrected proportion), or almost two out of three managers, consider themselves above average (very high/high) on Intuition, showing that it is viewed as a positive attribute by the Survey population.

The proportion of female managers rating themselves very high/high on Intuition is significantly larger than the corresponding proportion for male managers. This is quite in tune with the significant difference observed between these two groups in terms of the objective rating discussed earlier.

Table 5.4 Distribution based on self-rating on Intuition

Category*	Very high (%)	High (%)	Average (%)	Low (%)	Very low (%)	NR (%)
Sex						
Male	12.4	51.3	30.9	4.7	0.1	0.5
Female	18.2	62.2	19.1	0.4	–	–
Age						
Below 35	6.7	47.0	42.8	2.7	0.4	0.4
35–44	9.0	54.2	31.6	5.3	–	–
45–59	14.8	53.2	26.9	4.3	0.1	0.7
Over 59	27.3	47.8	23.7	0.2	–	1.0
Organization type						
Industry	12.5	52.2	30.1	4.0	–	1.1
Services	13.5	52.7	29.2	4.5	0.1	–
Management level						
Senior	11.7	50.4	32.0	5.4	–	0.5
Top	15.8	57.6	23.9	2.3	0.1	0.3
Intuition rating†						
Low	5.4	40.9	38.9	14.5	0.3	–
Medium	10.4	45.7	40.2	2.9	–	0.9
High	20.7	64.3	14.7	0.1	–	0.2
Country						
Austria	6.3	50.7	39.0	4.0	–	–
France	10.4	35.6	49.4	3.9	–	0.6
Netherlands	11.7	46.4	29.7	9.4	0.7	2.1
Sweden	8.5	49.7	34.3	6.5	0.5	0.5
UK	11.4	54.7	22.9	8.7	–	2.2
USA	16.9	61.8	19.3	2.0	–	–
Japan	13.8	38.6	41.3	6.3	–	–
Brazil	3.5	47.6	42.0	5.4	0.9	0.5
India	7.9	52.3	36.1	2.6	–	1.0
Total	13.4	52.2	29.7	4.2	0.1	0.4
(% corrected for NR)	(13.5)	(52.4)	(29.8)	(4.2)	(0.1)	–

*NR (= Not reported) omitted from all categories.
†Relates to objective rating presented in table 5.3.

It would appear that Intuition is viewed as a positive attribute to a larger extent by the relatively old managers (45 years or more) than the younger ones. This is further underlined by the fact that the proportion of top managers considering themselves very high/high on Intuition, at 73.4 per cent, is significantly larger than the corresponding proportion of 62.1 per cent for senior managers (correcting the proportion for 'Not reported' in both cases).

While the USA and the UK, which figure at the top in terms of objective rating (proportion of managers rated high), maintain their position in respect to self-rating as well (proportion of managers rating themselves very high/high), the other country in that group, Japan, is bracketed among the least Intuitive in terms of self-rating. On the other hand, Sweden, which has turned out to be the least Intuitive on the basis of objective rating, finds itself in the middle range in terms of self-rating.

Association Between Ratings

The association between the two rating systems can be tested statistically by forming the contingency table shown as table 5.5.

Table 5.5 Objective rating v. self-rating

	Self-rating			
Classification based on objective rating	Average or lower (number)	High (number)	Very high (number)	Total (number)
Low	185	145	20	350
Medium	253	265	36	554
High	91	230	57	378
Total	529	640	113	1282

Thirty managers whose classification is indeterminate in terms of either rating have been omitted from the above cross-tabulation.

It can be seen that the χ^2 (which will have 4 degrees of freedom) for the above contingency table works out to 79.67, which is significant even at the 1 per cent level, confirming the positive association between the two rating systems.

The contingency coefficient, C, works out to 0.24 as follows:

$$C = \sqrt{\frac{\chi^2}{\chi^2 + N}}$$

$$= \sqrt{\frac{79.67}{79.67 + 1282}}$$

$$= 0.24$$

Even allowing for the fact that the maximum value that can be attained by C for a 3×3 contingency table is only 0.82 ($\sqrt{2/3}$), the observed value of C should be considered rather low. This shows that while there is a positive association between the two rating systems, it is only of a moderate order.

What is Intuition?

Descriptions Given of Intuition

The questionnaire used for the Survey (see appendix 11) starts with an invitation to the respondent to describe Intuition as understood by him or her so as to get the top-of-the-mind opinion; that is, a response uninfluenced by the sequence of questions that follows in the questionnaire. This has led to diverse descriptions of Intuition, of which the following are the more important:

Description	%
Decision/perception without recourse to logical/rational methods	23.4
Inherent perception; inexplicable comprehension; a feeling that comes from within	17.1
Integration of previous experience; processing of accumulated information	16.8
Gut feeling	12.0
Decision/solution to problem, without complete data/facts	8.6
Sixth sense	7.4
Spontaneous perception/vision	7.3
Insight	6.7
Subconscious process	6.1
Instinct	5.7

Thus, the dominant perception is that Intuition is something of an antithesis to Logic/Reasoning. It will be noted that the list also includes popular notions like 'Gut feeling', 'Sixth sense' and 'Subconscious process'.

Graphic Expression

The percentage of managers giving graphic expression to their concept of Intuition is quite high at 77.6 per cent. This works out as follows for different categories:

Category	%
Male	77.0
Female	81.0
Industry	79.4
Services	76.5
Senior	77.3
Top	77.9
Low objective rating	74.8
Medium objective rating	77.6
High objective rating	79.3
Austria	69.6
France	77.3
Netherlands	84.7
Sweden	44.7
UK	70.2
USA	82.0
Japan	75.3
Brazil	84.3
India	71.5

There appears to be a positive association between Intuition orientation and readiness to express oneself graphically. This comes out not so much from the slight rise in the proportion from 74.8 per cent in the low group to 79.3 per cent in the high group as from the fact that the proportion is least for Sweden (44.7 per cent), which also has been adjudged as the least Intuitive on the basis of the objective rating discussed earlier.

Agreement with Specific Descriptions

The extent of agreement with three given descriptions of Intuition (obtained as three independent assessments and not as choice among three alternatives) can be seen from the distribution shown in table 5.6.

Table 5.6 Extent of agreement with three specific descriptions of Intuition

	Extent of agreement with		
Category*	a (%)	b (%)	c (%)
Sex			
Male	79.9	75.4	49.0
Female	64.3	92.1	73.6
Organization type			
Industry	80.8	73.3	50.5
Services	77.2	79.1	52.6
Management level			
Senior	81.4	81.0	49.7
Top	76.1	72.4	56.1
Intuition rating			
Low	76.7	67.1	45.7
Medium	74.0	75.5	45.3
High	83.5	84.8	61.0
Country			
Austria	63.6	87.1	38.6
France	62.6	75.4	48.5
Netherlands	70.3	66.6	34.9
Sweden	84.7	44.7	24.6
UK	84.6	74.9	45.5
USA	85.9	75.6	50.3
Japan	64.7	87.3	63.3
Brazil	79.3	72.1	56.4
India	79.3	80.6	52.3
Total	78.2	77.6	51.9

*NR (= Not reported) omitted from all categories.
(a) Spontaneous insight based on prior experience/expertise.
(b) Flash from 'subconscious levels'.
(c) Tuning into 'higher levels of consciousness'.

On an overall basis, the order of agreement with the three descriptions is as follows:

(a) & (b)* > (c)

This draws reasonable support from the pattern of responses to the open-ended question on the respondent's concept of Intuition, discussed earlier.

It will be noted that description (c) gets most agreement from the high group. Further, while descriptions (a) and (b) meet with more or

*> Denotes 'preferred over' (the inference being supported by statistical significance of the observed difference in the relevant proportions).

less the same degree of acceptance in the medium and high groups, managers in the low group seem to have a clear preference for description (a).

Perceived Relevance of Intuition

In Business Management

The perceived relevance of different functional areas of business/management to the application of Intuition can be seen from the following proportions relating to different areas:

	Area	%
1	Corporate strategy and planning	79.9
2	Investment/Diversification	59.7
3	Corporate acquisitions/mergers/alliances	55.3
4	Finance	31.1
5	Marketing	76.8
6	Public relations	64.3
7	Choice of technology/plant and equipment	35.4
8	Production/Operations	27.7
9	Materials management	24.4
10	Human resources development	78.6
11	Research and development	71.6

It will be seen that the following areas are perceived by the Survey population as the more important:

- corporate strategy and planning;
- marketing;
- public relations;
- human resources development (HRD);
- research and development (R&D).

One might have expected an area like corporate acquisitions/mergers/alliances to figure in the major areas of perceived importance, but this may have been taken to form part of corporate strategy and planning.

It will be noted that finance and production/operations are two major functional areas which rank among the least important in terms of perceived relevance.

In Other Fields

As regards fields other than business/management, the following are perceived to be the more important in terms of their relevance to application of Intuition:

Field	%
Specific disciplines (engineering, medicine, psychology, etc.)	18.8
Art, drama, music, literature, etc.	17.2
Sports	16.8
Education, teaching	15.1
Human/interpersonal relations	11.5
Love, marriage	9.3
Family (relations)	8.3
Politics, public life	8.0
Recreation, entertainment, etc.	5.2

It will be noted that the study of specific disciplines is considered most important as regards relevance to application of Intuition, and that this is followed by education and teaching in the fourth place. While the second and third spots go to fine arts and sports, which receive good attention in most of the Survey countries, interpersonal relations and allied areas (love, marriage and family relations) do figure among the other important responses.

How Does One Identify Intuition?

Stated Means of Identification

The query as to how Intuition could be identified elicited diverse responses, of which the following are the more important:

Response	%
Strong inner feeling, emotion	16.4
Inability to explain conclusion on the basis of available facts	14.0
Deviation of decision from logical reasoning	13.1
Spontaneous perception/vision	6.9

Thus, the emotional aspect is seen as the most important characteristic for identification of Intuition.

Associated Phenomena

The extent to which experience of Intuition is perceived to be accompanied by different phenomena can be seen from table 5.7.

Table 5.7 Associated phenomena

Category*	(a) Sensory (%)	(b) Physical (%)	(c) Mental (%)	(d) Emotional (%)
Sex				
Male	30.1	26.7	58.7	59.4
Female	43.5	28.8	55.9	58.4
Organization type				
Industry	30.0	24.7	57.8	62.3
Services	31.6	28.3	58.6	57.4
Management level				
Senior	34.0	25.8	60.4	63.2
Top	26.0	28.0	57.8	55.5
Intuition rating				
Low	23.9	23.3	60.8	59.4
Medium	27.9	28.4	52.6	53.9
High	40.6	26.2	61.5	62.5
Country				
Austria	25.8	30.2	46.0	68.0
France	20.0	12.4	45.6	65.0
Netherlands	20.2	28.1	42.5	80.1
Sweden	10.3	10.9	18.1	43.9
UK	28.6	18.9	55.2	78.1
USA	31.4	34.6	67.9	64.6
Japan	46.1	23.8	51.8	34.0
Brazil	23.0	17.2	41.0	54.1
India	26.6	23.1	62.8	60.2
Total	31.8	26.7	58.2	58.8

*NR (= Not reported) omitted from all categories.

Experience of Intuition is thus most perceived to be accompanied by changes in the mental and emotional aspects. This is consonant with the fact that the emotional aspect has been mentioned as the most important identifying characteristic for Intuition, as discussed earlier.

It may be noted that sensory and emotional aspects have been mentioned by senior managers to a significantly larger extent than by top managers.

Use of Intuition

In Professional Life

Only 7.5 per cent of the managers stated that they used more of Intuition in their professional life, as against 38.9 per cent using more of Logic/Reasoning. The remaining 53.6 per cent use Intuition and Logic/Reasoning in almost equal measure (see table 5.8).

Table 5.8 Extent of use of Intuition in professional life

Category*	More of Logic/ Reasoning (%)	Both in almost equal measure (%)	More of Intuition (%)
Sex			
Male	40.6	52.3	7.1
Female	29.1	62.9	8.0
Organization type			
Industry	38.2	55.5	6.3
Services	39.7	52.8	7.5
Management level			
Senior	42.0	51.8	6.1
Top	36.2	54.7	9.1
Intuition rating			
Low	55.7	41.5	2.8
Medium	45.7	51.4	2.8
High	24.1	61.2	14.7
Country			
Austria	46.0	49.3	4.8
France	32.7	61.9	5.4
Netherlands	45.7	45.6	8.7
Sweden	44.6	46.5	8.9
UK	33.3	59.2	7.5
USA	42.6	48.6	8.9
Japan	28.3	64.2	7.5
Brazil	53.5	42.1	4.4
India	44.0	51.4	4.6
Total	38.9	53.6	7.5

*NR (= Not reported) omitted from all categories.

It will be noted that the proportion of managers using more of Intuition in professional life is 14.7 per cent in the high group as against a mere 2.8 per cent in both low and medium groups. To look at it the other way, the proportion of managers using more of Logic/Reasoning drops significantly, from 55.7 per cent in the low group to 45.7 per cent in the medium group, and further to 24.1 per cent in the high group, pointing to a positive association between Intuition orientation and its use in professional life.

In Personal Life

The proportion of managers who stated that they use more of Intuition in their personal life is 30.6 per cent, as against the corresponding proportion of just 7.5 per cent for professional life. It can also be seen that there is a concomitant decline in the proportion of managers using more of Logic/Reasoning, from 38.9 per cent in the case of professional life to 16.2 per cent in the case of personal life. This pattern is in evidence whichever way the managers are classified (see table 5.9).

Table 5.9 Extent of use of Intuition in personal life

Category*	More of Logic/ Reasoning (%)	Both in almost equal measure (%)	More of Intuition (%)
Sex			
Male	17.0	55.1	27.9
Female	11.7	39.7	48.6
Organization type			
Industry	16.4	51.8	31.8
Services	17.1	54.5	28.4
Management level			
Senior	18.1	58.4	23.5
Top	15.5	45.9	38.6
Intuition rating			
Low	26.0	54.6	19.4
Medium	19.1	55.8	25.1
High	8.6	48.9	42.4
Country			
Austria	10.7	64.0	25.4
France	15.0	56.5	28.4
Netherlands	15.3	47.0	37.6
Sweden	16.6	55.2	28.2
UK	14.4	36.1	49.5
USA	19.7	55.8	24.5
Japan	3.9	57.6	38.5
Brazil	25.9	57.9	16.2
India	26.3	42.1	31.6
Total	16.2	53.1	30.6

*NR (= Not reported) omitted from all categories.

The proportion of managers using more of Intuition in their personal life increases from 19.4 per cent in the low group and 25.1 per cent in the medium group to a significantly higher level of 42.4 per cent in the high group. And, as in the case of professional life, there is a corresponding decline in the proportion of managers using more of Logic/Reasoning, from 26.0 per cent in the low group to 19.1 per cent in the medium group, and further to 8.6 per cent in the high group. This shows that there is a positive association between Intuition orientation and its use in personal life, just as in the case of professional life.

The use of Intuition in personal life seems to be most pronounced in the case of the UK, where the proportion of managers using more of Intuition is as high as 49.5 per cent. This is in tune with the fact that UK managers are among the most Intuitive of those of the Survey countries. However, the lowest proportion of 16.2 per cent for Brazil is not in keeping with the medium position occupied by this country in the ranking according to Intuition orientation.

Actual Instances

The proportion of managers who could cite specific instances where they had actually used Intuition in their professional/personal life is fairly high at 62.7 per cent. This proportion works out to 75.9 per cent for female managers, which is significantly higher than the corresponding proportion of 61.4 per cent for male managers. Considering that female managers have indeed been found to be more Intuitive than the male managers, this points to a positive association between Intuition orientation and the validated extent of its practical use.

This proportion is 76.3 per cent for the USA, whose managers are among the most Intuitive of those of the Survey countries. However, the inferred association is marred by the fact that the proportion for Japan, which also is in the top rung in terms of Intuition orientation, turns out to be the lowest at 31.9 per cent.

Opinions on Certain Notions

The respondents were asked to indicate to what extent they agree or disagree with each of ten given statements and the responses were obtained on a five-point scale, ranging from 'Strongly agree' to 'Strongly disagree'. Based on these responses, a composite index with range 0 to 100 was worked out by assigning values to different responses as follows:

Strongly agree	100
Agree	75
Can't say	50
Disagree	25
Strongly disagree	0

By choosing appropriate weighting factors, the index can be worked out for a given category as well as for the aggregate.

Aggregate indices worked out for different statements are as follows:

	Statement	*Index*
1	Many senior managers use Intuition in making decisions, at least to some extent.	79.0
2	Higher Intuitive capabilities would contribute to greater success in business.	77.9
3	Intuition contributes to harmonious interpersonal relationships.	71.0
4	Intuition is a characteristic associated more with women than with men.	53.0
5	Few managers who use Intuition would openly admit to the same.	52.0
6	The more Intuitive a person is, the more successful he or she will be in life.	58.1
7	Intuition cannot be blocked.	49.2
8	Intuition has a role to play in almost every facet of life.	79.4
9	Intuition can be cultivated/enhanced.	59.2
10	It is not safe to rely on Intuition in business/management.	40.3

Thus, there is a good measure of agreement* that:

- many managers use Intuition (1);
- Intuition contributes to success in business (2);
- Intuition contributes to harmonious interpersonal relationships (3);
- Intuition has a role to play in almost every facet of life (8).

*An index value of 65 or more has been taken to connote a 'good' measure of agreement.

It will be noted that the suggestion that Intuition contributes to success in life (6) does not meet with the same degree of acceptance as the more restrictive proposition that Intuition contributes to success in business (2). Thus, while the managers seem to believe that Intuition is more relevant to professional life, recalling the discussion in the previous section, the managers' claims indicate that they use Intuition to a larger extent in their personal life than in their professional life. This apparent contradiction probably has something to do with the way the propositions have been formulated: statement 6 is admittedly worded more sharply than statement 2.

Views on Certain Aspects

Views on certain aspects of Intuition were sought by ascertaining agreement with the following propositions, the figures alongside showing the proportions of managers in agreement:

Proposition	%
Dependence of Intuition on external environment	34.0
Possibility of inducing Intuition in others	30.4
Possibility of Intuition being a group process	37.7
Possibility of enhancing Intuition through specific types of practice/training	56.1

It will be noted that the proportion agreeing on the possible efficacy of training for enhancement of Intuition is fairly high at 56.6 per cent.

Proportions of managers who think that Intuition should form part of the curriculum at different levels of instruction are as follows:

Level	%
Primary school	38.5
Secondary school	42.9
College/University	53.6
Management institute	64.9

The proportion of managers supporting inclusion of Intuition in the curriculum thus rises progressively with the grade of institutions, reaching a high of 64.9 per cent in respect of study at the management institute level.

Interest in Further Participation

Proportions of managers indicating their willingness to participate further in this research through different means are as follows:

Means	%
Personal interviews	44·3
Experiential workshops	38.4
Seminars/Conferences	43·5

Having regard to the demands participation in research of this type makes on one's time, the above proportions may be taken to indicate a good degree of interest in the subject among managers constituting the Survey population.

6

Inter-Country Report: International Survey on Intuition

Profile of the Survey Population

A comparative picture of the profiles of managers in different Survey countries is given in table 6.1, from which the following can be seen:

Sex	The proportion of female managers ranges from 2.9 per cent in Brazil to 16.1 per cent in the USA, the median value of 7.5 per cent corresponding to Sweden.
Age	In France, the Netherlands, Brazil and India, the majority are aged below 45. In Austria, Sweden, the UK, the USA and Japan, the majority are aged 45 or more.
Organization type	The proportion of managers in the services sector ranges from 51.2 per cent in Austria to 64.9 per cent in the USA, with the median value of 58.1 per cent corresponding to France.
Management level	Classification of managers into senior and top groups is not available for Sweden. Among the other eight countries, the proportion of top managers varies from 25.1 per cent in the Netherlands to 61.2 per cent in the UK (which appears rather lopsided), with 32.4 per cent as the median value.

Table 6.1 Profiles of managers

Category	Austria (%)	France (%)	Netherlands (%)	Sweden (%)	UK (%)	USA (%)	Japan (%)	Brazil (%)	India (%)	Total (%)
Sex										
Male	93.0	88.6	92.8	92.5	92.0	83.9	87.9	97.1	95.0	87.9
Female	7.0	11.4	7.2	7.5	8.0	16.1	12.1	2.9	5.0	12.1
Age										
Below 35	5.2	13.0	11.8	6.2	4.0	5.2	7.5	11.7	18.2	7.7
35–44	29.7	46.6	42.8	38.8	31.4	30.5	36.8	47.8	37.9	35.0
45–59	62.8	33.6	45.4	49.6	58.9	52.2	51.9	35.6	37.5	49.3
Over 59	2.3	6.8	–	5.4	5.7	12.1	3.8	4.9	6.4	8.0
Organization type										
Industry	48.8	41.9	36.9	38.0	42.6	35.1	41.6	45.1	46.9	39.4
Services	51.2	58.1	63.1	62.0	57.4	64.9	58.4	54.9	53.1	60.6
Management level										
Senior	74.0	70.9	74.9	NA	38.8	64.5	65.8	69.5	60.8	62.8
Top	26.0	29.1	25.1	NA	61.2	35.5	34.2	30.5	39.2	37.2
Total	100.0	100.0	100.0	100.0	100.0	100.0	100.0	100.0	100.0	100.0

NA = Not available.
Proportions adjusted for NR (= Not reported) where necessary.

Intuition Ratings

Objective Rating

The proportion of managers rated high on the basis of an objective test carried out by the Survey (a three-way classification into low, medium and high groups: see appendix 11) ranges from 18.8 per cent in Sweden to 45.8 per cent in Japan:

Country	%*
Japan	45.8
USA	43.0
UK	41.5
Austria	37.1
Brazil	33.5
Netherlands	30.1
India	29.0
France	27.6
Sweden	18.8

*Proportions corrected for NR (= Not reported) where necessary.

On the above basis, the managers from the Survey countries can perhaps be categorized as follows:

More Intuitive	Japan, the USA and the UK
Average	Austria, Brazil, the Netherlands, India and France
Less Intuitive	Sweden

While not all the differences in the proportions are statistically significant, there is no doubt about Sweden's managers being the least Intuitive on the basis of the above yardstick.

Self-Rating

The proportion (corrected for 'Not reported') of managers rating themselves very high/high on Intuition (on a given five-point scale ranging from very high to very low) varies from 46.3 per cent in France to 78.7 per cent in the USA:

County	%
USA	78.7
UK	67.6

Country	%
India	60.8
Netherlands	59.4
Sweden	58.4
Austria	57.0
Japan	52.4
Brazil	51.4
France	46.3

Managers in the USA and the UK, which figure at the top of the above list, have been rated high on the basis of objective rating as well. However, managers in Japan, who top the list on the basis of objective rating, find themselves among the least Intuitive on the basis of self-rating. Likewise, managers in Sweden, who get the lowest rank on the basis of objective rating, figure in the middle range on the basis of self-rating. Thus, the association between the two ratings does not appear to be all that strong.

Association Between Ratings

The contingency coefficient between the two rating systems ranges from 0.17 for Sweden to 0.44 for the UK:

Country	*Contingency coefficient*
UK	0.44
France	0.41
USA	0.37
Austria	0.29
Netherlands	0.27
Japan	0.26
Brazil	0.21
Sweden	0.17
India	(Not calculated as χ^2 has turned out not to be significant)

The observations made earlier in respect of Japan and Sweden are borne out by the low value of their contingency coefficient, shown above. There seems to be nil or negligible association between the two rating systems in the case of India, where the χ^2 itself has been found not to be significant.

What is Intuition?

Descriptions Given of Intuition

As regards the managers' top-of-the-mind concept of Intuition, and taking the top three responses in respect to each country, a set of eight descriptions emerges (see table 6.2).

Table 6.2 Ranking of descriptions given of Intuition

Description	Austria	France	Netherlands	Sweden	UK	USA	Japan	Brazil	India	Total
Decision/perception without recourse to logical/rational methods	3	1	2	5	1	1	3	1	1	1
Inherent perception; inexplicable comprehension; a feeling that comes from within	4	4	1	1	3½	2		3	7	2
Integration of previous experience; processing of accumulated information	7	5	3	2	2	4	1	4	2	3
Gut feeling					3½	3			3	4
Spontaneous perception/vision	2	2	4	6	7½		6	5	4	7
(Powerful) inner voice; impulse	1				9		8		9	
Foresight; clairvoyance	5	3		3				2		
Spark; flash	6						2		10	

A blank indicates that either the description does not figure in the responses for the given country or the corresponding percentage is less than 5 per cent. Fractions indicate tied ranks.

Graphic Expression

The proportion of managers giving graphic expression to their concept of Intuition ranges from 44.7 per cent in the case of Sweden to 84.7 per cent in the case of the Netherlands:

Country	%
Netherlands	84.7
Brazil	84.3
USA	82.0
France	77.3

Country	%
Japan	75·3
India	71.5
UK	70.2
Austria	69.6
Sweden	44·7

The particularly low proportion for Sweden, which has been adjudged the least Intuitive among the Survey countries on the basis of the objective rating, suggests a positive association between Intuition orientation and the proneness to express oneself graphically on Intuition.

Agreement with Specific Descriptions

The extent of agreement with three given descriptions of Intuition shows that unambiguous ranking of these descriptions could be obtained only in four out of the nine Survey countries, as shown below:

(a) > (b) > (c)	Sweden and the USA
(b) > (a) > (c)	Austria and France
(a) & (b) > (c)	The Netherlands, the UK, Brazil and India
(b) > (a) & (c)	Japan

> Denotes 'preferred over' (the inference being supported by statistical significance of the observed difference in the relevant proportions).
(a) Spontaneous insight based on prior experience/expertise.
(b) Flash from 'subconscious levels'.
(c) Tuning into 'higher levels of consciousness'.

It will be seen that description (c) gets the lowest ranking everywhere (although in fact in Japan it ties with description (a)).

Perceived Relevance of Intuition

In Business/Management

Major areas of business/management perceived to be relevant to application of Intuition by managers in different Survey countries are shown in table 6.3.

Table 6.3 Major areas of perceived relevance in the field of business/management

Country	C	I	A	M	P	H	R
Austria	X			X	X	X	X
France	X			X		X	X
Netherlands	X			X	X	X	X
Sweden	X		X	X		X	
UK	X			X	X	X	X
USA	X			X		X	X
Japan	X	X		X		X	X
Brazil	X	X		X		X	X
India	X	X		X		X	X

X = Area figures in the list of major areas of perceived relevance for the given country.
C = Corporate strategy and planning
I = Investment/Diversification
A = Corporate acquisitions/mergers/alliances
M = Marketing
P = Public relations
H = Human resources development (HRD)
R = Research and development (R&D)

It will be seen that corporate strategy and planning, marketing and HRD are three functional areas which figure on the list of major areas for each of the Survey countries. R&D is a major area in all countries but Sweden. Sweden is also the only country where corporate acquisitions/mergers/alliances emerges as a major area of perceived relevance. Investment/diversification has been mentioned as one of the major areas in the case of Japan, Brazil and India, while public relations figures in the list for Austria, the Netherlands and the UK.

In Other Fields

Taking the top three responses in respect of each country, we get a list of eight fields outside the domain of business/management, perceived to be relevant to the application of Intuition (see table 6.4).

How Does One Identify Intuition?

Stated Means of Identification

Articulation on means of identification of Intuition was rather low. There are only four major responses (see table 6.5).

Table 6.4. Ranking of major areas of perceived relevance in other fields

Field	Austria	France	Netherlands	Sweden	UK	USA	Japan	Brazil	India	Total
Specific disciplines	4	12	1	4	1	2	5	2	10	1
Art, drama, music, literature	1	5½			2	3	2	8	4	2
Sports	3	1	5	2	3	4	1	3	9	3
Education, teaching	5		7		9	1		5	11	4
Human/interpersonal relations	8	2½	3	1	4	12½	3	4	1	5
Love, marriage	7	7	4	5	7	10½	4		3	6
Family (relations)	9	4	6		5½	6		1	5	7
Politics, public life	2	10	2	3	5½	7½		6	2	8
Recreation, entertain-ment, etc.	6	9				8			8	9

Fractions indicate tied ranks.

Table 6.5 Ranking of stated means of identification of Intuition

Means	Austria	France	Netherlands	Sweden	UK	USA	Japan	Brazil	India	Total
Strong inner feeling, emotion	3	2	3	2	1	1	3	3	2	1
Inability to explain conclu-sion on the basis of avail-able facts	2	3	1	1	3	2	5		3	2
Deviation of decision from logical reasoning	1	1	2	3	2	3	1	1	1	3
Spontaneous perception/ vision	4	4			4	4	2	2	4	4

A blank indicates that either the concerned means does not figure in the responses for the given country or the corresponding proportion is less than 5 per cent.

It will be noted that although deviation of decision from logical reasoning gets the first rank in five out of the nine Survey countries, the top rank on a global basis goes to strong inner feeling, emotion, which is accorded the first rank in the UK and the USA, since these countries carry higher weightings in arriving at the global averages.

Associated Phenomena

Responses to the query on different phenomena accompanying experience of Intuition show that the first two ranks are shared by the emotional and mental aspects and the last two by the sensory and physical aspects, except that in the case of Japan the second rank goes to sensory aspects and the third to emotional aspects (see table 6.6).

Table 6.6 Ranking of associated phenomena

Aspect	Austria	France	Netherlands	Sweden	UK	USA	Japan	Brazil	India	Total
Emotional	1	1	1	1	1	2	3	1	2	1
Mental	2	2	2	2	2	1	1	2	1	2
Sensory	4	3	4	4	3	4	2	3	3	3
Physical	3	4	3	3	4	3	4	4	4	4

Use of Intuition

In Professional Life

In five out of the nine Survey countries, the majority of the managers have given a specific indication on whether they use more of Logic/Reasoning or more of Intuition in their professional life:

Specific indication	Austria, the Netherlands, Sweden, the USA and Brazil
Use both in almost equal measure	France, the UK, Japan and India

The proportion of managers using more of Intuition in their professional life ranges from 4.4 per cent in the case of Brazil to 8.9 per cent in the case of Sweden and the USA, the median value of 7.5 per cent corresponding to the UK and Japan:

Country	%
Sweden	8.9
USA	8.9
Netherlands	8.7
UK	7.5
Japan	7.5

Country	%
France	5.4
Austria	4.8
India	4.6
Brazil	4.4

In Personal Life

Only in three out of the nine Survey countries have the majority of the managers given a specific indication on whether they use more of Logic/Reasoning or more of Intuition in their personal life:

Specific indication	The Netherlands, the UK and India
Use both in almost equal measure	Austria, France, Sweden, the USA, Japan and Brazil

The proportion of managers using more of Intuition in their personal life ranges from 16.2 per cent in the case of Brazil to 49.5 per cent in the case of the UK, the median value of 28.4 per cent corresponding to France:

Country	%
UK	49.5
Japan	38.5
Netherlands	37.6
India	31.6
France	28.4
Sweden	28.2
Austria	25.4
USA	24.5
Brazil	16.2

Actual Instances

The proportion of managers who could cite specific instances where they had actually used Intuition in their professional/personal life ranges from 31.9 per cent in the case of Japan to 76.3 per cent in the case of the USA, the median value of 63.9 per cent corresponding to India:

Country	%
USA	76.3
Netherlands	71.6
Austria	71.4
UK	65.7
India	63.9
Brazil	61.6
France	60.8
Sweden	51.8
Japan	31.9

Opinions on Certain Notions

Of the ten statements on which opinion was elicited in the form of extent of agreement/disagreement and the responses converted into a composite index with range 0 to 100, there is a good measure of agreement* on the following three propositions in all countries:

- many senior managers use Intuition in making decisions, at least to some extent;
- higher Intuitive capabilities would contribute to greater success in business;
- Intuition has a role to play in almost every facet of life.

Another proposition which meets with a good measure of agreement in all countries but Austria and Japan is:

- Intuition contributes to harmonious interpersonal relationships.

Other statements which have met with a good degree of acceptance in selected countries are as follows:

• Intuition cannot be blocked.	India
• Intuition can be cultivated/enhanced.	The UK and the USA
• It is not safe to rely on Intuition in business/management.	Sweden

*An index value of 65 or more has been taken to connote a 'good' measure of agreement.

Views on Certain Aspects

As regards the extent of agreement with certain other propositions, the range and median value in different cases are as follows:

Proposition		
Dependence of Intuition on external environment	Range:	21.1 per cent (Japan) to 49.8 per cent (France)
	Median:	38.3 per cent (Austria)
Possibility of inducing Intuition in others	Range:	21.1 per cent (India) to 42.3 per cent (Austria and the UK)
	Median:	31.4 per cent (France and the USA)
Possibility of Intuition being a group process	Range:	24.4 per cent (India and Japan) to 49.8 per cent (the USA)
	Median:	27.0 per cent (Brazil)
Possibility of enhancing Intuition through specific types of practice/training	Range:	31.5 per cent (Sweden) to 63.6 per cent (the USA)
	Median:	49.1 per cent (Brazil)

Ranges and medians corresponding to proportions of managers who think that Intuition should be included in the curriculum at different levels of instruction are as follows:

Level		
Primary school	Range:	11.5 per cent (Sweden) to 46.7 per cent (Japan)
	Median:	29.8 per cent (the UK)
Secondary school	Range:	25.2 per cent (Sweden) to 54.9 per cent (the USA)
	Median:	30.6 per cent (Austria)
College/University	Range:	30.1 per cent (Japan) to 67.3 per cent (the USA)
	Median:	49.0 per cent (India)
Management institute	Range:	36.5 per cent (France) to 80.9 per cent (the USA)
	Median:	64.1 per cent (India)

Interest in Further Participation

Statistics relating to proportions of managers indicating willingness to participate further in this research by different means are as follows:

Personal interviews	Range: 20.5 per cent (Japan) to 69.4 per cent (India) Median: 48.8 per cent
Experiential workshops	Range: 28.3 per cent (Japan) to 60.2 per cent (India) Median: 35.5 per cent
Seminars/Conferences	Range: 30.9 per cent (Austria) to 69.9 per cent (Brazil) Median: 36.9 per cent

As these responses could not be obtained for Sweden, the above statistics relate to only eight countries and the median does not correspond to any country.

Conclusion

This chapter and the preceding one have summarized the results of the International Survey on Intuition at both the global and inter-country levels. One critical finding is that Intuition is perceived as playing a major role in the professional lives of the responding managers, with 53.6 per cent using both Intuition and Logic/Reasoning in almost equal measure and a further 7.5 per cent stating they actually use more of Intuition. Furthermore, almost 80 per cent believe that Intuition has relevance in corporate strategy and planning – the highest percentage accorded to any of the functional areas.

The final two chapters focus on vision and visioning in corporate settings and show how intuition can be operationalized in the process of corporate strategy formulation and implementation.

7

Applying Intuition: Vision and Visioning

A man to carry on a successful business must have imagination. He must see things in a vision, a dream of the whole thing.

Charles M. Schwab (1862–1939)
American steel magnate,
first President of US Steel Corporation

For a decade or two a new concept has been expounded in the strategic management literature and invoked repeatedly by many business leaders, namely the concept of corporate vision. The fervour and intensity of the public discussion create the impression that, at least in some quarters, corporate vision is seen as the magic word which unfailingly opens the door to hidden treasures of business success, a kind of modern 'Open Sesame!' transplanted into the business arena. Its popularity seems to have its roots at least partly in the expectation that it responds better to the planning needs of our times than the traditional strategic planning approaches. Corporate vision promises to provide a means by which we can revitalize our maturing companies boldly and forcefully.

While we believe that some of the hopes pinned to the concept may be exaggerated, we are at the same time convinced that the concept of vision and the process of visioning hold substantial promise. It is not just the proverbial new wine in old bottles. Most of the present discussion has, however, two major shortcomings. First, the majority of the discussants do not realize that a vision can hardly be created solely with the help of the traditional incremental and analytical way of thinking (the Cartesian approach), which has dominated our strategic planning practices during the last three decades. Second, even those followers of the vision concept who realize that other, non-rational (for instance, intuitive) approaches have a major role to play in creating a vision frequently do not understand the phenomenon of intuition deeply enough to make its use operational in a company.

On the basis of our research we have developed the concept of intuition described in the earlier chapters. This has enabled us to create a process which allows us to tap the intuitive capabilities of managers when developing a vision. This approach has been tested successfully in companies as well as in senior management learning events and workshops. In order to prepare the ground for a discussion of that approach, we will first have to develop our overall concept of vision and visioning.

A Vision Defined

At the moment, a corporate vision is widely understood to be an image of a desired future organizational stage.[1] 'When a manager or a whole organization holds a reasonably clear image of a desirable future, that's vision', suggests Hal Leavitt. He calls visionary managers pathfinders and writes: 'The futures that interest pathfinders are imagined, not predicted.'[2] In very practical terms, a vision is an answer to the question: 'What do we want to create?'[3] The following examples may help to illustrate what is meant by a vision.

In 1928, at the age of 27, William Paley took over CBS. The company then had no radio stations of its own, did not figure large in the industry (which was dominated by NBC) and was in fact making losses. Within a span of ten years. Paley had built up a network of 114 stations, and the company produced $28 million in profits a year. Four decades later – with Paley still heading CBS – the company was the key player in the broadcasting industry.[4] The role vision played in this phenomenal success is well described by David Halberstam:

What [Paley] had from the start was a sense of vision, a sense of what might be. It was as if he could sit in New York in his tiny office with his almost bankrupt company and see not just his own desk, or the row of potential advertisers outside along Madison Avenue, but millions of American people out in the hinterland, so many of them out there, almost alone, many of them in homes as yet unconnected to electricity. People alone with almost no form of entertainment other than radio. It was his sense, his confidence that he could reach them, that he had something for them that made him different. He could envision an audience when there was in fact no audience. He not only had the vision, he knew how to harness it.[5]

In 1963, Martin Luther King, the founder and leader of the Southern Christian Leadership Conference (which became a mass movement preaching active non-violence to free the oppressed American minorities), led the historic march on Washington which culminated in his speech, 'I have a dream . . .' at the Mall before an inter-racial audience estimated at 200,000 people. In this speech, he described in beautiful language an America worth living in (and in his case even dying for). This landmark speech, which without any doubt entered history as one of the great speeches of the twentieth century, today still moves people deeply.

In another case taken from business, Theodore Vail, chair of AT&T, had a vision of a universal telephone service in the United States. It took fifty years to realize his dream, but as a result of it, there is at least one telephone in each American household.[6]

When asked what role vision plays in his life as an executive, Jan Carlzon, the CEO of SAS (who some years ago turned the company around), answered that to have a vision, to be able to see the whole picture, to see the forest despite the many trees is his responsibility. He feels equally responsible for communicating this: 'in this phase . . . I am a preacherman'. Carlzon does not believe that it is his job to conduct the everyday airline business. He sees his task rather as preparing a situation in which business can best be carried out in the company. In this respect, 'I am working a lot with visions', he states.[7]

Steve Jobs, who had earlier founded the Apple Computer Company, described the vision for his new computer NeXT in the following way to his staff:

> We wanted to start a company that had a lot to do with education and in particular higher education, colleges and universities. So, our vision is that there's a revolution in software going on now on college and university campuses. And it has to do with providing two types of breakthrough software. One is called simulated learning environments. You can't give a student in biology a five million dollar recombinant DNA laboratory. But you can simulate those things, you can simulate them on a very powerful computer. It is not possible for students to afford those things. It is not possible for most faculty members to afford those things. So if we take what we can do best, which is to find really great technology and pull it down to a price point that is affordable to people, if we can do the same thing for this type of a computer,

which is maybe ten times as powerful as a personal computer, that we did for personal computers; then I think we can make a real difference in the way the learning experience happens in the next five years. And that's what we are trying to do . . . [and] one of my largest wishes is that we build NeXT from the heart. And the people that are thinking about coming to work for us or buying our products, or who want to sell us things, feel that we're doing this because we have a passion about it. We're doing this because we really care about the higher education process, not because we want to make a buck.[8]

Characteristics of a Good Vision

What are some of the characteristics these visions have in common?

Good visions are *inspiring* – they are exhilarating. To ask employees, even managers, year after year for '10 per cent plus' (in profits or sales, for instance) hardly motivates people any more; they have been through that exercise too many times. Visions, in contrast, create the spark of excitement that lifts the organization out of the mundane.

Unlike the incremental approach to planning ('*x* per cent a year will get us there in year *y*'), what all these visions have in common is that they represent a discontinuity, a step function, a *jump ahead*. To take an example from the business sphere: the authors of a business vision describe in it what they want the company to be – not to become – in, say, five years' time, and then look back and ask what their organization would have to do today to arrive at the desired future state in due time. This means these companies do not work towards a vision, they rather work from a vision.

Good visions *align* people in an organization. By creating a common identity and a shared sense of purpose, a vision provides a first step in allowing people to work together who may not have trusted each other before. Such an alignment frees energies which up to then may have been eaten up by internal friction and in-fighting.

Good visions are *competitive, original and unique*. 'Powerful visions are statements of intent that create an obsession with winning throughout the organization.'[9] By focusing attention on a desired leadership position, and continually searching for new ways to gain competitive advantages, the actions and aspirations mean more than merely striving to catch up to competition and to match best practices.

At the same time, good visions *make sense in the marketplace*; that is, they are not utopian in the word's negative meaning. Unfortunately, this economic sense is often difficult to document with hard facts at the outset. This very point is frequently the source of friction between traditional, analytical (Cartesian) managers and entrepreneurial visionaries. Analytical managers insist on data; for them, propositions which cannot be substantiated with hard facts are half-baked ideas. Visionaries, however, as they typically enter uncharted territory, do not have facts and figures to prove that their idea is going to pay off. A good case in point is Steve Jobs and the founding of Apple. When he tried to convince several of the large traditional computer companies of his vision – to put computing power into the hand of large portions of the population – the established firms, citing their own market research (facts and figures!), told him that in their view there was no market to speak of for personal computers out there. This brings up a major characteristic of a vision and of visioning: the hallmark of the true visionary is that he or she reads the environment differently from 'the pack' and, as a result, comes up with unique business ideas.

Being immersed in a vision also fosters *risk-taking and experimentation*. The existence and the widespread understanding of a vision instil in an organization a sense of direction. Such an umbrella provides members of even complex organizations with rules of inclusion and exclusion, and by doing so allows them to take risks, develop initiatives and take decisions on their own. As an example, Stamford Raffles, the founder of Singapore, comes to mind. Raffles was an officer of the British East India Company stationed in the Far East, which meant he was so far away from headquarters in London (or his immediate superior in India) that any communication would have taken months. At one point, Raffles in a surprise coup created a settlement at the tip of the Malay Peninsula right at the edge of the Straits of Malacca and on the site of the ancient city of Sinhapura. This was in the middle of a territory which the Dutch claimed as their sphere of interest. The settlement, which later became Singapore, prevented the Dutch from getting a stranglehold on the route to China. How did Raffles know how to function in such a remote place? There was a vision of the British Empire in which he was fully immersed. It was clear to him that in order to realize that vision, the British would need a stepping stone to the Far East. When the opportunity offered itself, Raffles acted relatively autonomously (and, as the records show, to the horror of headquarters, which feared a war with the Dutch over Singapore). History, however, has vindicated Raffles – at least from a business point of view.[10]

The parallel of this situation with today's broadly based companies – product-wise as well as geographically – is obvious. If top management in such a vast company wants to promote entrepreneurial behaviours in its rank and file, it has to make sure the managers down the line are guided by a powerful vision, otherwise these eager beavers are all over the map with their activities. So, to sum up: good vision empowers and enables people.

A good vision also fosters *long-term thinking*. Senge, who stresses this point particularly, posits that it simply may not be possible to convince human beings rationally to take a long-term view. He argues that in every instance where one finds a long-term view actually operating in human affairs, there is a long-term vision at work appealing to the guts of people: 'The cathedral builders of the Middle Ages laboured a life time with the fruits of their labours still a hundred years into the future.'[11]

There is an additional indispensable characteristic of a vision: its integrity, in at least two respects. First, a vision has to be truly *genuine*, 'which proves crucial to visionary leadership'.[12] Employees recognize very soon to what extent management really stands behind a vision, not only with their minds but also with their hearts. The very moment the employees start doubting the seriousness of top management, cynicism is invariably the consequence.

There is, however, a further aspect to be taken into consideration: a vision is a *powerful tool*, and like any tool it can be used for the benefit of people or abused terribly. As in every aspect of human life, a good vision has to be governed by ethical principles. After all, Martin Luther King's great rhetorical gifts could have been abused for demagogical purposes; only the morality of his cause justified his method of raising the expectations of the masses by creating an incredible tension among his listeners that day in Washington. The same holds true, of course, for a business vision.

Last but not least, it should be mentioned that good visions are *shared visions*.[13] This is such a pivotal characteristic that we will come back to it in detail. To prepare the ground for that discussion, we have first to look into the question of what actually constitutes a vision and how one creates a vision statement.

Elements of a Good Vision Statement

What are the elements of a good vision statement? Westley and Mintzberg have shed some light on this question. Using their insights, one can identify two constituent parts of a vision: the content of a vision statement, and its context.

The Content

'Vision may focus on products, services, markets or organizations or even ideals. These aspects are the strategic component, the central image which drives a vision; we refer to the core', write Westley and Mintzberg.[14] Day strikes a similar note: 'Vision is a guiding theme that articulates the nature of the business and its intentions for the future.'[15]

In addition to having a core, Westley and Mintzberg believe that every vision is surrounded 'by a kind of halo designed to gain its acceptance. It is this component, comprising its symbolic aspects of rhetorical and metaphorical devices, which we refer to as its circumference'.[16] The process of creating this 'circumference' Conger calls 'rhetorical crafting'. It heightens the vision's motivational appeal and determines whether it will be sufficiently memorable to influence the day-to-day decision-making of an organization.[17] Some of the main tools in this context are metaphors, analogies and organization stories. The power of metaphor and analogies comes from their ability to capture and illustrate an experience of reality by appealing simultaneously to the various aspects of the listener – to the emotions, to the intellect, to imagination, and to values.[18] Conger echoes here a thought by José Ortega y Gasset, who once said, 'The metaphor is probably the most fertile power possessed by man.'

One should note that the value added by the visionary may lie in the circumference alone, in the core alone or in the core and the circumference in combination, with the last of these obviously representing the most exciting situation.

A vision statement to be practical and effective must address itself to the following content dimensions:

- the basic idea on which the business is built. Why should a customer come to our doorstep? A good business idea has three major elements to it. The first two are closely related: a strong, enduring *customer problem* in the market the company has identified as its territory on the one hand and a unique, attractive and *acceptable solution* to that problem offered by the company on the other. If one or both of these factors show any weakness, the attractiveness of the business idea is reduced. This idea is usually made concrete with the help of the product and/or service offered by a business as well as with the help of the market to be served.[19]
- the *business system* – the third major element of a business idea. There is more to a business than a product, and a market; 'there is in

fact an entire chain of activities from product design to product utilization by the final customer, that must be mobilized to meet certain market expectations. The most commonly accepted term to designate this chain of activites is the business system', write Gilbert and Strebel.[20] Parts of this system are the organization structure, the resources, the organized knowledge, the leadership style (including major values), the links to subcontractors and the reward system.

As can be seen from the above, a vision is a contemplated future image of the total organization, 'a dream of the whole thing', to quote the epigraph to this chapter by Charles M. Schwab. A vision statement describes these dimensions in an exciting manner at a given point in time, say, five years into the future. The earlier mentioned 'rhetorical crafting' certainly has its place here.

The Context

As was mentioned above, the second constituent element of a vision is its context. Obviously a wide variety of contexts is conceivable: the nature of the organization itself can vary in ownership, in structure, in size, in development stage, in being public or private, in its infancy or maturity, etc. The industry and the broader environment may also vary, for example, from traditional mass production to contemporary high technology.[21] In each and every one of these cases the specific context influences a vision (and for that matter a visioning process) substantially.

The Physiology of Visioning

We now have to look into the question of how to create a vision and translate it into action – we have to turn to process aspects, the physiology of a visioning, so to speak. As in the previous section, we will stay on the conceptual level for the time being.

The creation of a vision is always the result of some process, even if it seems to be a very short or ill-structured one. Attempts to structure and apply such a process run the serious risk of robbing this highly creative, entrepreneurial activity of its vitality.[22] We believe we must live with this risk, as we have to try to give the practising manager some guidance in creating and applying a vision. Before embarking on the discussion of such a process, we would like to inject a word of caution. There is obviously no formula for how to find a vision. There are, however, certain principles and guidelines for building a vision. A discipline of establishing a vision is emerging and so are tools for working with visions.[23]

Generic Approaches to Visioning

All modes of vision-building observed in practice as well as in the literature can be placed on a continuum, which is based on the mental origin of a vision and its evolution (see figure 7.1).

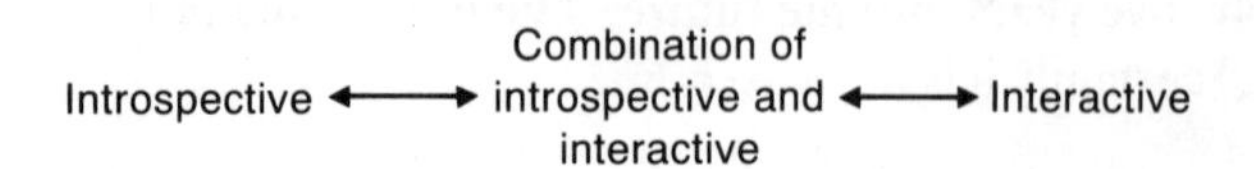

Figure 7.1 Continuum of approaches to visioning

At one end of the continuum are highly introspective approaches to visioning. In these cases a strong, pathfinding leader creates a vision essentially through introspection. Frequently these cases represent genuine 'Road to Damascus' experiences the leader has – they appear suddenly like visitations. Major inventions or technological breakthroughs are linked to visions of this nature, particularly if the person spearheading the invention is a charismatic leader.

At the other extreme of the spectrum one finds ways to create a vision which are essentially interactive. Members of a group – sometimes at the helm of a unit – in intense discussions hammer out a shared vision for their organization. It may well be that the articulation of that vision, the pulling together of the results of the discussion, is left to one person.

In the majority of cases of building a vision, an approach is used which would have to be placed somewhere in the middle of the continuum. In these situations, the two pure modes are mixed; that is, in the process of establishing a vision, introspective periods (during which the participating persons work individually) are followed by highly interactive stretches of discussion among a group of people, and vice versa. As this hybrid approach is so prominent and frequent, we would like to see it as a third mode of vision-building. To support our argument and to imbue figure 7.1 with some life, we would like to give a few practical cases.

As an example of an essentially introspectively established vision, Westley and Mintzberg use the invention of the Polaroid camera by Edwin Land. They quote his own description of the way it all started:

One day when we were vacationing in Sante Fe in 1943, my daughter Jennifer, who was then 3, asked me why she could not see the picture I had taken of her. As I walked around that charming town, I undertook the task of solving the puzzle she had set for me. Within the hour, the camera, the film and the physical chemistry become so clear that with a great sense of excitement I hurried to the place where a friend was staying to describe to him in detail a dry camera which would give a picture immediately after exposure. In my mind it was so real that I spent several hours on that description.[24]

Stories of this nature may easily create the impression that an idea like the one leading to the creation of the Polaroid camera springs fully blown from nowhere. Such an assumption underestimates how many years Land spent in 'perfecting the polarization process, schooling his scientific and inventive abilities, practicing and repeating, learning his craft'.[25] Leavitt argues along similar lines when he points out that creativity in individuals is enhanced by depth and breadth of knowledge and experience. 'People who know a lot of things are more likely to put together new combinations of ideas than are people who don't have much knowledge to put together', he insists.[26] This does not take away anything from the fact that the discovery of the Polaroid camera was a genuine breakthrough, a real creative act. It represented a step-function in the development of photography.

Land himself was unclear about the sources of his creativity; he suggests that impulses of this nature are ill understood. It seems to us that one of the key roots of creative outbursts of this kind is human intuition, the non-rational part of human nature. Albert Einstein, who, of course, lived through similar experiences, saw this link between creativity and intuition, as one of his most frequently quoted statements shows: 'I believe in intuition and inspiration . . . at times I feel certain that I am right while not knowing the reason . . . Imagination is more important than knowledge. For knowledge is limited, whereas imagination embraces the entire world, stimulating progress, giving birth to evolution.'

Can a performance like that of Edwin Land be programmed? Certainly not. Some would argue that the best companies can do in this respect is to let it happen. 'A manager can't make a new idea spring up within the organization. He cannot create the creative team. Like saboteurs, creative people hatch their own plot and form their own little cells. A manager can't control it; he can only help', Nayak and Ketteringham found in their research on breakthroughs.[27] We know today quite well how to structure an environment which is favourable to fostering innovative behaviour.[28] We would even go a step further and argue that we now know much more about what Land described as these 'ill-understood sources' of this type of creativity, which Einstein called 'intuition' and 'imagination'. We even believe that we have distinctly improved our chances of tapping these intuitive sources of the human mind, as we will show later.

An example of a visioning process which would have to be placed more towards the middle of our continuum is Jan Carlzon's, which was actually two-pronged. On the one hand, he put great emphasis on the Euroclass, SAS's version of business class; by doing so, he banked on the essentially price-insensitive business traveller (in contrast to other airlines, which courted the basically very cost-conscious tourist). On the other hand, he stressed process and organization structure as key elements of his vision, a fact which makes his approach particularly interesting. His novel insights were into the nature of service itself and of the organizational structure most likely to deliver it. His organization blueprint included:

> making the frontline workers – ticket agents and stewardesses in particular – into 'managers', giving them the authority to respond to the needs and problems of individual customers. Middle Managers are transformed from supervisors into resources for the frontline workers. They are reprimanded for inhibiting these people's initiatives.[29]

Carlzon describes a process of arriving at his vision which is quite different from that of Land. Rather than an outburst of creativity resulting in a complete, holistic design, Carlzon claims that his organizational blueprint grew out of a number of small insights and discrete moments of inspiration, which he discussed again and again with his co-managers and then pieced together into a whole. His account is echoed by Hal Leavitt:

> Vision does not spring fully grown from Adam's rib. It usually starts in a fumbling, groping way, reaching toward some shadow dream that cannot easily be verbalised or defined. Whether it was Mao's vision for a new China, Robert Hutchins' vision for a new University of Chicago, or a start-up founder's vision for a new company, each was surely continuously shaped, reshaped and clarified.[30]

These visioning processes in the central part of the continuum in figure 7.1 may appear quite messy to the outsider. Sir John Harvey-Jones, when he was still chairman and CEO of ICI, once made a remark about this:

> I believe we need a clearer understanding of the role of corporate vision or, as I prefer to denote it, a corporate dream . . . The dreams have to be the product of those at the top and will result only from the expenditure of a great deal of time and effort. But it needs to be time and effort in sweat shirts, with cans of beer, sandwiches and flip charts, rather than in business suits, with a coffee and computer graphics.[31]

We know also of cases where visions are established in an approach which would have to be located pretty much to the right of the continuum in figure 7.1; that is, they are established in an almost totally interactive way. For example, in 1961, John Kennedy articulated a vision that had been emerging for many years among leaders within America's space programme: to have man on the moon by the end of the decade. Was Kennedy the creator of that vision? He certainly was not, although he played a major part in the process. In other cases of approaches to visioning in the right-hand portion of figure 7.1, visions 'just bubble' up from people interacting at many levels. Interestingly enough, these might well be people who are not necessarily in positions of authority.[32]

Cutting through all these approaches to visioning captured in figure 7.1, there is one indispensable requirement: visions not only have to be communicated effectively to others in the organization, they must be shared by them. It is to this aspect we would like to turn now.

Communicating and Sharing

As mentioned earlier, the communication and sharing of a vision are of paramount importance to the concept. Let us start discussing this aspect by first taking a look at those cases where the creation of a vision is largely a top-down process; that is, examples taken from the left-hand side of the continuum in figure 7.1.

Such a strong top-down characteristic makes the effective communication of the vision particularly important. We simply have to realize that a vision as a private mental image of a desired future state of the organization is at best incomplete, if not worthless. Even in the most top-down company, headed by a charismatic leader, such an image must be embraced by the rest of the organization if it is to serve its purpose. One prerequisite for achieving this sharing is a skilful communication of that vision by the charismatic leader to the rank and file. The leader actually has to make them 'see' it. Like General Patton, visionaries have to have the gift of creating in their people the readiness to follow them into battle, so to speak. Visionaries who are not able to perform this task are forgotten as dreamers. We should therefore not be surprised to find that successful visionaries are also very adept at using language in communicating their vision. Language has the ability to stimulate and motivate, not only through appeals to logic, but also through appeals to emotions.[33]

This latter aspect is of particular importance. In many cases, visions require a change of behaviour in the organization. At the same time, 'every thing the social sciences know about changing behaviour says that people change for emotional reasons far more than for rational reasons. It's love, hate, greed, loyalty, jealousy and passion much more than cool pure reason that drive us to change our ways', Leavitt stresses.[34] In their efforts to get to the guts of people, good visionaries usually very skilfully employ symbols and metaphors in communicating their vision. Jan Carlzon used the metaphor of 'moments of truth' to describe the significance of every contact of his 'frontline managers' with customers. It is also fascinating to examine what Martin Luther King did in his speech, 'I have a dream . . .'; he used most naturally (it seems) a large number of metaphors and symbols to describe to his audience a desirable future America.

> We attribute the utmost significance to this duality in visionaries. We do not hesitate to say that how successfully a vision is communicated is as important as the image that is actually communicated. By wedding perception to symbols, the leader creates a vision and the vision, by evoking an emotional response, forms a bridge between leader and follower as well as between idea and action.[35]

This interaction between visionaries and their audience is not only significant for building support for the vision, but also impacts on the vision itself. It helps to shape it. To underline this point, Westley and Mintzberg compare the visioning process to a drama performance. The power of work and gesture of an actor is not enough for a great performance – such a performance cannot occur with the actor alone in a room. Actors need an audience to co-create with them. The relationship between the stage and the spectators is vital for a great performance: the audience can either make actors fly or rather effectively clip their wings.

The same holds true for visionaries and visions. Like a drama performance, vision occurs in a two-way current – it comes alive only if it is shared.[36] And like an actor, a visionary may well have a bad house. The case of Charles Parry is an example. He became CEO of Alcoa in 1983, but was soon deposed because his vision was rejected by a deep-seated conservative company culture. As Day reports:

For years Alcoa, the largest US producer of aluminium, had suffered through boom–bust cycles in the industry. By the early eighties the combination of chronic excess capacities to produce ingots, and several state-owned competitors who were more concerned with job protection than profits, reduced the profits to a break-even level. In response Parry articulated a vision of Alcoa as the preeminent producer of highly engineered alloys using ceramics, composites and plastics. His eventual aim was to derive 50 percent of revenues from non-aluminium markets. Unfortunately, Parry had already alienated most of his management with a series of shutdowns to cut costs . . . Meanwhile the board, which generally endorse the need to reduce dependency on primary aluminium, were uneasy with the 50 percent goal . . . They were further disenchanted with the logic of the acquisitions being proposed, and by 1987 they withdrew their support.[37]

To this discussion of the communication of the vision should be added a dimension which is particularly pertinent for approaches to visioning at the centre or to the right of the continuum in figure 7.1. A shared vision emerges from personal visions:

Organizations intent on building shared visions continually encourage members to develop their personal visions. If people do not have their own vision, all they can do is sign up for somebody else's. The result is compliance, never commitment. On the other hand people with a strong sense of personal direction can join together to create a powerful synergy towards what I/we truly want.[38]

A vision is not a truly shared vision until it connects with the personal visions of people throughout the organization. Visions that are genuinely shared take time to emerge. They grow almost as a by-product of interactions between individual visions. In this experience, truly shared visions require ongoing conversations where individuals not only feel free to express their dreams, but learn how to listen to each other's dreams. Out of this listening, new insights into what is possible emerge.

The result of such a process is worth the effort. As Senge stresses:

> A shared vision is not an idea . . . It is rather a force in people's hearts, a force of impressive power. It may be inspired by an idea, but once it goes further – if it is compelling enough to acquire the support of more than one person – then it is no longer an abstraction. It is palpable. People begin to see it as if it exists. Few, if any, forces in human affairs are as powerful as a shared vision.[39]

A similarly strong statement was made by Sir John Harvey-Jones. In the above-mentioned speech he gave in St Gallen (Switzerland) a few years ago, he said:

> Dreams do not have to be demonstrably achievable although it helps if there is some broad indication of scale. They must not be precise, but they have to be ambitious far beyond the capabilities of day to day operations . . . they have to attract the hearts and the minds of people who have to have to accomplish them.[40]

Conclusion

The purpose of this chapter was to clarify the concept of vision. As vision and visioning are still relatively young approaches to formal planning, this exploration was necessary. This chapter thus becomes a stepping stone to the final one, where we want to explore much more deeply how our understanding of intuition can be practically applied. In the next chapter, visioning will be used as a vehicle to demonstrate a practical application of intuition in one aspect of strategic management, namely the effort to create a challenging, desirable and exciting future image of a given corporation. Was not Robert Browning right after all when he said: 'A man's reach should exceed his grasp, / Or what's a heaven for?'

Notes

1 Bernard M. Bass, 'Charismatic and inspirational leadership: what's the difference?', *Proceedings of Symposium on Charismatic Leadership in Management*, McGill University, Montreal, 1987, p. 51.
2 Harold J. Leavitt, *Corporate Pathfinders* (Homewood, Ill.: Dow Jones-Irwin, 1986), p. 62.

3 Peter M. Senge, *The Fifth Discipline: The Art and Practice of the Learning Organization* (New York: Doubleday, 1990), p. 206.
4 Warren Bennis and Burt Nanus, *Leaders* (New York: Harper & Row, 1985), p. 87.
5 David Halberstam, *The Powers That Be* (New York: Dell, 1979), p. 40.
6 Senge, *Fifth Discipline*, p. 207.
7 Interview by Sandra Vandermerwe, Faculty Member at IMD, Lausanne, with Jan Carlzon on 3 March 1987.
8 Jay A. Conger, 'Inspiring others: the language of leadership', *Academy of Management Executive*, 1991, vol. 5, no. 1, pp. 32–3.
9 George S. Day, *Market Driven Strategy* (New York: The Free Press, 1990), p. 17. Gary Hamel and C. K. Prahalad, 'Strategic intent', *Harvard Business Review*, May–June 1989, p. 64.
10 Maurice Collins, *Raffles* (London: Century, 1988).
11 Senge, *Fifth Discipline*, p. 210.
12 Frances Westley and Henry Mintzberg, 'Visionary leadership and strategic management', *Strategic Management Journal*, 1989, vol. 10, p. 21.
13 Senge, *Fifth Discipline*, pp. 205–32; Day, *Market Driven Strategy*, p. 16; Westley and Mintzberg, 'Visionary leadership', pp. 18–21.
14 Westley and Mintzberg, 'Visionary leadership', p. 22.
15 Day, *Market Driven Strategy*, p. 15.
16 Westley and Mintzberg, 'Visionary leadership', p. 22.
17 Conger, 'Inspiring others', p. 32.
18 Ibid., p. 39.
19 F. Friedrich Neubauer, *Portfolio Management* (Deventer: Kluwer, 1990), pp. 8–9.
20 Xavier Gilbert and Paul Strebel, 'Developing competitive advantage', in James Brian Quinn, Henry Mintzberg and Robert M. James (eds), *The Strategy Process* (Englewood Cliffs: Prentice-Hall, 1988), p. 70.
21 Westley and Mintzberg, 'Visionary leadership', p. 22.
22 Ibid., p. 17; Leavitt, *Corporate Pathfinders*, p. 39.
23 Senge, *Fifth Discipline*, p. 211,
24 E. Land, 'The most basic form of creativity', *The Times*, 26 June 1972, p. 84.
25 Westley and Mintzberg, 'Visionary leadership', p. 19.
26 Leavitt, *Corporate Pathfinders*, p. 64.
27 P. Ranganath Nayak and John M. Ketteringham, *Breakthroughs!* (New York: Rawson Associates, 1986), pp. 338–9.
28 Leavitt, *Corporate Pathfinders*, p. 63.
29 Westley and Mintzberg, 'Visionary leadership', p. 29 (quoting from *Moments of Truth* by Jan Carlzon).
30 Leavitt, *Corporate Pathfinders*, p. 62.
31 Sir John Harvey-Jones, speech given at the St Gallen Symposium, Switzerland, 17 May 1988.
32 Senge, *Fifth Discipline*, p. 214.
33 Westley and Mintzberg, 'Visionary leadership', p. 20.
34 Leavitt, *Corporate Pathfinders*, p. 6.

35 Westley and Mintzberg, 'Visionary leadership', p. 20.
36 Ibid., p. 21.
37 Day, *Market Driven Strategy*, pp. 16–17.
38 Senge, *Fifth Discipline*, p. 211.
39 Ibid., p. 206.
40 Harvey-Jones, speech, p. 6.

8

The Practice of Visioning (The PN Model)

Good business leaders create a vision, articulate the vision, passionately own the vision, and relentlessly drive it to completion.

Jack Welsh,
CEO of General Electric

The vast majority of the conceptual considerations on visioning discussed in the previous chapter has been incorporated by two of the authors in our own visioning process. The main aim in creating this process was to make the concept operational. We shall now have a closer look at it.

The essence of the PN (Parikh–Neubauer) Model of Corporate Visioning is captured in figure 8.1. As can be seen, the approach starts out with two strands of visioning, namely *reflective visioning* and *intuitive visioning*. Both streams are eventually combined to form an *integrative vision*, which serves as a powerful basis for action plans. Figure 8.1 also implies that visioning is an ongoing process. As shown there at the right-hand side, the integrative vision and the current reality of the business are reviewed on an ongoing basis. If need be, the vision is modified.

Reflective Visioning

In order to explain the steps in the reflective visioning process (see the upper left-hand part of figure 8.1), we assume that the group going through the process represents a general management group – the top management of a corporation, of a division or of a major, relatively independent subsidiary. (The process can, however, also be applied to

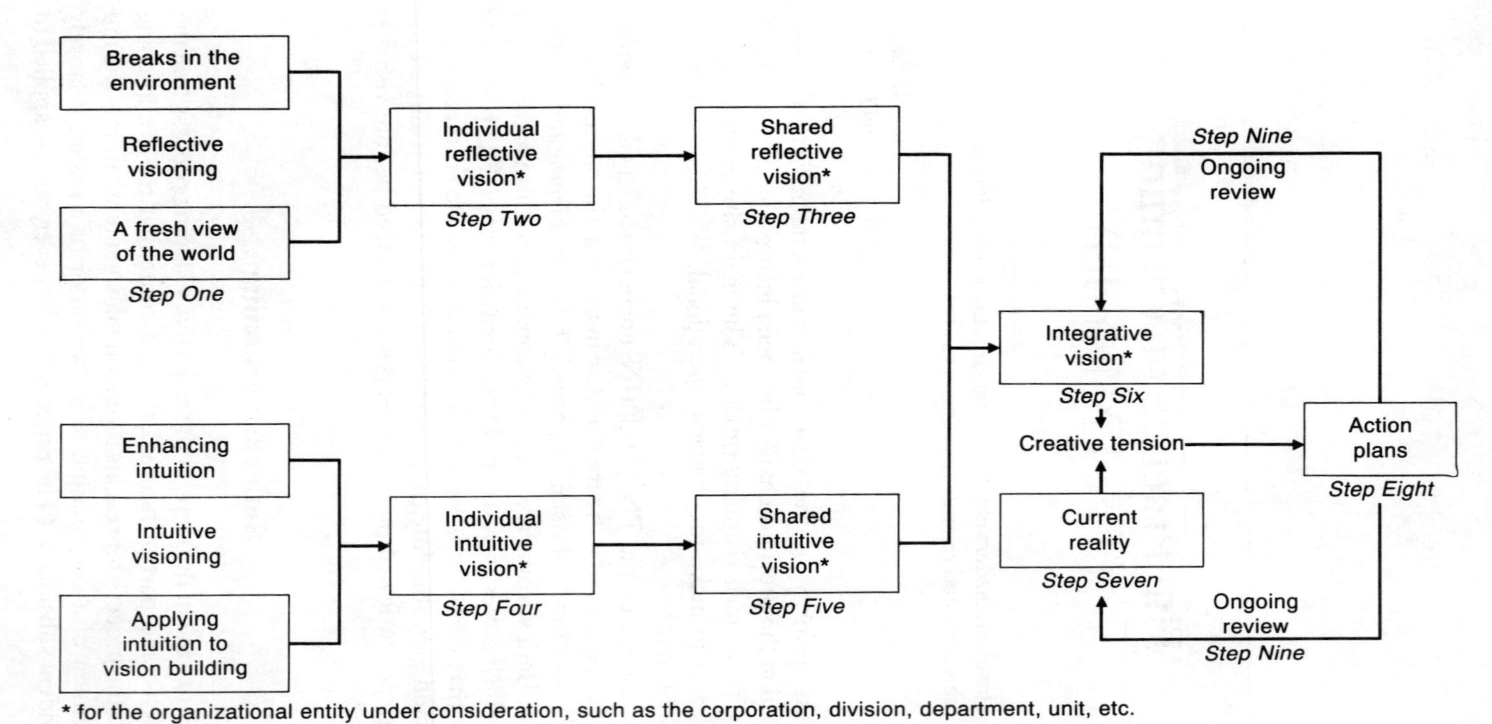

* for the organizational entity under consideration, such as the corporation, division, department, unit, etc.

Figure 8.1 Vision-building process: the PN model

functional areas in a company, such as an R&D or human resources department, etc.)

Before entering the first step of the process, the group is familiarized with the concept of a vision and of visioning pretty much along the lines discussed in the previous chapter. One of the main aims of this presentation is to impress on the group that they will have to avoid the temptation of falling back into some of the familiar routines of traditional, incremental strategic planning. After this introduction, the group is invited to begin the reflective visioning process proper.

Step One

As stated earlier, the creation of a vision depends heavily on two major aspects:

- a break (or discontinuity) in the environment and/or a new way of 'reading' that environment, and
- the ability to create 'an image of a desired future organizational state' of the unit under consideration.

In Step One the first of these two aspects is dealt with.

In order to familiarize the managers with the forefront of developments in the different environmental domains, they are exposed to short, pointed presentations by experts on the economic, technological, social and political environments in which the company is living. The emphasis of these brief presentations is on observed or expected discontinuities, convergences or undercurrents. Examples of such developments could be the expected future regionalism in Europe, the globalization of capital markets, the possible eclipse of the public corporation, etc.

As we have pointed out earlier, the hallmark of visionaries, of entrepreneurial managers, is their ability to read these events and developments differently from the pack; that is, differently from the way other managers would interpret them. The following example illustrates this point. During the years of the independence movements in black Africa, Europeans who had established their business there in the colonial days became nervous about their future, fearing that the 'hotheads' in the new administrations would push through threats to nationalize foreign-owned assets. In contrast, Tiny Rowland, the head of the British mining finance house Lonrho, sensed that the new black African leaders wanted to reassure world opinion as to their stability and responsibility. While the other European business people moved out as fast as they could sell, he moved in forcefully by offering them low cash multiples, mopping up valuable earnings and debt-free assets at knock-down prices.[1] Was Tiny Rowland privy to information other business people in black Africa did not have? He was not. He just read the environment differently from the others. The essence of this part of the visioning exercise is well captured in a sentence from Marcel Proust: 'To go on a voyage of discovery you don't need new landscapes, you need fresh eyes.'

In order to make it easier for the managers participating in the process to look at those environments with fresh eyes, they are exposed to creativity-based techniques in the course of this step. In this context, one can for instance use techniques Edward de Bono has introduced into the literature (and business practice).[2] The aim of this step is to come up with options for exciting and (hopefully) fresh business ideas, as we have defined them earlier.

Step Two

In the second step, the managers are asked to do individual work. On the basis of the inputs provided in Step One, they are requested to create their personal vision of the company, say, five years on. In order to give them some guidance on how to perform this task, we use the time-honoured technique of asking them: 'What would you like *Fortune* magazine to write about your company five years from now?' (If the company is not active internationally, we replace *Fortune* with any other prominent national business magazine that the participants know and appreciate.)

In our guidelines we ask the participants explicitly to write a lively, journalistic story, one they would use to lure the cream of the crop of graduating university students to their organization. This request forces the participants to abandon the terse outline with bulleted points they typically use when they make presentations to peers and superiors.[3]

We urge them equally explicitly to jump ahead in this thinking and compose the story with no strings attached (further on, there will be ample opportunity to add water to the wine of this optimistic thinking). At a later point in the process we make them work from their vision; that is, to put themselves mentally in the future state described by the vision and ask what they would have to do today to arrive at that state.

Some practitioners resist trying this approach. We ask them to suspend their disbelief at least and to reserve their criticism for the outcome. This usually works. In the end, executives with whom we have interacted have enjoyed visioning the desired future state of their organization.

Very similar to the '*Fortune*' approach is the 'visioning the ideal' approach, of which Tichy gives the following example.[4] In 1985, Clark Equipment and AB Volvo created a new company by merging Clark Michigan with Volvo's BM division. There resulted one of the largest construction and mining equipment manufacturers in the world. Two years earlier, Clark had found itself in great difficulties. In addition, there had been no way to generate the resources to redirect its future in the time available. Rather than give up in despair, Clark Michigan took several unusual steps:

- They encouraged management to come up with an unconstrained design of an ideal competitor to the two giants in the industry, Caterpillar and Komatsu.
- Again without constraints, Clark Michigan's management considered which companies in the industry together with itself would most closely approximate the ideal company they had designed. Three organizations were identified as potential partners.
- Armed with this concept, they first approached Daimler-Benz and acquired their Euclid Truck subsidiary, a company specializing in off-road vehicles (used in open-pit mining, for instance). They furthermore opened discussion with Volvo BM, the construction equipment division of Volvo, suggesting a joint venture to them. The idea met with a friendly reception, but one manager insisted on some in-depth analyses to understand the merits of the case fully. Teams were formed which looked into the matter and discovered that the project would create advantages for both companies. In the autumn of 1984, presentations were made to the boards and the commitment to the joint venture was reached by the end of that year.

When the Clark managers looked back at the process and compared the outcome to the ideal they had envisioned, they had to admit to themselves that they had got most of what they had wanted. What happened at Clark would have been hardly achievable with conventional planning.

In our work with practitioners we find it helpful to combine the two approaches. When the participants write their *Fortune* article, we ask them to compose a story in which they envisage their company as an ideal competitor in their industry. As this task may awe some of the practitioners, we suggest that they break it up into more manageable sub-tasks.

One of the sub-tasks would be to answer the question: 'Envisage the ideal version of your product. How would it look?' Under normal circumstances, time allows us only to solicit the participants' opinion. If the process were stretched out over a longer period, one might even confront key customers and distributors with this question and use their reaction when describing an ideal product. The same holds true, of course, for services the company offers. Jan Carlzon's 'passenger pleasing plane' is an example. Carlzon's vision is a craft of unorthodox design with 75–80 per cent of the interior volume of the fuselage allocated to passenger comfort and cabin baggage storage, compared to the 35 per cent traditionally allocated. Here is his explanation of this dream: 'For the 1990s our starting point is that we need an aircraft which the passenger wants. Then we can add on engines and the cockpit, not the other way around.' In a news conference, Carlzon picked up a model of a narrow-bodied plane, turned it on its side and said: 'This is what I see. The floor (of the Passenger Pleasing Plane) is lower; the roof higher. Seating would be no more than two seats abreast with an aisle. Belly space for the baggage would be reduced because there would be wardrobes for the traveller. Businessmen don't want to wait for their luggage.'[5]

Another sub-task to use in envisaging an ideal competitor would be to ask: 'What would be the ideal distribution system in your industry? If you could start all over again, how would you set it up?' A good example in this context would be the method Citicorp invented in 1986 to help Americans select their mortgage loans. In 1981, Citicorp was not even in the top one hundred mortgage lenders in the US. To change the situation, they dreamed up a new distribution system:

> Simply described, Citicorp has strung together three thousand real estate brokers, lawyers, and insurance agents into a thirty-seven-state referral network. To qualify for Mortgage Power (the name of the program) and receive a loan for an origination fee 1.5% below what one would get by going directly to Citicorp, the home buyer must go through a Citicorp agent. The agents, in turn, are paid by the home buyer a broker's fee of 0.5%. The positioning of the mortgage is not the lowest cost in the market, but a hassle-free one that will be approved (or not) within fifteen days, with very little paperwork.[6]

Further sub-tasks would include answering questions like: 'What would be the ideal organization structure for your company?', or: 'In your opinion, what would be the ideal management style?' (The answer to the last question would also express an opinion on a desirable culture and the basic values on which it rests.) Other sub-task questions which could be raised in this context are: 'If we could start all over again, what would be the ideal business system for our company? What stage in the value chain should we concentrate on? Could we leave out stages that do not add value?'

A good example in this context would be IKEA, the international home furnishings retailer of Swedish origin. When enormous obstacles in Swedish furniture manufacturing and trade (such as a high degree of cartelization) hampered the growth of his budding company, Ingvar Kamprad, the founder of IKEA, dreamed up a modified form of the business system. IKEA eliminated or modified the activities that increased the delivery cost and did not add essential perceived value from the consumer point of view. Gilbert and Strebel describe Kamprad's concept in the following way:

> Carefully monitoring sub-contracting of production to specialized manufacturers ensured quality at a lower cost. The furniture was no longer assembled, but flat-packed. It was not displayed in city-center stores but in hyper-stores outside cities. A trade-off was made between minimum inventories, to decrease delivered cost, and immediate availability. Furthermore, by doing its own product design, IKEA could insure a low delivered cost consistency throughout its business system. On the other hand, perceived value was added where this could be done for a low delivered cost. A very wide range of home products was offered under the same roof and could be looked at and tried by the consumer in the display section of the stores, rather than only seen in different stores or in catalogs. The furniture was normally available immediately and could be taken back home by car. Doing its own design IKEA could offer a homogeneous, modular product range. The desirable image of Scandinavian furniture was skilfully exploited to add perceived value. Last not least, by redesigning its entire business system, IKEA built an additional powerful competitive advantage: the know-how necessary to operate this formula.[7]

Their unique approach made IKEA into the world's largest home furnishings retailer by the end of the 1980s.

The sub-tasks mentioned above are meant only to be indicative. Other aspects have to be added to round out the picture. These partial stories have to be combined and homogenized, so that they result in a cohesive story.

We consider Step Two (which is done individually) an extremely important one in the process. As artists always have an image of the work they want to create in their minds, so visionary managers have to be able to create for themselves their personal image of a desired future state of their organization. As Bennis and Nanus have said:

> If there is a spark of genius in the leadership function at all, it must lie in this transcending ability . . . to assemble – out of all the variety of images, signals, forecasts and alternatives – a clearly articulated vision of the future that is at once simple, easily understood, clearly desirable and energizing.[8]

Step Three

In order to serve its purpose, a vision has to be a shared vision, as we said earlier. This sharing among the top management group is done in Step Three in a plenary session of the team. During this session, the managers jointly study the individual vision statements, discuss them in considerable depth, identify areas which they have in common as well as outlying ideas. In this intensive session (in 'sweat shirts, with cans of beer, sandwiches and flip charts', to repeat John Harvey-Jones's words), and under the guidance of experienced process facilitators, a shared reflective vision is hammered out – in all the specificity needed to make it meaningful. A vision statement is, of course, never finished. Nevertheless one has to push it to a certain completeness at this stage, otherwise one has problems in the remaining steps of the exercise. (If the company happens to have several rather heterogeneous divisions, one might proceed in stages, by first going through the process on the divisional level, creating a shared divisional vision, and then converting these various visions into a shared, corporate vision.)

As can be seen from this description of the first three steps, our process allows us to employ all the generic modes of visioning we have – individual approaches as well as interactive, sharing ways.

The reflective visioning process has been made part of the exercise for a number of reasons. Although it breaks in several respects with the traditional planning approaches, it is still a rational way of proceeding. This means it offers managers a rod to hold on to; that is, they find themselves on a largely familiar terrain. This eases them into our visioning process. We feel we have to provide this comfort before breaking even more radically with the traditional approaches by using non-rational, intuitive processes. These intuitive approaches are, however, needed to get the full benefit of the visioning process.

Intuitive Visioning

The basic difference between reflective visioning and intuitive visioning is that while pursuing reflective visioning, one is responding to the question, 'What can I get?' While this does not imply merely an incremental projection of growth and does enable a jump ahead of the conventional vision statement, it is still basically an intellectual or rational process – in other words, it is the maximum possible stretching of one's imagination into the future, but inevitably tempered with realism. The process of intuitive visioning, on the other hand, implies responding to the question, 'What do I really want?' While answering this, one does not keep the frame of reference of current reality or even what may be considered as realistic future possibility. It implies total resonance within oneself with whatever it is that one is up to in one's life, with whatever are one's basic urges and uncontaminated inner dreams. In other words, after one intellectually, rationally or realistically arrives at a maximum stretch of one's imagination in the context of real-world possibilities – that is, in developing the reflective vision – one should go into another level of mental activity, namely the intuitive level, and access one's own inner world through some specific mental ('intuitive') processes for creating an intuitive vision.

As mentioned above, at the intuitive level one is not locked into either linear thinking or blocked by any so-called rational constraints. Intuitive vision therefore is not only a much bigger leap – a quantum leap – from the current reality, but also qualitatively different from the reflective vision. In other words, in the process of reflective visioning one is still constrained by logical realism; in intuitive visioning, one has no such constraints. The intuitive visioning process facilitates the release of one's innate creativity, unfettered by rational, analytical or linear thinking or one's existing mind-sets. It enables one to break the connections with one's conventional pattern of thinking and experience a different kind or level of perception or insight about possibilities in the future. This enhances the ability to develop some totally new and different kinds of connection or linkage. Finally, this process also helps to generate hitherto unthought-of applications or innovative ideas.

The underlying assumption here is that our education, experience and expertise, while we have acquired through them certain kinds of knowledge and skill which enable us to intensify our depth of thinking, have usually tended to restrict the breadth or the width of our imagination and creativity. Modern education seems to have affected adversely our natural rounded sensibilities and narrowed them down into a square hole of the Cartesian model. Moreover, being 'realistic' also implies remaining linked with the existing, established paradigm or learnt viewpoint of what reality in the world of business is about. When we go deep inside us, beyond this frame of reference, through intuitive processes, then we have no such limiting factors, which helps in 'rounding the square'. In other words this process enables one to go beyond one's ordinary, conscious, logical, rational, somewhat simplistic mental state to the exploration of deeper and more complex patterns at subconscious levels. This facilitates expansion or enlargement of the context in our thinking, making it more holistic, macroscopic and synthesizing.

There are also suggestions that in such an intuitive process, when one is in a very relaxed and receptive state of mind or begins to get in touch with a deeper and expanded state of consciousness, the constraints and barriers of our rational, egoistic, skin-encapsulated thinking begin to soften and become dormant. One's consciousness in a sense gets connected and in tune with larger systems and enables the reception of information from sources outside one's own self. This phenomenon is also generally described as extrasensory perception (ESP). This is supposed to be basically of three varieties:

1 our minds connecting and tapping other minds – telepathy;
2 our minds interacting with matter, seeing or touching other objects, articles, etc., and through them receiving some information – clairvoyance;
3 our minds going beyond time and space coordinates and even supposedly tapping into the future – premonition.

Now from a business point of view, no matter what the processes are and what their descriptions are, it is of immense value to develop a condition within oneself which enables one to expand the arena and sources of information. This helps in cultivating the ability (and therefore the possibilities it brings) to have the different kinds of insight and innovative connection which surface in our minds as intuition.

However, one has to be careful and vigilant about ensuring that one is able, over a period of time, to cultivate the sensitivity and ability to distinguish between one's instinctive drives or impulsive desires, or what may be commonly described as wishful thinking, from authentic intuition, as described in chapter 3. What happens ordinarily is that one experiences these inner compulsive urges but suppresses them in the context of realistic lifestyles. Therefore, these urges remain suppressed at a subconscious level – the level which can be described, among other things, as that of unarticulated dreams. In a paradigm governed by rational, logical, analytical processes, one usually believes that one should not be carried away by one's dreams for fear of getting out of touch with reality. While this is basically correct, there is a tendency to overdo it. To redress the balance, we need more systematically to explore our inner dynamics, as described earlier.

To put it in rather simplistic terms, keeping in mind the emerging scenarios in business – characterized by accelerating change, complexity, uncertainty and conflict – we need to think not only from our heads, but also from our guts, and to develop the combination so as to reflect from our hearts. In other words, it is absolutely necessary to have our heads high up in the sky (but not lost in the clouds) and at the same time to have our feet firmly on the ground (but not stuck in the mud).

While the essence and basis of the intuitive vision is intuition, and the intuitive visioning process involves accessing intuition, it implies an ongoing interaction with one's reasoning abilities as well as the energy of one's emotion. It is an ongoing synthesis of all three (intuition, reason and emotion), leading to an ongoing virtuous spiral of analysis, imagination and innovation (see figure 8.2).

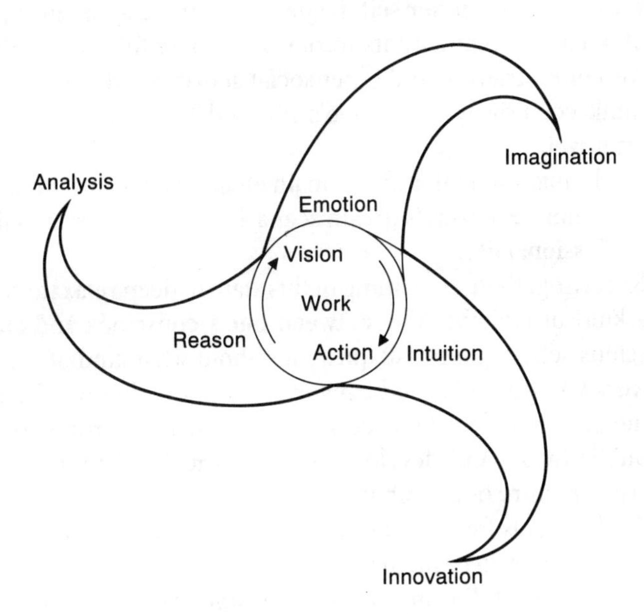

Figure 8.2 Work as a vision made visible

It is through such interaction, triggered off by the intuitive processes, that one can create an intuitive vision on an individual basis as well as a shared vision within an organization. The process of sharing one's intuitive vision generates a deeper understanding within the organization and a sense of common belonging and bonding. This releases positive energy and ongoing action to implement and actualize the shared vision. Work, in this way, is vision made visible.

Step Four

A brief description of the sequence involved in this highly creative and exciting intuitive process is given below (see also chapter 4):

1 *Relaxing*: the first and the most important step is to be totally relaxed, in terms of body, mind and emotion. There are specific relaxation processes which give one the experience of being 'centred'.
2 *Imaging*: then go into the processes of imaging, and guide oneself to a deeper inner level of awareness, leading to an imaginary retreat, detached and disconnected from the external environment.
3 *Symbolizing*:
   (a) Personal life:
   Receiving: having reached such a state of being totally absorbed with one's own inner self, begin to 'dream' and create a picture of what one really wants in one's personal life, family life, life with one's friends, and other social activities. Allow the mind to think cognitively about one's life and to create visual images intuitively.
   Analysing: then identify the main elements that are dominant in these images or one's dream scenarios in one's personal life.
   (b) Professional life:
   Receiving: then, remaining in this state of deep relaxation and in a kind of twilight zone between one's conscious and subconscious self, begin to ask questions about what kind of activity or work you would like to be involved with. In other words, answer the question, 'What do I really want to do in my professional and public lives?' and develop a dream articulated into a vision: a visual picture or a symbol.
   Analysing: as for one's personal life, identify the elements of the dream scenario or picture.
   Verbalizing: following the same sequence, articulate a verbal vision statement of one's professional life.

This process leading to a picture or symbol is useful and exciting in several ways. First, it enables one to become aware of one's inner dynamics. Frequently it is quite surprising to get in touch with one's innermost urges and get an insight into what one is really up to in one's life. Second, it trains one to develop 'total thinking' by learning the visual language of creating images, pictures and symbols, and balancing or synthesizing them with one's conventional, rational and analytical thinking. Above all, it is also a very enjoyable and energizing process (see figure 8.3).

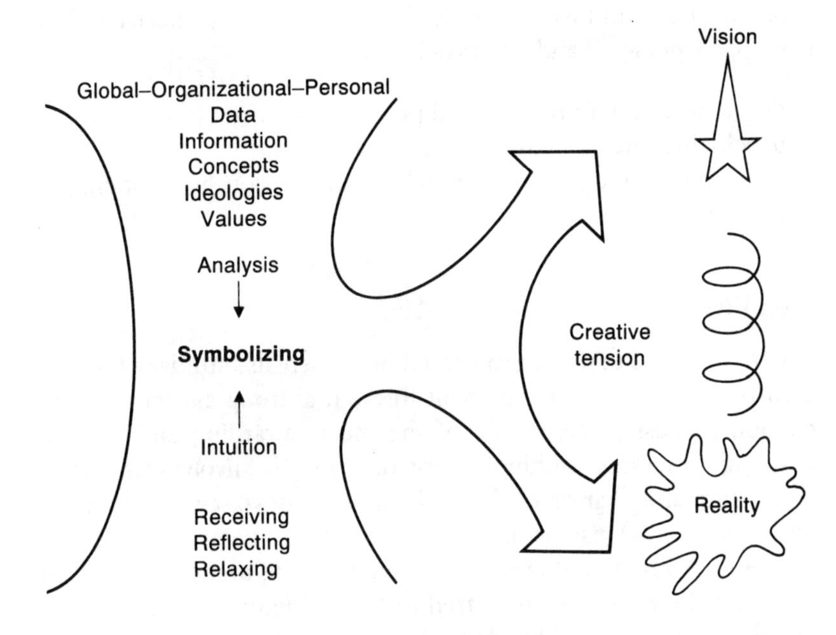

Figure 8.3 Intuitive vision-building

However, the next stage in Step Four is a crucial one: after having articulated a vision and a verbal statement about one's personal life, as well as about one's professional life, one has to compare the two – the personal and the professional vision. One usually finds some convergence as well as some discrepancies between them. While one is generally aware of this situation, one has not usually gone into a systematic process of identifying, crystallizing and balancing in a conscious manner these complementarities and divergencies. These, therefore, are frequently manifested as an ongoing tension and even conflict between one's personal and family life on the one hand, and one's professional and business life on the other. While such tension and conflict cannot be totally avoided or resolved, one can certainly minimize them through a conscious and deliberate effort to bring about an alignment between the two visions and even convert such tension into a creative energy, thereby transforming one's negative emotions into positive ones. At a deeper level, this also enables one to transform one's posture from a reactive to a more proactive one. This is of growing importance not only in one's personal life but also in one's business or corporate life.

In other words, there are three stages involved in Step Four in the creation of an intuitive aligned vision – that is, a synthesized vision from one's personal and professional visions:

1 developing an intuitive attuned personal vision;
2 developing one's intuitive professional vision;
3 developing an aligned individual intuitive vision by balancing the above two.

Step Five

The next step is to develop a shared or consensus intuitive vision and a corresponding verbal statement through a group sharing and discussion process. This is one of the most rewarding and powerful bonding processes within an organization. It involves multistage interaction and sharing of the individual, intuitive, aligned (personal and professional) visions in small groups. It can begin at any level, at the top or bottom, and percolate throughout the organization. There will rarely be a completely shared or totally identical vision throughout the organization. However, there will at least be a broad consensus about the major elements and direction in the vision.

The really important thing in Step Five is the process. While sharing the visual images or symbols, there is so much fun as well as insight, so much resonance experienced with the colleagues at a deeper level while articulating a verbal statement, that a deeper-level, finer tuning takes place. This process of evolving a shared vision becomes a kind of common thread, or understanding, that brings all the diverse pulls and forces within an organization into a common track and direction.

In summary, to every vision – personal life vision; professional life vision; aligned, individual, intuitive vision; and shared, intuition vision – there are three aspects:

1 an image, picture or symbol;
2 the main elements in these visuals;
3 a verbal statement incorporating these elements.

Integrative Visioning

Step Six

Having developed the shared reflective and intuitive visions, we have now to go beyond this and integrate them by comparing and synthesizing or balancing them. The resulting vision is the integrative vision. This then becomes one's driving force in life and also indicates the relevant activity and priorities for the immediate future (see figures 8.4 and 8.5 below).

As shown in figure 8.4, the entire process of developing an integrative vision is essentially one of learning, and enables the individual to develop a learning culture within one's self, one's family and any organization. While the process of developing a reflective vision stimulates one's intellectual and imaginative faculties, it is still within the framework of a 'responsible' view of reality and future possibilities. The intuitive processes free one from this state and facilitate a kind of creative or quantum leap. The real challenge is to engage, on an ongoing basis, in the process of learning to integrate the two levels of visioning. As in the case of synthesizing one's personal and professional intuitive visions, there will be a continuing creative tension between the intuitive and reflective visions.

Step Seven

Now, the most interesting part, namely Step Seven, is to use the visioning and symbolizing process to influence the existing situation or the current reality in a manner that helps move the current reality towards the vision of the desired future state. This involves three stages of symbolization:

1 symbols of the desired future (which we call vision);
2 symbols of the current reality;
3 symbols of the various intermediate stages, each one indicative of the shifts in each stage over the years, through which current reality could be pulled towards the envisioned state.

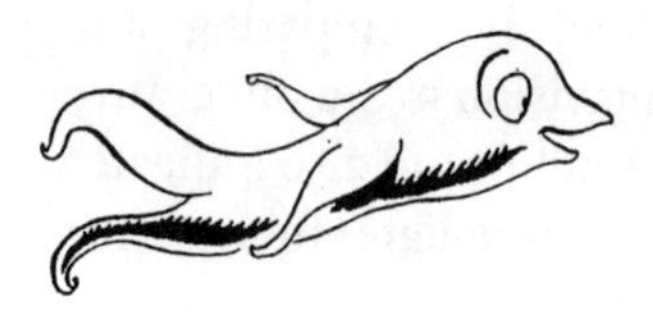

Current reality

Vision (future state)

Current reality

Vision

Current reality

Vision (future state)

Current reality

Vision

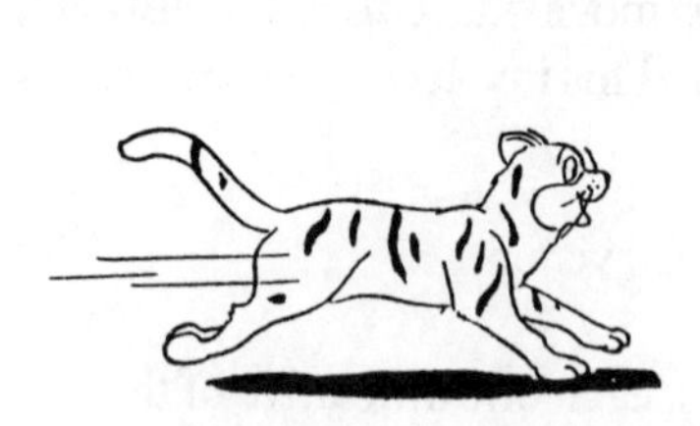

Current reality

Vision (future state)

Current reality

Vision

There will be a time frame for each stage.

The ultimate objective is to take this entire process throughout the organization at all levels. Whatever level you are at, you enrol the teams or units or divisions or departments – whatever there may be in the organization – so that ultimately there is an ongoing, shared vision at the corporate level. This becomes the real driving energy, the forceful thrust throughout the organization. In other words, basically two things happen. First, the corporation is positioned *vis-à-vis* the external environment, consisting of customers and competitors, in a way much different from that which one usually arrives at through the conventional planning processes. Second, the entire corporation is galvanized into a single-purpose, single-minded, united drive towards actualizing the corporate vision.

Keeping in mind the relevance, significance and even urgency of this process in contemporary management, one would like to coin a special word for it and call it 'visionance'. It should be the organizing principle of business, or any organized activity. It really brings a kind of romance into management and is the essence of excellence – durable excellence.

In other words, it generates a resonance (attunement) with oneself, and a congruence (alignment within one's personal and professional lives and sharing with one's colleagues) in the family and/or at work. It also creates the basis for empowerment within the entire organization, ultimately leading to higher performance and a sense of fulfilment (see figure 8.4).

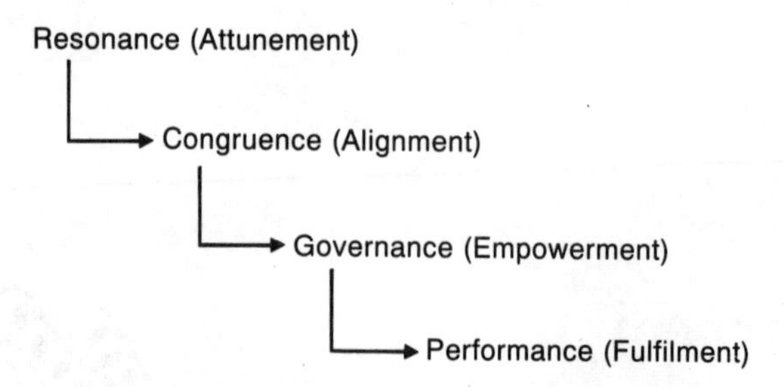

Figure 8.4 Developing an integrative vision

Step Eight

The next step is to translate the shared integrated vision into a plan of action, which should clearly indicate who should do what by what time and with what resources. This step is clearly the most crucial one and has to be processed with maximum possible participation and commitment at all levels.

Step Nine: A Never-Ending Process

The real dynamics within the organization – in a sense the main 'theme' of the organization – would therefore be an ongoing review of the shared vision of the future, of the view of current reality from the perspective of that vision and the relevant plan of action. Vision is not a solution to a problem. If it is seen in that light, when the problem of low morale or unclear strategic direction goes away, the energy behind the vision will also go away. Building shared vision must be seen as a central element of the daily work of leaders. It is ongoing and never-ending.[9] The continuous nature of this process is emphasized in figure 8.1. A vision, this journey into an unknown, uncharted territory, has to be recalibrated again and again. This requires business acumen, strength of character and courage. This has been true for pathfinders throughout the ages. As George Santayana once said: 'Columbus found a new world, and had no chart save one that Faith had deciphered in the skies.'

Conclusion

All this may appear, at first sight, rather complex and may even overwhelm. However, after one has gone through a few rounds of this process, it becomes very lucid, natural, and almost automatic. It is just a question of learning a new skill. Like any other skill it takes a little time and effort, but if one does this with a full faith and trust in the process and with a sense of determination and commitment, it takes much less time and effort than one may imagine at the outset. Eventually it can become a natural way of thinking, a way of life.[10]

The three processes – reflective, intuitive and integrative visioning – in combination lead to sustainable peak performance, which is the goal of any organization. Figure 8.5 shows the vision stages as an ongoing virtuous spiral: first, developing an understanding of whatever is in *sight* in the external environment, then looking inside one's own internal environment, or inner dynamics, and developing what one may call *in*sight; and then integrating with this *in*sight one's in*sight*. The combination or synthesis of these two will generate what one may call *insight*. Remaining in touch with this insight, one develops an *outlook* in the context of the external environment, and functions in one's life with that outlook.

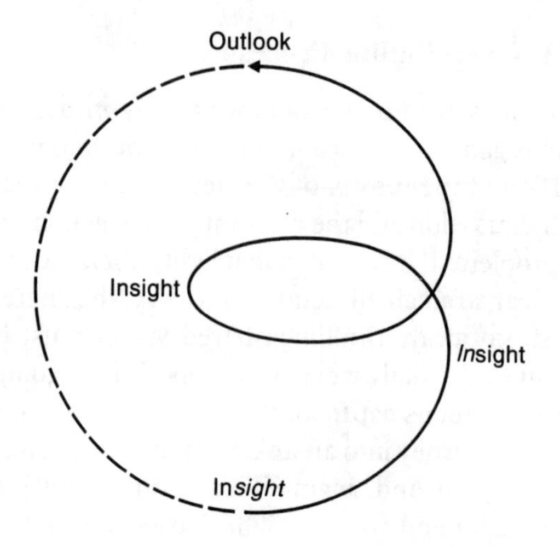

Figure 8.5 Vision stages

The interesting point is that one's outlook or the governing attitude with which one functions in the outer world is not a reactive or *ad hoc* approach, but a proactive one. It is a deep-rooted, connected and integrated attitude based on a more creative (rather than reactive) perception, connection and application of one's desires and directions in life.

To repeat a well-known metaphor: at a construction site, where there were several workers cutting stone, an ordinary conventional stone-cutter would say, 'I am cutting stone'; a more intelligent, well-trained, expert worker would say, 'I am converting stone into specific shapes'; a visionary worker would say 'I am building a cathedral.' One can easily surmise the significant difference this vision-driven performance would make to the quality of the work as well as to the feeling of the worker during and after the work. It is possible to have a vision of the cathedral even while pursuing a relatively dull work like that of cutting stone, through the kinds of processes that are described so far. Even more powerful is the well-known story of Michelangelo and his statue of David. On being questioned as to how he created such a masterpiece out of an ordinary marble rock, he is supposed to have said that it was very simple: all that happened was that while looking at the marble he had a vision of David, and after that all he did was to cut or sculpt away all that was 'not David'.

It is also important to note that this process of intuitive visioning, if pursued on an ongoing basis, does lift us from the stage of 'having' a vision to a level of intensely getting absorbed and identified with it, or shall we say 'becoming' our vision. Taking this further to the corporate level, in such identification with the corporate shared vision one perceives one's own vision as a part of the corporate one, and therefore perceives oneself functioning in the corporation as a facilitative instrument for actualizing the corporate vision. This is a very significant shift – from the posture of operating towards a vision to that of operating from a vision. This is, in a true sense, making a real difference. It is a transformative shift from a problem-driven, conventional, organizational culture getting caught within the problem/solution cycle to one which can be described as a vision-driven culture, where problems appear as opportunities through the enlargement of the context – in a sense, making limitations or adversity work for you. This is a shift from what one may call organization development to organizational transformation, from a problem-ridden 'disease' mode to a vision-driven 'health' mode (see figure 8.6).

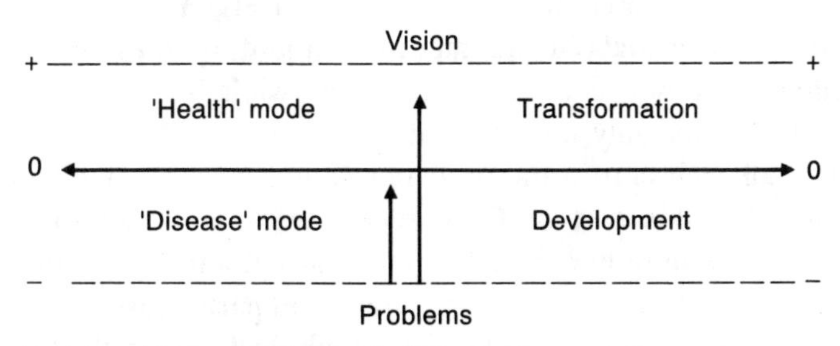

Problem-driven: Confinement within problem–solution cycle
Propensity for problematizing

Vision-driven: Problems seen as opportunities
Enlarging context
Making limitations irrelevant
Making adversity work for you

Figure 8.6 Transformative shift

Another important issue is that one's perception of the current reality itself changes if one is operating from a vision. Through the optics of the vision of the future, the view of the current reality begins to appear different from the one which one ordinarily perceives through problem-solving lenses. Thinking again of the story about Michelangelo, one can easily see the difference between the ordinary way of looking at a marble rock and viewing the same rock from the vision of seeing David in it. This is transformative in a true sense: in terms of perception of the rock, of the connection between one's work (creating a David) and the current reality (ordinary rock), and of application and direction of one's energy (strategies and tools).

Moreover, not only is the current reality viewed differently from an individual's viewpoint, but in a corporate setting, through this process, one can and should also develop a consensus or shared view of the current reality. Frequently, the frustrating problem faced by many managements today is that there are almost irreconcilable differences, even at the top management level, in perception, interpretation and judgement about the current reality, and as to what the strengths and weakness, opportunities and threats in the current situation of the organization are. With the process mentioned above, these are minimized. In fact, a constructive consensus happens about the perceived convergencies as well as divergencies in various viewpoints about the current reality. The attempt, then, with the vision-driven energy, which becomes a team work, is constantly to enhance the convergence and overcome or minimize the divergence.

It is not unlikely that one may face inner doubts or questions such as the following about this process, which, while being interesting, appears to be not only unusual but in a sense also 'far out'. Is this process really relevant in the hard-nosed and hard-headed world of business? Can this sort of thing really work? Is it not too much dreaming or being rather too soft? Does it also not imply spending too much time on such processes? In business and particularly in our fast-moving world, we have to make very quick decisions with very little data, and is this process not too slow? Even if one may feel interested in it, is it not a kind of a luxury which we can ill afford these days? Moreover, it does not seem to be grounded enough and perhaps it may take us too far out.

If one brushes aside all such doubts, one may still tell oneself: even if this thing works, so what? I have been successful so far with the way in which I have been thinking and functioning, so why go into any such thing, which appears to be rather risky and may even endanger my success path if I do something so different from what I have been used to so far? Another source of reinforcement to such a negative response is the notion that one is not able to create a real visual image in one's mind, or even articulate and visualize clearly what one really wants. Therefore, 'This is not for me.'

These are quite understandable thoughts, questions and concerns that may arise in anyone's mind, but then we are talking about the importance of making a difference. This is learning with a difference, and is it not true to say that if we want to make a real difference, then we have to think and function differently? Doing more of the same and expecting different results has been considered as another definition of insanity. In other words, unless we develop courage and the capacity of thinking differently, there are greater chances of remaining stuck with a very limited perception in a fast-changing world. We will remain where we are, but the world will move on. Therefore, perhaps the greatest risk today is not to take such a step.

If nothing else, this process of visioning at least creates a greater amount of clarity and direction within one's own self, and a deeper understanding of our inner dynamics. At the next stage, in the process of shared vision-building within one's own family, it creates a deeper feeling of caring and connection within the family. When this is extended to one's arena of work in a corporate setting, then the process of shared visioning also helps generate a deeper rapport, a kind of bonding among the members of the organization, and a genuine feeling of mutual trust among them rather than a fear of threat from each other. This process, therefore, results in the creation of shared meaning and purpose in one's work life with colleagues, a kind of reassuring resonance with each other. This is the essence of authentic and durable team building. In other words, a shared vision develops a strong feeling of co-ownership of, and responsibility for, the purpose and the processes within the organization.

This is the essence of the emerging concept of leadership in creating and facilitating success. This is also a most natural and organic way of converting what otherwise has been an arena of adversarial and conflicting cultures, which inevitably results in negative stress and frustrations, into an affectionate atmosphere, a healing climate of genuine partnership in progress. This is not only more authentic and durable; it is above all very pleasant and fulfilling. The least, therefore, that this process of visioning can contribute is to bring some enjoyment, some fun, some joy into the arena of work. In other words, it enables one to move from functioning with a fear of losing into a posture of performing with the joy of doing. To do so requires accessing and implementing our intuitive potential in addition to putting our reflective capacities to work.

Notes

1 Derek F. Channon and David Robinson, *The London and Rhodesian Mining Company Ltd*, case study (Manchester: Manchester Business School, 1973).
2 Edward de Bono, *Six Thinking Hats* (Boston: Little, Brown and Company, 1985).
3 Noel M. Tichy and Mary Ann Devanna, *The Transformational Leader* (New York: John Wiley, 1986), p. 142.
4 Ibid., pp. 140ff.
5 Scandinavian Airlines System SAS (A), case study by Sandra Vandermerwe, IMD, 1989, p. 10.
6 James F. Bandrowski, *Corporate Imagination Plus* (New York: The Free Press, 1990), p. 34. By 1988, Citicorp had become the nation's biggest mortgage lender.
7 Xavier Gilbert and Paul Strebel, 'Developing competitive advantage', in James Brian Quinn, Henry Mintzberg and Robert M. James (eds), *The Strategy Process* (Englewood Cliffs: Prentice-Hall, 1988), p. 79.
8 Warren Bennis and Burt Nanus, *Leaders* (New York: Harper & Row, 1985), p. 103.
9 Peter M. Senge, *The Fifth Discipline: The Art and Practice of the Learning Organization* (New York: Doubleday, 1990), p. 214.
10 Jagdish Parikh, *Managing Your Self* (Oxford: Blackwell, 1991).

Appendix 1 International Survey on Intuition

Universe for the Survey

The universe for the Survey has been taken to comprise all top/senior managers in private sector organizations conforming to certain minimum criteria in terms of size in nine selected countries.

Though the public sector has a significant presence in the economies of most countries, it is known that decision-making in this sector is far from streamlined, subject as it is to constant interference or pressures from bureaucrats, arbitrary ministerial directives, political compulsions, etc. It was therefore decided to exclude this sector from the purview of this Survey.

It was felt that even within the private sector, certain minimum criteria needed to be laid down with regard to the size of the organization so as to ensure a measure of homogeneity. The Survey has been conducted in the following nine countries, of which seven are from the industrial market economies, one is from middle-income developing countries (Brazil) and the other from low-income developing countries (India):

1 Austria
2 France
3 the Netherlands
4 Sweden
5 the United Kingdom
6 the United States of America
7 Japan
8 Brazil
9 India

In view of the wide disparity of the economic levels of the different countries, it was not possible to lay down uniform criteria regarding the size of organizations. In the case of the USA, the threshold level was around $500 million in terms of annual sales turnover, while in India the corresponding level was Rs500 million ($20 million). In Sweden, it was specified in terms of the minimum number of persons employed: 100 for industrial organizations and 50 for service organizations.

It will be noted that the USA, Japan and the five European countries (which provide a good cross-section of Europe) are among the most industrialized countries of the world, while Brazil and India represent two different levels of economic development among the developing countries. It will also be seen that in terms of geographical coverage, Europe, North America, South America, the Far East and South Asia find representation in the Survey.

The nine Survey countries account for about 30 per cent of the world population and their share of the world GNP is about 60 per cent.

On the basis of available data on civilian employment and proportions of labour force employed in the industry and services sectors in different countries (data available for 1987/8 have been suitably projected for 1990), and on certain assumptions, the Survey population has been estimated at 1.463 million (as of 1990), with the breakdown shown in table A1.1.

Table A1.1 Survey population

Country	Industry (000s)	Services (000s)	Total (000s)
Austria	8.4	8.8	17.2
France	44.5	61.7	106.2
Netherlands	11.7	20.0	31.7
Sweden	9.3	15.2	24.5
UK	62.0	83.4	145.4
USA	224.5	414.2	638.7
Japan	124.2	174.2	298.4
Brazil	36.3	44.1	80.4
India	56.6	64.2	120.8
Total	577.5	885.8	1463.3

Detailed working is shown in table A1.2. The estimates given may not be precise but certainly serve to indicate the order of magnitude of the population of different countries. Such indications about the relative proportions are necessary for working out meaningful averages for the population as a whole (which may be referred to as global averages).

Sample Design

It was proposed to follow a stratified, multistage sample design, viewing each of the Survey countries as a stratum and attempting a four-way sub-stratification as follows:

Type of activity	Industry/Services
Size of organization	Medium/Large

A finer substratification was to be attempted at the next stage on the basis of area of responsibility and sex, as follows:

Area of responsibility	General management/Finance/ Marketing/Production (Operations)/ Human resources development (HRD)/ Other
Sex	Male/Female

It was also provided that both the organizations and the managers would be selected on SRS (simple random sampling) basis from appropriate sampling frames to be developed for the purpose.

The above guidelines, together with the judgement of the Coordinators in different countries, constituted the basis for selection of the sample from the Survey population.

In all, 1312 managers responded to the survey, with the following breakdown:

Austria	114
France	118
Netherlands	89
Sweden	456
UK	52
USA	143
Japan	56
Brazil	204
India	80
Total	1312

Questionnaire

A structured, self-administrated questionnaire was developed for the Survey, which is reproduced in appendix 11. In countries where English is not the first language, translated versions of the questionnaire were used and the responses obtained were translated back into English.

Table A1.2 Basis for estimation of population totals for different countries, 1990

Category	Unit	Austria	France	Netherlands	Sweden	UK	USA	Japan	Brazil	India	Total
Population (1990)	Millions	7.6	56.2	14.9	8.4	57.1	250.4	123.8	153.8	830.0	1502.2
Civilian employment	Millions	3.4	21.2	6.1	4.7	27.2	120.7	60.9	53.8	290.5	588.5
Industry											
% employed	%	41	35	32	33	38	31	34	27	13	
Number employed	K	1394	7420	1952	1551	10 336	37 417	20 706	14 526	37 765	133 067
Relevant proportion*	%	60	60	60	60	60	60	60	25	15	
Relevant employment	K	836	4452	1171	931	6202	22 450	12 424	3632	5665	57 763
Senior/top managers as % of relevant employment	%	1.0	1.0	1.0	1.0	1.0	1.0	1.0	1.0	1.0	1.0
Number of senior/top managers	K	8.4	44.5	11.7	9.3	62.0	224.5	124.2	36.3	56.6	577.5
Services											
% employed	%	50	56	63	62	59	66	55	42	17	
Number employed	K	1700	11 872	3843	2914	16 048	79 662	33 495	22 596	49 385	221 515
Relevant proportion*	%	40	40	40	40	40	40	40	15	10	
Relevant employment	K	680	4749	1537	1166	6419	31 865	13 398	3389	4938	68 141
Senior/top managers as % of relevant employment	%	1.3	1.3	1.3	1.3	1.3	1.3	1.3	1.3	1.3	
Number of senior/top managers	K	8.8	61.7	20.0	15.2	83.4	414.2	174.2	44.1	64.2	885.8
Survey population (industry + services)	K	17.2	106.2	31.7	24.5	145.4	638.7	298.4	80.4	120.8	1463.3

K = 1000
*Relevant proportion = Proportion reckoned to be employed in organizations conforming to the Survey specifications.

Data on population has been extracted from *World Almanac and Book of Facts 1991*, except in the case of India, where the basis has been the census figure for 1991 as adjusted backwards for the estimated growth during the intervening period (at the time of writing) of about eight months.

The source for data on civilian employment for six countries – France, the Netherlands, Sweden, the UK, the USA and Japan – is *Statistical Abstract of the US: 1990* (10th edition), US Department of Commerce, Bureau of the Census. This publication provides the figures up to 1988; the figures for 1990 shown in the table are projections based on the observed average growth during 1986–8.

In the case of Austria, civilian employment has been taken to constitute 45 per cent of the population, while the proportion has been reckoned at 35 per cent for Brazil and India.

Data on proportions of labour force employed in industry and services has been extracted from *World Development Report 1988*, New York, Oxford University Press.

Proportions of civilian employment in industry and services sectors relevant for the study have been estimated on the basis of certain auxiliary information obtained in respect of some of the Survey countries.

Tabulation and Analysis

In the detailed computer tabulation brought out for each of the Survey countries (see appendices 2–10) and in chapters 5–6, the following sets have been used as background data:

Sex	Male
	Female
Age	Below 35
	35–44
	45–59
	Over 59
Organization type	Industry
	Services
Functional area	General management
	Finance
	Marketing
	Production/Operations
	HRD
	Other
Management level	Senior
	Top
Intuition rating	Low
	Medium
	High

An additional background relating to the nine Survey countries has been used in respect of the tabulation for 'All countries' (chapters 5–6), besides the six sets listed above.

While the industry/services classification was used for sample selection, the others are post-sampling classifications. Estimated population totals, together with the industry/services breakdown (as shown in table A1.2), have been used as the basis for working out the weighting factors. This applies to the global ('All countries') tables as well as to individual country tabulations.

The classification of medium/large organizations was not used as part of the background sets, as this could not be obtained in all cases and, where such classification was available, analysis showed no significant differences on the basis of it.

Managers at the level of chair, board director, president, chief executive (CEO), group vice president, etc., have been classified as top managers, and others such as vice-presidents and general managers have been grouped as senior managers. (We sought to exclude managers belonging to the middle and lower levels from the purview of the Survey.)

The Intuition rating has been based on an objective score developed by the Survey for each manager (see question 2 of the questionnaire in appendix 11) as follows:

Rating	*Score*
Low	0.0–3.5
Medium	4.0–6.0
High	6.5–10.0

By and large, only statistically significant differences have been commented upon in the chapters and appendices devoted to the Survey (judged by significance at the 5 per cent level).

Appendix 2 Report for Austria

Profile of Managers

The sample for Austria comprises 114 managers representing an estimated 17 200 managers in the country conforming to the Survey specifications. A profile of the Austrian managers, as drawn up by the Survey, is given in table A2.1.

Table A2.1 Profile of the Austrian managers in the Survey population

Category	Sample count	Estimated population (000s)	%	% corrected for NR*
Sex				
Male	104	15.9	92.4	93.0
Female	9	1.2	7.0	7.0
NR*	1	0.1	0.6	
Age				
Below 35	6	0.9	5.2	5.2
35–44	33	5.1	29.7	29.7
45–59	73	10.8	62.8	62.8
Over 59	2	0.4	2.3	2.3
Organization type				
Industry	44	8.4	48.8	48.8
Services	70	8.8	51.2	51.2
Functional area				
General management	32	4.3	25.0	31.6
Finance	13	2.0	11.6	14.7
Marketing	19	3.2	18.6	23.5
Production/Operations	5	1.0	5.8	7.4
Human resources development	7	1.1	6.4	8.1
Other	12	2.0	11.6	14.7
NR*	26	3.6	20.9	
Management level				
Senior	62	9.7	56.4	74.0
Top	23	3.4	19.8	26.0
NR*	29	4.1	23.8	
Total	114	17.2	100.0	100.0

*NR = Not reported.

It will be seen that:

- 7.0 per cent of the managers are females;
- 65.1 per cent or nearly two-thirds of the managers are relatively advanced in age, being 45 years old or more;
- 26.0 per cent of the managers belong to the top level (proportion corrected for the large complement of NR).

Intuition Ratings

Objective rating

Paired alternatives

Responses to the query regarding choice between ten given pairs of alternatives (where one of the terms is taken to indicate orientation towards Intuition and the other towards Logic/Reasoning) yield the distribution shown in table A2.2.

Table A2.2 Choice between paired alternatives

Intuition-oriented		Logic/Reasoning-oriented		Extent of non-expression of preference (%)
Description	Extent of preference (%)	Description	Extent of preference (%)	
1 Invent	43.4	Build	55.1	1.5
2 Vision	55.2	Common sense	44.8	–
3 Abstract	21.0	Concrete	75.7*	3.3
4 Innovative	90.5*	Conventional	8.1	1.5
5 Creative	66.9*	Analytical	27.9	5.1
6 Ideas	76.5*	Facts	22.4	1.1
7 Imaginative	46.7	Realistic	50.0	3.3
8 Ingenious	46.0	Practical	52.9	1.1
9 Fascinating	34.9	Sensible	63.2*	1.8
10 Spontaneous	55.5	Systematic	42.3	2.2

*The observed preference is statistically significant (at the 5 per cent level).
The two alternatives in each pair were presented to the respondent in a predetermined random sequence (see question 2 of the questionnaire in appendix 11).

It will be seen that of the five cases where the observed differences are statistically significant, in three cases the term associated with Intuition was preferred over its counterpart associated with Logic/Reasoning while it is the other way about in the remaining two cases. This indicates *prima facie* that the Intuition orientation of the Austrian managers may not be of a high order. A more comprehensive rating of the managers on this dimension is attempted later in this section.

Overall Intuition score

By assigning 1 to the choice indicating orientation towards Intuition and 0 to the one towards Logic/Reasoning, an overall score has been computed for each responding manager. Where there was no indication of preference for one term over the other in a given pair (evidenced by the respondent ticking both the alternatives or leaving the section blank), a score of ½ has been awarded; however, where no clear preference was indicated in respect even one of the ten given pairs, it has been treated as a case of 'Not reported' (NR). It is clear that the overall score ranges from 0 to 10 in steps of ½.

Classification

Based on the overall Intuition score, a three-way classification of managers has been devised as follows:

Score	*Category*
0.0–3.5	L: Low orientation
4.0–6.0	M: Medium orientation
6.5–10.0	H: High orientation

It will be noted that this classification has been used as one of the standard backgrounds in tabulation of the Survey responses. This is referred to as 'objective rating' as distinct from the 'self-rating' carried out by the respondents, which is discussed later.

Distribution

The above classification has led to the distribution shown in table A2.3.

It will be seen that, on an overall basis, the proportion of managers rated high works out to 37.1 per cent, which is better than had been suggested earlier by the preliminary inference based on choice between paired alternatives.

Self-Rating

Self-rating by the managers regarding Intuition on a given five-point scale (ranging from very high to very low) has yielded the distribution shown in table A2.4.

Table A2.3 Distribution based on objective rating on Intuition

Category	Low (%)	Medium (%)	High (%)
Sex*			
Male	20.7	41.9	37.4
Female	52.5	10.5	37.0
Age			
Below 35	13.2	13.2	73.5
35–44	21.0	44.5	34.5
45–59	25.2	40.1	34.7
Over 59	–	50.0	50.0
Organization type			
Industry	13.6	47.7	38.6
Services	31.4	32.9	35.7
Management level*			
Senior	19.5	41.9	38.6
Top	24.0	50.1	25.9
Total	22.7	40.1	37.1

*NR (= Not reported) omitted from classification.

Table A2.4 Distribution based on self-rating on Intuition

Category	Very High (%)	High (%)	Average (%)	Low (%)	Very low (%)
Sex*					
Male	6.8	51.4	37.5	4.4	–
Female	–	37.0	63.0	–	–
Age					
Below 35	–	79.9	20.1	–	–
35–44	4.9	44.5	42.0	8.6	–
45–59	7.7	52.9	37.1	2.3	–
Over 59	–	–	100.0	–	–
Organization type					
Industry	6.8	50.0	40.9	2.3	–
Services	5.7	51.4	37.1	5.7	–
Management level*					
Senior	3.3	52.9	39.2	4.6	–
Top	9.3	49.9	33.4	7.4	–
Intuition rating†					
Low	4.9	29.0	56.4	9.6	–
Medium	–	54.1	41.3	4.6	–
High	13.8	60.3	25.8	–	–
Total	6.3	50.7	39.0	4.0	–

*NR (= Not reported) omitted from classification.
†Relates to objective rating presented in table A2.3.

It will be seen that the majority (57.0 per cent) of the managers have rated themselves very high/high on Intuition, suggesting that Intuition is generally viewed by the Austrian managers as a positive attribute.

The proportion of managers rating themselves very high/high on Intuition rises from 33.9 per cent in the low group and 54.1 per cent in the medium group to a significantly higher level of 74.1 per cent in the high group, indicating a positive association between the two rating systems. Other observed differences are not statistically significant.

Association Between Ratings

The association between the two rating systems can be tested statistically by forming the contingency table shown as table A2.5.

Table A2.5 Objective rating v. self-rating

	Self-rating		
Classification based on objective rating	Average or lower (number)	Very high/high (number)	Total (number)
Low	18	10	28
Medium	20	24	44
High	11	31	42
Total	49	65	114

It can be seen that the χ^2 (which will have 2 degrees of freedom) for table A2.5 works out to 10.12, which is significant even at the 1 per cent level, confirming the positive association between the two ratings.

The contingency coefficient, C, works out to 0.29 as follows:

$$C = \sqrt{\frac{\chi^2}{\chi^2 + N}}$$

$$= \sqrt{\frac{10.12}{10.12 + 114}}$$

$$= 0.29$$

This value of C may be taken as a measure of the association between the two rating systems.

What is Intuition?

Descriptions Given of Intuition

The questionnaire used for the Survey (see appendix 11) starts with an invitation to the respondent to describe Intuition as understood by him or her so as to get the top-of-the-mind opinion; that is, a response uninfluenced by the sequence of questions that follows in the questionnaire. This has led to diverse descriptions of Intuition, of which the following are the more important:

Description	%
(Powerful) inner voice; impulse	49.7
Spontaneous perception/vision	29.4
Decision/perception without recourse to logical/rational methods	27.2
Inherent perception; inexplicable comprehension; a feeling that comes from within	25.0
Foresight; clairvoyance	15.0
Spark; flash	6.3
Integration of previous experience; processing of accumulated information	5.9

It will be seen that nearly half the Austrian managers described Intuition as '(Powerful) inner voice; impulse'. There are three other prominent descriptions that centre on spontaneity, antithesis of logic and inherent perception respectively.

It will be noted that the list also includes: 'Spark; flash' and 'Foresight; clairvoyance'.

Graphic Expression

The proportion of managers giving graphic expression to their concept of Intuition is fairly large at 69.6 per cent, pointing to the keen interest evinced in the subject by the Austrian managers. This proportion works out as follows for different categories of managers:

Category	%
Male	68.6
Female	79.0
Industry	84.1
Services	55.7

Category	%
Senior	79.2
Top	72.3
Low	45.2
Medium	77.1
High	76.3

The proportion of 84.1 per cent for the industry sector is significantly higher than that of 55.7 per cent for the services sector. Further, the proportion rises from 45.2 per cent in the low group to a significantly higher level of 77.1 per cent in the medium group and 76.3 per cent in the high group, suggesting a positive association between Intuition orientation and propensity to give graphic expression.

Other observed differences are not statistically significant.

Agreement with Specific Descriptions

The extent of agreement with three given descriptions of Intuition (obtained as three independent assessments and not as choice among three alternatives) can be seen from the distribution shown in table A2.6.

Table A2.6 Extent of agreement with three specific descriptions of Intuition

	Extent of agreement with		
Category	a (%)	b (%)	c (%)
Sex*			
Male	64.1	87.7	39.1
Female	52.5	79.0	26.5
Organization type			
Industry	61.4	88.6	43.2
Services	65.7	85.7	34.3
Management level*			
Senior	60.8	93.5	43.2
Top	66.7	81.4	33.3
Intuition rating			
Low	72.6	82.3	22.6
Medium	66.0	86.2	32.1
High	55.5	91.1	55.5
Total	63.6	87.1	38.6

*NR (= Not reported) omitted from classification.
(a) Spontaneous insight based on prior experience/expertise.
(b) Flash from 'subconscious levels'.
(c) Tuning into 'higher levels of consciousness'.

The observed differences between the extents of agreement with the different descriptions are statistically significant, resulting in an unambiguous order of acceptance of these descriptions as follows:

(b) > (a) > (c)

> Denotes 'preferred over'.

It may be noted that description (b) comes out on top despite the facts that 'Spark; flash' figures far down the list of responses to the open-ended question on the respondent's concept of Intuition, and that 'Subconscious' does not find a place at all in the major responses to this question (see 'Descriptions Given of Intuition'). On the other hand, though the second most important response to this question centres on spontaneity, description (a) gets only the second rank in terms of the extent of acceptance.

Perceived Relevance of Intuition

In Business/Management

The perceived relevance of different functional areas of business/management to the application of Intuition can be seen from the following proportions relating to different areas:

	Area	%
1	Corporate strategy and planning	74.3
2	Investment/Diversification	43.4
3	Corporate acquisitions/mergers/alliances	42.7
4	Finance	14.3
5	Marketing	78.3
6	Public relations	66.5
7	Choice of technology/plant and equipment	31.3
8	Production/Operations	19.5
9	Materials management	15.1
10	Human resources development	70.2
11	Research and development	68.8

Thus, the following are perceived as the major areas of application for Intuition in the field of business/management (no order of importance

intended):

- corporate strategy and planning;
- marketing;
- public relations;
- human resources development (HRD);
- research and development (R&D).

One might have expected areas like investment/diversification and corporate acquisitions/mergers/alliances to figure in the major areas of perceived importance, but these may have been taken to form part of corporate strategy and planning.

It will be noted that finance and production/operations are two major functional areas which rank among the least important in terms of perceived relevance.

In Other Fields

As regards fields other than business/management, the following are perceived to be the more important in terms of their relevance to application of Intuition:

Field	%
Art, drama, music, literature, etc.	33.8
Politics, public life	17.6
Sports	14.4
Specific disciplines (engineering, medicine, psychology, etc.)	14.3
Education, teaching	13.6
Recreation, entertainment, etc.	12.5
Love, marriage	10.3
Human/interpersonal relations	8.5
Family (relations)	7.0
Military/police affairs	5.5
Personal career/life	5.5

While fine arts claim the top spot, followed by politics/public life, it is significant that the study of specific disciplines and education/teaching figure fairly prominently in the other fields perceived to be relevant to the application of Intuition.

How Does One Identify Intuition?

Stated Means of Identification

The query as to how Intuition could be identified elicited diverse responses, of which the following are the more important:

Response	%
Deviation of decision from logical reasoning	21.3
Inability to explain conclusion on the basis of available facts	14.7
Strong inner feeling, emotion	10.3
Spontaneous perception/vision	7.0
Rapidity with which a decision is taken	5.9

It will be recalled that deviation of decision from logical reasoning, which tops the list here, also figures as a prominent response to the open-ended question on the meaning of Intuition (see 'Descriptions Given of Intuition'). However, 'spontaneous perception/vision', which figures as an equally prominent response to this question, is not viewed as a major identifying characteristic of Intuition.

Associated Phenomena

The extent to which experience of Intuition is perceived to be accompanied by different phenomena can be seen from table A2.7.

Table A2.7 Associated phenomena

Category	(a) Sensory (%)	(b) Physical (%)	(c) Mental (%)	(d) Emotional (%)
Sex*				
Male	25.5	29.9	47.9	68.5
Female	21.0	26.5	26.5	58.0
Organization type				
Industry	31.8	40.9	56.8	65.9
Services	20.0	20.0	35.7	70.0
Management level*				
Senior	34.7	40.6	41.3	60.8
Top	9.3	20.5	55.7	76.0
Intuition rating				
Low	11.3	11.3	29.2	63.0
Medium	29.4	35.0	39.5	66.9
High	30.7	36.7	63.4	72.2
Total	25.8	30.2	46.0	68.0

*NR (= Not reported) omitted from classification.

Experience of Intuition is thus most perceived to be accompanied by changes in the emotional aspects (followed by mental aspects), though emotion does not quite figure as a major response to the question on means of identification discussed earlier.

Use of Intuition

In Professional Life

Nearly half the managers stated that they use Intuition and Logic/Reasoning almost to the same extent in their professional life. As for the others, the proportion of managers reportedly using more of Intuition is a mere 4.8 per cent, as against 46.0 per cent using more of Logic/Reasoning, as may be seen from table A2.8.

Table A2.8 Extent of use of Intuition in professional life

Category	More of Logic/Reasoning (%)	Both in almost equal measure (%)	More of Intuition (%)
Sex*			
Male	45.8	49.0	5.2
Female	42.0	58.0	–
Organization type			
Industry	47.7	50.0	2.3
Services	44.3	48.6	7.1
Management level*			
Senior	46.4	50.3	3.3
Top	48.3	40.7	11.1
Intuition rating			
Low	59.6	37.1	3.2
Medium	50.5	44.9	4.6
High	32.7	61.4	5.9
Total	46.0	49.3	4.8

*NR (= Not reported) omitted from classification.

It will be noted that the proportion of managers using more of Logic/Reasoning drops from 59.6 per cent in the low group to 50.5 per cent in the medium group and further to 32.7 per cent in the high group. These differences are not statistically significant but may be taken to be indicative of a positive association between Intuition orientation and the extent of its use in professional life.

In Personal Life

A good majority (64.0 per cent) of the Austrian managers stated that they use Intuition and Logic/Reasoning in almost equal measure in their personal life. The proportion of managers using more of Intuition is significantly high at 25.4 per cent as compared to the corresponding proportion of 4.8 per cent in respect of use in professional life. There is a concomitant drop in the proportion of managers using more of Logic/Reasoning from 46.0 per cent in the case of professional life to 10.7 per cent in the case of personal life. This pattern is in evidence whichever way the managers are classified (see table A2.9).

Table A2.9 Extent of use of Intuition in personal life

Category	More of Logic/Reasoning (%)	Both in almost equal measure (%)	More of Intuition (%)
Sex*			
Male	11.6	62.6	25.9
Female	–	79.0	21.0
Organization type			
Industry	11.4	63.6	25.0
Services	10.0	64.3	25.7
Management level*			
Senior	9.8	63.4	26.8
Top	22.2	46.4	31.4
Intuition rating			
Low	12.9	75.8	11.3
Medium	14.7	66.9	18.4
High	5.0	53.5	41.5
Total	10.7	64.0	25.4

*NR (= Not reported) omitted from classification.

The proportion of managers using more of Intuition is significantly large at 41.5 per cent in the high group as compared to 11.3 per cent in the low group and 18.4 per cent in the medium group. This shows that, just as in the case of professional life, managers with better Intuition orientation reportedly use Intuition in their personal life to a larger extent than those with a low orientation.

It may also be noted that, unlike managers in the other categories, a majority (53.6 per cent) of the top managers could state in clear terms whether they use more of Logic/Reasoning or Intuition in their personal life.

Actual Instances

The proportion of managers who could cite specific instances where they had actually used Intuition in their professional/personal life is quite high at 71.4

per cent. This proportion rises from 54.9 per cent in the low group to 79.9 per cent in the medium group and 72.4 per cent in the high group, offering additional evidence of the association between Intuition orientation and the extent of its actual use in professional/personal life.

Opinions on Certain Notions

The respondents were asked to indicate to what extent they agree or disagree with each of ten given statements and the responses were obtained on a five-point scale, ranging from 'Strongly agree' to 'Strongly disagree'. Based on these responses, a composite index with range 0 to 100 was worked out by assigning values to different responses as follows:

Strongly agree	100
Agree	75
Can't say	50
Disagree	25
Strongly disagree	0

By choosing appropriate weighting factors, the index can be worked out for a given category as well as for the aggregate.

Aggregate indices worked out for different statements are as follows:

	Statement	*Index*
1	Many senior managers use Intuition in making decisions, at least to some extent.	77.1
2	Higher Intuitive capabilities would contribute to greater success in business.	72.4
3	Intuition contributes to harmonious interpersonal relationships.	67.7
4	Intuition is a characteristic associated more with women than with men.	41.1
5	Few managers who use Intuition would openly admit to the same.	59.9
6	The more Intuitive a person is, the more successful he or she will be in life.	52.0
7	Intuition cannot be blocked.	51.5

8	Intuition has a role to play in almost every facet of life.	74.2
9	Intuition can be cultivated/ enhanced.	65.4
10	It is not safe to rely on Intuition in business/management.	48.1

Thus, there is a good measure of agreement* that:

- many managers use Intuition (1);
- Intuition contributes to success in business (2);
- Intuition has a role to play in almost every facet of life (8).

There are two other notions on which there is reasonable agreement:

- Intuition contributes to harmonious interpersonal relationships (3);
- Intuition can be cultivated/enhanced (9).

It will be noted that the suggestion that Intuition contributes to success in life (6) does not meet with the same degree of acceptance as the more restrictive proposition that Intuition contributes to success in business (2). Thus, while the managers seem to believe that Intuition is more relevant to professional life, recalling the discussion in the previous section, the managers' claims indicate that they use Intuition to a larger extent in their personal life than in their professional life. This apparent contradiction probably has something to do with the way the propositions have been formulated: statement 6 is admittedly worded more sharply than statement 2.

Views on Certain Aspects

Views on certain aspects of Intuition were sought by ascertaining agreement with the following propositions, the figures alongside showing the proportions of managers in agreement:

Proposition	%
Dependence of Intuition on external environment	38.3
Possibility of inducing Intuition in others	42.3
Possibility of Intuition being a group process	39.0
Possibility of enhancing Intuition through specific types of practice/ training	45.3

*An index value of 65 or more has been taken to connote a 'good' measure of agreement.

It is a little odd that although there is reasonable agreement that Intuition can be cultivated/enhanced (statement 9 in the previous section), the last proportion above concerning the scope for enhancing Intuition through training is not particularly high.

Proportions of managers who think that Intuition should form part of the curriculum at different levels of instruction are as follows:

Level	%
Primary school	25.7
Secondary school	30.6
College/University	34.6
Management institute	60.0

The proportion of managers supporting inclusion of Intuition in the curriculum thus rises progressively with the grade of institutions, reaching a reasonably good level of 60.0 per cent in respect of study at the management institute stage.

Interest in Further Participation

Proportions of managers indicating their willingness to participate further in this research through different means are as follows:

Means	%
Personal interviews	26.1
Experiential workshops	33.5
Seminars/Conferences	30.9

The above proportions are somewhat low in comparison with other Survey countries, but it should be noted that participation in research of this type does make considerable demands on a participant's time.

Appendix 3 Report for France

Profile of Managers

The sample for France comprises 118 managers representing an estimated 106 200 managers in the country conforming to the Survey specifications. A profile of the French managers, as drawn up by the Survey, is given in table A3.1.

Table A3.1 Profile of the French managers in the Survey population

Category	Sample count	Estimated population (000s)	%	% corrected for NR*
Sex				
Male	106	94.1	88.6	88.6
Female	12	12.1	11.4	11.4
Age				
Below 35	16	13.8	13.0	13.0
35–44	54	49.5	46.6	46.6
45–59	41	35.7	33.6	33.6
Over 59	7	7.2	6.8	6.8
Organization type				
Industry	65	44.5	41.9	41.9
Services	53	61.7	58.1	58.1
Functional area				
General management	30	27.7	26.1	27.1
Finance	19	17.3	16.3	16.9
Marketing	19	16.4	15.4	16.0
Production/Operations	7	5.3	5.0	5.2
Human resources development	16	14.3	13.5	14.0
Other	22	21.3	20.1	20.8
NR*	5	3.9	3.7	
Management level				
Senior	81	71.7	67.5	70.9
Top	31	29.4	27.7	29.1
NR*	6	5.1	4.8	
Total	118	106.2	100.0	100.0

*NR = Not reported.

It will be seen that:

- 11.4 per cent of the managers are females;
- the majority (59.6 per cent) of the managers are relatively young, being less than 45 years old;
- 29.1 per cent of the managers belong to the top level (proportion corrected for NR).

Intuition Ratings

Objective Rating

Paired alternatives

Responses to the query regarding choice between ten given pairs of alternatives (where one of the terms is taken to indicate orientation towards Intuition and the other towards Logic/Reasoning) yield the distribution shown in table A3.2.

Table A3.2 Choice between paired alternatives

Intuition-oriented		Logic/Reasoning-oriented		Extent of non-expression of preference (%)
Description	Extent of preference (%)	Description	Extent of preference (%)	
1 Invent	26.3	Build	68.0*	5.7
2 Vision	29.3	Common sense	66.2*	4.6
3 Abstract	16.8	Concrete	79.9*	3.3
4 Innovative	67.8*	Conventional	27.7	4.6
5 Creative	41.3	Analytical	52.9	5.9
6 Ideas	53.2	Facts	41.8	5.0
7 Imaginative	38.3	Realistic	57.8*	3.9
8 Ingenious	38.0	Practical	57.4*	4.6
9 Fascinating	25.5	Sensible	69.5*	5.0
10 Spontaneous	52.3	Systematic	43.1	4.6

*The observed preference is statistically significant (at the 5 per cent level).
The two alternatives in each pair were presented to the respondent in a predetermined random sequence (see question 2 of the questionnaire in appendix 11).

It will be seen that of the seven cases where the observed differences are statistically significant, in only one case was the term associated with Intuition preferred over its counterpart associated with Logic/Reasoning, while it is the other way about in the remaining six cases. This indicates *prima facie* a comparatively low orientation towards Intuition among the French managers. A more comprehensive rating of the managers on this dimension is attempted later in this section.

Overall Intuition score

By assigning 1 to the choice indicating orientation towards Intuition and 0 to the one towards Logic/Reasoning, an overall score has been computed for each responding manager. Where there was no indication of preference for one term over the other in a given pair (evidenced by the respondent ticking both the alternatives or leaving the section blank), a score of ½ has been awarded; however, where no clear preference was indicated in respect of even one of the ten given pairs, it has been treated as a case of 'Not reported' (NR). It is clear that the overall score ranges from 0 to 10 in steps of ½.

Classification

Based on the overall Intuition score, a three-way classification of managers has been devised as follows:

Score	*Category*
0.0–3.5	L: Low orientation
4.0–6.0	M: Medium orientation
6.5–10.0	H: High orientation

It will be noted that this classification has been used as one of the standard backgrounds in tabulation of the Survey responses. This is referred to as 'objective rating' as distinct from the 'self-rating' carried out by the respondents, which is discussed later.

Distribution

The above classification has led to the distribution shown in table A3.3.

It will be seen that, on an overall basis, only 27.6 per cent of the managers merited a rating above average, confirming the preliminary inference drawn earlier on the basis of choice between paired alternatives.

The observed differences between different groupings are not statistically significant, but there is a broad indication that male managers have a better orientation towards Intuition than female managers and that Intuition bears a positive association with age. Likewise, managers in the industry sector appear to be more Intuitive than their counterparts in the services sector, while top managers seem to score over senior ones.

Self-Rating

Self-rating by the managers regarding Intuition on a given five-point scale (ranging from very high to very low) has yielded the distribution shown in table A3.4.

Table A3.3 Distribution based on objective rating on Intuition

Category	Low (%)	Medium (%)	High (%)	NR (%)
Sex				
Male	42.5	27.4	29.4	0.7
Female	34.7	46.0	9.7	9.7
Age				
Below 35	54.9	28.2	16.8	–
35–44	48.8	21.9	27.0	2.4
45–59	29.7	38.1	30.3	1.9
Over 59	25.7	41.9	32.4	–
Organization type				
Industry	33.8	33.8	30.8	1.5
Services	47.2	26.4	24.5	1.9
Management level*				
Senior	48.0	26.3	24.7	1.0
Top	26.8	38.5	30.8	4.0
Total	41.6	29.5	27.1	1.7
(% corrected for NR)	(42.3)	(30.1)	(27.6)	

*NR (= Not reported) omitted from classification.

Table A3.4 Distribution based on self-rating on Intuition

Category	Very high (%)	High (%)	Average (%)	Low (%)	Very low (%)	NR (%)
Sex						
Male	9.3	38.2	48.1	3.7	–	0.7
Female	19.3	15.3	59.7	5.7	–	–
Age						
Below 35	–	40.1	46.5	13.4	–	–
35–44	19.7	37.3	40.7	2.4	–	–
45–59	3.8	30.3	60.7	3.3	–	1.9
Over 59	–	41.9	58.1	–	–	–
Organization type						
Industry	9.2	43.1	44.6	1.5	–	1.5
Services	11.3	30.2	52.8	5.7	–	–
Management level*						
Senior	10.3	32.3	53.2	4.2	–	–
Top	10.3	43.4	42.4	4.0	–	–
Intuition rating*†						
Low	13.6	26.2	52.2	7.9	–	–
Medium	2.2	21.2	74.5	2.2	–	–
High	11.2	65.6	20.9	–	–	2.4
Total	10.4	35.6	49.4	3.9	–	0.6
(% corrected for NR)	(10.5)	(35.8)	(49.7)	(4.0)	–	

*NR (= Not reported) omitted from classification.
†Relates to objective rating presented in table A3.3.

The proportion of managers who have rated themselves very high/high on Intuition is rather low at 46.0 per cent, suggesting that the French managers not only are comparatively low in terms of Intuition orientation but do not generally perceive it as much of a positive attribute either.

The proportion of top managers rating themselves very high/high works out to 53.7 per cent, significantly higher than the corresponding proportion of 42.6 per cent for senior managers. Likewise, a larger proportion of 47.8 per cent (as corrected for NR) of males rate themselves thus, as compared to 34.6 per cent of female managers, though the difference is not statistically significant.

The proportion of managers rating themselves very high/high on Intuition is significantly large at 78.7 per cent (as corrected for NR) in the high group, as compared to 39.8 per cent in the low group and 23.4 per cent in the medium group (the difference between the low and medium groups is not statistically significant), indicating a positive association between the two rating systems.

Association Between Ratings

The association between the two ratings can be tested statistically by forming the contingency table shown as table A3.5.

Table A3.5 Objective rating v. self-rating

	Self-rating		
Classification based on objective rating	Average or lower (number)	Very high/high (number)	Total (number)
Low	28	19	47
Medium	27	9	36
High	6	26	32
Total	61	54	115

Three managers whose classification is indeterminate in terms of either of the rating systems have been omitted from the above cross-tabulation.

It can be seen that the χ^2 (which will have 2 degrees of freedom) for table A3.5 works out to 22.86, which is significant even at the 1 per cent level, confirming that there is a good positive association between the two rating systems.

The contingency coefficient, C, works out to 0.41 as follows:

$$C = \sqrt{\frac{\chi^2}{\chi^2 + N}}$$

$$= \sqrt{\frac{22.86}{22.86 + 115}}$$

$$= 0.41$$

This value of C may be taken as a measure of the association between the two rating systems, in line with the inference drawn in the preceding subsection.

What is Intuition?

Descriptions Given of Intuition

The questionnaire used for the Survey (see appendix 11) starts with an invitation to the respondent to describe Intuition as understood by him or her so as to get the top-of-the-mind opinion; that is, a response uninfluenced by the sequence of questions that follows in the questionnaire. This has led to diverse descriptions of Intuition of which the following are the more important:

Description	%
Decision/perception without recourse to logical/ rational methods	42.9
Spontaneous perception/vision	20.2
Foresight; clairvoyance	16.8
Inherent perception; inexplicable comprehension; a feeling that comes from within	11.3
Integration of previous experience; processing of accumulated information	9.7
Decision/solution to problem, without complete data/facts	8.9

Thus, the dominant perception appears to be that Intuition is something of an antithesis to Logic/Reasoning, while spontaneity and foresight also come out prominently in the responses.

Graphic Expression

The proportion of managers giving graphic expression to their concept of Intuition is quite high at 77.3 per cent, pointing to the keen interest evinced in the subject by the French managers. This proportion is significantly higher in the industry sector than in the services sector. It is also higher among female managers than male managers (though not to a significant extent) and appears to bear a positive association with Intuition orientation:

Category	%
Male	75.6
Female	90.3
Industry	87.7
Services	69.8
Low	70.1
Medium	84.5
High	79.1

Agreement with Specific Descriptions

The extent of agreement with three given descriptions of Intuition (obtained as three independent assessments and not as choice among three alternatives) can be seen from the distribution shown in table A3.6.

Table A3.6 Extent of agreement with three specific descriptions of Intuition

	Extent of agreement with		
Category	a (%)	b (%)	c (%)
Sex*			
Male	62.3	76.2	47.6
Female	65.3	69.3	55.7
Organization type			
Industry	63.1	75.4	47.7
Services	62.3	75.5	49.1
Management level*			
Senior	63.4	76.0	46.6
Top	65.3	77.9	49.0
Intuition rating*			
Low	57.1	80.6	52.9
Medium	68.3	61.8	49.3
High	66.5	84.8	43.9
Total	62.6	75.4	48.5

*NR (= Not reported) omitted from classification.
(a) Spontaneous insight based on prior experience/expertise.
(b) Flash from 'subconscious levels'.
(c) Tuning into 'higher levels of consciousness'.

Broadly, the order of acceptance of the three descriptions is as follows:

(b) $>$ (a) $>$ (c)

$>$ Denotes 'preferred over'.

Considering that neither 'flash' nor 'subconscious' figures in the major responses to the open-ended question on the respondent's concept of Intuition, it is rather surprising that description (b) should have met with the largest extent of acceptance. On the other hand, the observed extent of agreement with description (a) is fully supported by the pattern of responses to the open-ended question.

It may be noted that while description (b) gets the highest degree of acceptance in the low and high groups, the preference of managers in the medium group appears to be for description (a).

Perceived Relevance of Intuition

In Business/Management

The perceived relevance of different functional areas of business/management to the application of Intuition can be seen from the following proportions relating to different areas:

Area	%
1 Corporate strategy and planning	74.8
2 Investment/Diversification	54.4
3 Corporate acquisitions/mergers/alliances	57.3
4 Finance	19.5
5 Marketing	71.2
6 Public relations	57.8
7 Choice of technology/plant and equipment	25.1
8 Production/Operations	19.1
9 Materials management	14.5
10 Human resources development	84.1
11 Research and development	68.9

Thus, the following four are perceived as the major areas of application for Intuition in the field of business/management (no order of importance

intended):

- corporate strategy and planning;
- marketing;
- human resources development (HRD);
- research and development (R&D).

One might have expected an area like corporate acquisitions/mergers/alliances to figure in the major areas of perceived importance, but this may have been taken to form part of corporate strategy and planning.

It will be noted that finance and production/operations are two major functional areas which rank among the least important in terms of perceived relevance.

In Other Fields

As regards fields other than business/management, the following are perceived to be the more important in terms of their relevance to application of Intuition:

Field	%
Sports	14.1
Human/interpersonal relations	10.8
Friendship	10.8
Family (relations)	9.5
Arts, drama, music, literature, etc.	9.1
Personal life	9.1
Love, marriage	8.3
Children (bringing up children, children's education, etc.).	7.8
Recreation, entertainment, etc.	7.6
Politics, public life	6.9
Speculation (covering stockmarkets, gambling, etc.)	5.9
Specific disciplines (engineering, medicine, psychology, etc.)	5.4

It will be noted that while the top spot goes to sports, which is in keeping with the importance given to this activity in the Western countries, family, friendship and interpersonal relations figure prominently in the responses. (Given all the popular association of romance with the French, it is ironic that love/marriage should come far down the list.)

How Does One Identify Intuition?

Stated Means of Identification

The query as to how Intuition could be identified has elicited diverse responses, of which the following are the more important:

Response	%
Deviation of decision from logical reasoning	21.7
Strong inner feeling, emotion	12.6
Inability to explain conclusion on the basis of available facts	12.6
Spontaneous perception/vision	7.2

It will be seen that deviation of decision from Logic/Reasoning is perceived as the most important among the identifying characteristics of Intuition.

Associated Phenomena

The extent to which experience of Intuition is perceived to be accompanied by different phenomena can be seen from table A3.7.

Table A3.7 Associated phenomena

Category	(a) Sensory (%)	(b) Physical (%)	(c) Mental (%)	(d) Emotional (%)
Sex				
Male	21.3	10.8	45.5	63.7
Female	9.7	25.0	46.0	75.0
Organization type				
Industry	21.5	13.8	53.8	66.2
Services	18.9	11.3	39.6	64.2
Management level*				
Senior	24.1	13.2	47.5	65.6
Top	7.0	4.0	44.1	66.2
Intuition rating*				
Low	25.1	9.5	42.3	60.2
Medium	12.4	12.4	52.8	65.5
High	21.6	17.6	41.6	72.0
Total	20.0	12.4	45.6	65.0

*NR (= Not reported) omitted from classification.

Consistently with the pattern of responses on means of identification discussed earlier, experience of Intuition is most perceived to be accompanied by changes in the emotional and mental aspects.

Use of Intuition

In Professional Life

The proportion of managers using Intuition and Logic/Reasoning in almost equal measure in their professional life is fairly high at 61.9 per cent. As for the others, only 5.4 per cent of the managers stated that they use more of Intuition, as against 32.7 per cent using more of Logic/Reasoning, as may be seen from table A3.8.

Table A3.8 Extent of use of Intuition in professional life

Category	More of Logic/Reasoning (%)	Both in almost equal measure (%)	More of Intuition (%)
Sex			
Male	31.9	65.2	2.9
Female	38.6	36.4	25.0
Organization type			
Industry	23.1	69.2	7.7
Services	39.6	56.6	3.8
Management level*			
Senior	37.8	58.4	3.8
Top	19.6	70.2	10.3
Intuition rating*			
Low	47.1	52.9	–
Medium	36.2	57.2	6.5
High	8.8	82.4	8.8
Total	32.7	61.9	5.4

*NR (= Not reported) omitted from classification.

It will be noted that the majority of female managers, unlike their male counterparts, have stated in clear terms whether they use more of Intuition or Logic/Reasoning in their professional life. There is evidence of greater use of Intuition by managers in the industry sector (as compared to those in the services sector) and by top managers (as compared to senior managers).

It will also be noted that managers professing to use more of Intuition are all located in the medium and high groups. Looking at it the other way, the proportion of managers using more of Logic/Reasoning drops from 47.1 per cent in the low group and 36.2 per cent in the medium group to a significantly lower level of 8.8 per cent in the high group. This suggests that the managers identified by the study as having better Intuition orientation reportedly use Intuition in their professional life to a larger extent than those with a comparatively low orientation.

In Personal Life

The majority (56.5 per cent) of the French managers stated that they use Intuition and Logic/Reasoning in almost equal measure in their personal life. The proportion of managers using more of Intuition is significantly high at 28.4 per cent, as compared to a mere 5.4 per cent for such corresponding use in professional life. There is a corresponding drop in the proportion of managers using more of Logic/Reasoning from 32.7 per cent in the case of professional life to 15.0 per cent in the case of personal life. This pattern is evident whichever way the managers are classified (see table A3.9).

Table A3.9 Extent of use of Intuition in personal life

Category	More of Logic/Reasoning (%)	Both in almost equal measure (%)	More of Intuition (%)
Sex			
Male	14.5	58.6	26.9
Female	19.3	40.3	40.3
Organization type			
Industry	12.3	53.8	33.8
Services	17.0	58.5	24.5
Management level*			
Senior	18.7	55.3	26.0
Top	8.6	60.6	30.8
Intuition rating*			
Low	17.8	58.1	24.0
Medium	17.7	63.3	19.0
High	8.8	48.0	43.2
Total	15.0	56.5	28.4

*NR (= Not reported) omitted from classification.

The proportion of managers using more of Intuition in their personal life is significantly large at 43.2 per cent in the high group, as compared to 24.0 per cent in the low group and 19.0 per cent in the medium group. This shows that, just as in the case of professional life, managers with better Intuition orientation professedly use Intuition in their personal life to a larger extent than those with a relatively low orientation.

Actual Instances

The proportion of managers who could cite specific instances where they had actually used Intuition in their professional/personal life is fairly high at 60.8 per cent. This proportion is significantly higher in the industry sector (69.2 per cent) than in the services sector (54.7 per cent). Top managers (66.2 per cent) have also evinced a higher proportion than senior managers (61.9 per cent), though the difference in this case is not statistically significant.

Opinions on Certain Notions

The respondents were asked to indicate to what extent they agree or disagree with each of ten given statements and the responses were obtained on a five-point scale, ranging from 'Strongly agree' to 'Strongly disagree'. Based on these responses, a composite index with range 0 to 100 was worked out by assigning values to different responses as follows:

Strongly agree	100
Agree	75
Can't say	50
Disagree	25
Strongly disagree	0

By choosing appropriate weighting factors, the index can be worked out for a given category as well as for the aggregate.

Aggregate indices worked out for different statements are as follows:

	Statement	*Index*
1	Many senior managers use Intuition in making decisions, at least to some extent.	79.2
2	Higher Intuitive capabilities would contribute to greater success in business.	76.2
3	Intuition contributes to harmonious inter-personal relationships.	74.7
4	Intuition is a characteristic associated more with women than with men.	60.8
5	Few managers who use Intuition would openly admit to the same.	55.4
6	The more Intuitive a person is, the more successful he or she will be in life.	60.0
7	Intuition cannot be blocked.	52.5
8	Intuition has a role to play in almost every facet of life.	77.8
9	Intuition can be cultivated/enhanced.	55.1
10	It is not safe to rely on Intuition in business/management.	37.3

Thus, there is a good measure of agreement* that:

- many managers use Intuition (1);
- Intuition contributes to success in business (2);
- Intuition contributes to harmonious interpersonal relationships (3);
- Intuition has a role to play in almost every facet of life (8).

It will be noted that the suggestion that Intuition contributes to success in life (6) does not meet with the same degree of acceptance as the more restrictive proposition that Intuition contributes to success in business (2). Thus, while the managers seem to believe that Intuition is more relevant to professional life, recalling the discussion in the previous section, the managers' claims indicate that they use Intuition to a larger extent in their personal life than in their professional life. This apparent contradiction probably has something to do with the way the propositions have been formulated: statement 6 is admittedly worded more sharply than statement 2.

It will also be seen that the negative suggestion that it is not safe to rely on Intuition in business/management (statement 10) has been virtually rejected, reinforcing the inference on the perceived relevance of Intuition in this domain.

Views on Certain Aspects

Views on certain aspects of Intuition were sought by ascertaining agreement with the following propositions, the figures alongside showing the proportions of managers in agreement:

Proposition	%
Dependence of Intuition on external environment	47.1
Possibility of inducing Intuition in others	31.4
Possibility of Intuition being a group process	25.5
Possibility of enhancing Intuition through specific types of practice/training	37.1

The proportions are relatively low. In particular, the low proportion corresponding to the possibility of enhancing Intuition through training is consistent with the ambivalence noted in the responses to the two statement

*An index value of 65 or more has been taken to connote a 'good' measure of agreement.

questions touching on this aspect (statement 7 on blocking and statement 9 on enhancing Intuition).

Proportions of managers who think that Intuition should form part of the curriculum at different levels of instruction are shown below:

Level	%
Primary school	32.5
Secondary school	30.1
College/University	41.3
Management institute	36.5

There is thus a good measure of agreement that Intuition is a fit subject for inclusion in the curriculum at different levels.

Interest in Further Participation

Proportions of managers indicating willingness to participate further in this research through different means are as follows:

Means	%
Personal interviews	33.2
Experiential workshops	35.2
Seminars/Conferences	36.7

If interest in further participation is not exactly overwhelming, this probably has something to do with the nature of the investigation, which does make considerable demands on a participant's time.

Appendix 4 Report for the Netherlands

Profile of Managers

The sample for the Netherlands comprises 89 managers representing an estimated 31 700 managers in the country conforming to the Survey specifications. A profile of the Dutch managers, as drawn up by the Survey, is given in table A4.1.

Table A4.1 Profile of the Dutch managers in the Survey population

Category	Sample count	Estimated population (000s)	%	% corrected for NR*
Sex				
Male	83	28.4	89.6	92.8
Female	4	2.2	6.9	7.2
NR*	2	1.1	3.5	
Age				
Below 35	9	3.6	11.4	11.8
35–44	31	13.0	41.0	42.8
45–59	46	13.8	43.5	45.4
Over 59	–	–	–	–
NR*	3	1.3	4.1	
Organization type				
Industry	52	11.7	36.9	36.9
Services	37	20.0	63.1	63.1
Functional area				
General management	37	11.7	36.9	39.9
Finance	9	3.0	9.5	10.2
Marketing	7	2.5	7.9	8.5
Production/Operations	13	6.1	19.2	20.8
Human resources development	6	2.0	6.3	6.8
Other	12	4.0	12.6	13.7
NR*	5	2.4	7.6	
Management level				
Senior	56	21.8	68.8	74.9
Top	27	7.3	23.0	25.1
NR*	6	2.6	8.2	
Total	89	31.7	100.0	100.0

*NR = Not reported.

It will be seen that (correcting the proportions for NR):

- 7.2 per cent of the managers are females;
- the majority (54.6 per cent) of the managers are relatively young, being less than 45 years old;
- 25.1 per cent of the managers belong to the top level.

Intuition Ratings

Objective Rating

Paired alternatives

Responses to the query regarding choice between ten given pairs of alternatives (where one of the terms is taken to indicate orientation towards Intuition and the other towards Logic/Reasoning) yield the distribution shown in table A4.2.

Table A4.2 Choice between paired alternatives

Intuition-oriented		Logic/Reasoning-oriented		Extent of non-expression of preference (%)
Description	Extent of preference (%)	Description	Extent of preference (%)	
1 Invent	46.4	Build	49.4	4.1
2 Vision	46.9	Common sense	49.0	4.1
3 Abstract	31.4	Concrete	68.6*	–
4 Innovative	80.1*	Conventional	19.9	–
5 Creative	62.6*	Analytical	34.9	2.4
6 Ideas	60.2*	Facts	35.9	3.8
7 Imaginative	34.4	Realistic	64.2*	1.4
8 Ingenious	26.0	Practical	72.3*	1.7
9 Fascinating	34.7	Sensible	62.9*	2.4
10 Spontaneous	45.2	Systematic	54.1	0.7

*The observed preference is statistically significant at the 5 per cent level.
The two alternatives in each pair were presented to the respondent in a predetermined random sequence (see question 2 of the questionnaire in appendix 11).

It will be seen that of the seven cases where the observed differences are statistically significant, in three instances the term associated with Intuition has been preferred to its counterpart associated with Logic/Reasoning, while it is the other way about in the other four cases. This indicates *prima facie* that the Intuition orientation of the Dutch managers may not be of a high order. A more comprehensive rating of the managers on this dimension is attempted later in this section.

Overall Intuition score

By assigning 1 to the choice indicating orientation towards Intuition and 0 to the one towards Logic/Reasoning, an overall score has been computed for each responding manager. Where there was no indication of preference for one term over the other in a given pair (evidenced by the respondent ticking both the alternatives or leaving the section blank), a score of ½ has been awarded; however, where no clear preference was indicated in respect of even one of the ten given pairs, it has been treated as a case of 'Not reported' (NR). It is clear that the overall score ranges from 0 to 10 in steps of ½.

Classification

Based on the overall Intuition score, a three-way classification of managers has been devised as follows:

Score	*Category*
0.0–3.5	L: Low orientation
4.0–6.0	M: Medium orientation
6.5–10.0	H: High orientation

It will be noted that this classification has been used as one of the standard backgrounds in tabulation of the Survey responses. This is referred to as 'objective rating' as distinct from the 'self-rating' carried out by the respondents, which is discussed later.

Distribution

The above classification has led to the distribution shown in table A4.3.

The proportion of 30.1 per cent relating to managers with high orientation is moderate, confirming the preliminary inference based on choice between paired alternatives, which has been discussed earlier.

The proportion of female managers with high orientation is 50.0 per cent, as against 29.7 per cent for male managers, and this rises from 21.2 per cent in the age below 35 group to 36.8 per cent in the age 45–59 group, but these differences are not statistically significant.

Self-Rating

Self-rating by the managers regarding Intuition on a given five-point scale (ranging from very high to very low) has yielded the distribution shown in table A4.4.

It will be seen that the majority (59.4 per cent, using the corrected proportion) of the managers rated themselves very high/high, showing that Intuition is generally viewed as a positive attribute by the Dutch managers.

Table A4.3 Distribution based on objective rating on Intuition

Category	Low (%)	Medium (%)	High (%)	NR (%)
Sex*				
Male	31.5	38.8	29.7	–
Female	25.0	25.0	50.0	–
Age*				
Below 35	6.2	72.5	21.2	–
35–44	43.4	28.1	28.5	–
45–59	26.4	36.8	36.8	–
Over 59	–	–	–	–
Organization type				
Industry	21.2	48.1	30.8	–
Services	35.1	35.1	29.7	–
Management level*				
Senior	33.5	34.4	32.1	–
Top	30.1	45.4	24.5	–
Total	30.0	39.9	30.1	–

*NR (= Not reported) omitted from classification.

Table A4.4 Distribution based on self-rating on Intuition

Category	Very high (%)	High (%)	Average (%)	Low (%)	Very low (%)	NR (%)
Sex*						
Male	11.1	46.0	29.3	10.4	0.8	2.4
Female	25.0	50.0	25.0	–	–	–
Age*						
Below 35	15.0	42.5	36.3	6.2	–	–
35–44	8.3	59.7	23.6	8.3	–	–
45–59	13.4	35.5	32.6	12.1	1.6	4.9
Over 59	–	–	–	–	–	–
Organization type						
Industry	3.8	51.9	25.0	11.5	1.9	5.8
Services	16.2	43.2	32.4	8.1	–	–
Management level*						
Senior	14.9	45.3	29.6	9.1	–	1.0
Top	6.1	48.5	25.8	13.5	3.1	3.1
Intuition rating†						
Low	8.1	33.2	37.9	18.5	2.4	–
Medium	14.6	48.8	23.5	9.6	–	3.6
High	11.3	56.6	29.7	–	–	2.4
Total	11.7	46.4	29.7	9.4	0.7	2.1
(% corrected for NR)	(11.9)	(47.5)	(30.3)	(9.6)	(0.7)	

*NR (= Not reported) omitted from classification.
† Relates to objective rating presented in table A4.3.

The proportion of managers rating themselves very high/high on Intuition rises from 41.3 per cent in the low group to 65.8 per cent in the medium and 69.6 per cent in the high group (correcting the proportion for 'Not reported' in the last two groups), indicating a positive association between the two rating systems.

Association Between Ratings

The association between the two rating systems can be tested statistically by forming the contingency table shown as table A4.5.

Table A4.5 Objective rating v. self-rating

	Self-rating		
Classification based on objective rating	Average or lower (number)	Very high/high (number)	Total (number)
Low	15	9	24
Medium	12	24	36
High	8	18	26
Total	35	51	86

Three managers in the medium and high groups whose classification is indeterminate in terms of self-rating have been omitted from the cross-tabulation.

It can be seen that the χ^2 (which will have 2 degrees of freedom) for table A4.5 works out to 6.59, which is significant at the 5 per cent level, confirming positive association between the objective rating and self-rating.

The contingency coefficient, *C*, works out to 0.27 as follows:

$$C = \sqrt{\frac{\chi^2}{\chi^2 + N}}$$

$$= \sqrt{\frac{6.59}{6.59 + 86}}$$

$$= 0.27$$

This value of *C* may be taken as a measure of association between the two rating systems.

What is Intuition?

Descriptions Given of Intuition

The questionnaire used for the Survey (see appendix 11) starts with an invitation to the respondent to describe Intuition as understood by him or her so as to get the top-of-the-mind opinion; that is, a response uninfluenced by the sequence of questions that follows in the questionnaire. This has led to diverse descriptions of Intuition, of which the following are the more important:

Description	%
Inherent perception; inexplicable comprehension; a feeling that comes from within	21.0
Decision/perception without recourse to logical methods	14.6
Integration of previous experience; processing of accumulated information	8.1
Spontaneous perception/vision	6.5
Decision/solution to problem, without complete data/facts	6.2

The Dutch managers were comparatively less articulate in their responses to this query.

Graphic Expression

The proportion of managers giving graphic expression to their concept of Intuition is quite high at 84.7 per cent. This works out as follows for different categories of managers:

Category	%
Male	82.9
Female	100.0
Industry	76.9
Services	89.2
Low	83.9
Medium	88.6
High	80.2

The difference between the proportions corresponding to male and female managers is significant, but not so the other differences.

Agreement with Specific Descriptions

The extent of agreement with three given descriptions of Intuition (obtained as three independent assessments and not as choice among three alternatives) can be seen from the distribution shown in table A4.6.

Table A4.6 Extent of agreement with three specific descriptions of Intuition

Category	Extent of agreement with		
	a (%)	b (%)	c (%)
Organization type			
Industry	75.0	55.8	34.6
Services	67.6	73.0	35.1
Management level*			
Senior	69.4	66.7	38.3
Top	69.9	72.4	30.1
Intuition rating			
Low	72.5	67.8	27.5
Medium	68.7	63.3	34.2
High	70.3	69.8	43.4
Total	70.3	66.6	34.9

*NR (=Not reported) omitted from classification.
In this and the subsequent tables, the sex classification has been omitted in view of the low sample count corresponding to the female managers.
(a) Spontaneous insight based on prior experience/expertise.
(b) Flash from 'subconscious levels'.
(c) Tuning into 'higher levels of consciousness'.

On an overall basis, the order of agreement with the three descriptions is as follows:

(a) & (b) > (c)

> Denotes 'preferred over'.

This does not draw much support from the pattern of responses to the open-ended question on the respondent's concept of Intuition, where much articulation was not in evidence in any case.

It may be noted that the extent of agreement with description (c) rises progressively from the low group to the high group, though the observed differences are not statistically significant.

Perceived Relevance of Intuition

In Business/Management

The perceived relevance of different functional areas of business/management to the application of Intuition can be seen from the following proportions relating to different areas:

	Area	%
1	Corporate strategy and planning	79.3
2	Investment/Diversification	52.3
3	Corporate acquisitions/ mergers/alliances	48.7
4	Finance	24.3
5	Marketing	76.8
6	Public relations	66.6
7	Choice of technology/plant and equipment	24.6
8	Production/Operations	12.2
9	Materials management	10.8
10	Human resources development	80.1
11	Research and development	62.1

Thus, the following are perceived as the major areas of application for Intuition in the field of business/management (no order of importance intended):

- corporate strategy and planning;
- marketing;
- public relations;
- human resources development (HRD);
- research and development (R&D).

One might have expected an area like corporate acquisitions/mergers/alliances to figure in the major areas of perceived importance, but this may have been taken to form part of corporate strategy and planning.

It will be noted that finance and production/operations are two major functional areas which rank among the least important in terms of perceived relevance.

In Other Fields

As regards fields other than business/management, the following are perceived to be the more important in terms of their relevance to application of Intuition:

Field	%
Specific disciplines (engineering, medicine, psychology, etc.)	24.6
Politics, public life	16.6
Human/interpersonal relations	15.2
Love, marriage	12.6
Sports	11.8
Family (relations)	8.2
Education, teaching	8.0
Personal life	7.0
Friendship	5.8

It will be seen that while study of specific disciplines comes out on top, the other responses revolve around interpersonal relations to a large extent.

How Does One Identify Intuition?

Stated Means of Identification

The query as to how Intuition could be identified elicited diverse responses, of which the following are the more important:

Response	%
Inability to explain conclusion on the basis of available facts	13.2
Deviation of decision from logical reasoning	11.8
Strong inner feeling, emotion	9.4
Strong urge/impulse to take a particular decision	5.2

It will be noted that the emotional aspect is also seen as an important characteristic for identifying Intuition.

Associated Phenomena

The extent to which experience of Intuition is perceived to be accompanied by different phenomena can be seen from table A4.7.

Experience of Intuition is thus most perceived to be accompanied by changes in the emotional aspects (followed by the mental aspects), which have figured as an identifying characteristic, but not very prominently, in the responses to an earlier query on the subject.

Table A4.7 Associated phenomena

Category	(a) Sensory (%)	(b) Physical (%)	(c) Mental (%)	(d) Emotional (%)
Organization type				
Industry	26.9	34.6	59.6	69.2
Services	16.2	24.3	32.4	86.5
Management level*				
Senior	20.7	29.8	47.0	81.8
Top	19.6	30.1	38.0	75.5
Intuition rating				
Low	16.1	12.8	39.3	80.1
Medium	27.0	35.0	42.0	74.7
High	15.1	33.5	46.2	87.3
Total	20.2	28.1	42.5	80.1

*NR (= Not reported) omitted from classification.

Use of Intuition

In Professional Life

Only 8.7 per cent of the managers stated that they use more of Intuition in their professional life, as against 45.7 per cent using more of Logic/Reasoning, the balance of 45.6 per cent using both Intuition and Logic/Reasoning in almost equal measure, as may be seen from table A4.8.

Table A4.8 Extent of use of Intuition in professional life

Category	More of Logic/Reasoning (%)	Both in almost equal measure (%)	More of Intuition (%)
Organization type			
Industry	50.0	40.4	9.6
Services	43.2	48.6	8.1
Management level*			
Senior	40.2	49.3	10.6
Top	65.0	28.8	6.1
Intuition rating			
Low	57.3	42.7	–
Medium	52.3	33.8	13.9
High	25.5	64.2	10.4
Total	45.7	45.6	8.7

*NR (= Not reported) omitted from classification.

It will be noted that the proportion of managers using more of Intuition works out to 13.9 per cent and 10.4 per cent in the medium and high groups, as against nil in the low group. To look at it the other way, the proportion of managers using more of Logic/Reasoning drops from 57.3 per cent in the low group and 52.3 per cent in the medium group to a significantly lower level of 25.5 per cent in the high group, indicating a positive association between Intuition orientation and the stated extent of its use in professional life.

In Personal Life

The proportion of managers who stated that they use more of Intuition in their personal life works out to 37.6 per cent, as against the corresponding proportion of a mere 8.7 per cent in respect of use in professional life. There is a concomitant decline in the proportion of managers using more of Logic/Reasoning from 45.7 per cent in the case of professional life to 15.3 per cent in the case of personal life. This pattern is in evidence whichever way the managers are classified (see table A4.9).

Table A4.9 Extent of use of Intuition in personal life

Category	More of Logic/Reasoning (%)	Both in almost equal measure (%)	More of Intuition (%)
Organization type			
Industry	23.1	44.2	32.7
Services	10.8	48.6	40.5
Management level*			
Senior	15.7	48.7	35.6
Top	19.6	52.8	27.6
Intuition rating			
Low	23.2	52.6	24.2
Medium	13.2	42.0	44.8
High	10.4	48.1	41.5
Total	15.3	47.0	37.6

*NR (= Not reported) omitted from classification.

The proportion of managers using more of Intuition increases from 24.2 per cent in the low group to 44.8 per cent and 41.5 per cent in the medium and high groups. Likewise, the proportion of managers using more of Logic/Reasoning drops from 23.2 per cent in the low group to 13.2 per cent and 10.4 per cent respectively in the medium and high groups. None of these differences is statistically significant, but there is reasonable indication of a positive association between Intuition orientation and the professed extent of its use in personal life.

Actual Instances

The proportion of managers who could cite specific instances where they had actually used Intuition in their professional/personal life is quite high at 71.6 per cent. This proportion rises progressively from 59.7 per cent in the low group to 73.0 per cent in the medium group and further to 81.6 per cent in the high group, offering additional support to the inference drawn earlier regarding a positive association between Intuition orientation and its use in practice.

Opinions on Certain Notions

The respondents were asked to indicate to what extent they agree or disagree with each of ten given statements and the responses were obtained on a five-point scale, ranging from 'strongly agree' to 'strongly disagree'. Based on these responses, a composite index with range 0 to 100 was worked out by assigning values to different responses as follows:

Strongly agree	100
Agree	75
Can't say	50
Disagree	25
Strongly disagree	0

By choosing appropriate weighting factors, the index can be worked out for a given category as well as for the aggregate.

Aggregate indices worked out for different statements are as follows:

	Statement	*Index*
1	Many senior managers use Intuition in making decisions, at least to some extent.	74.1
2	Higher Intuitive capabilities would contribute to greater success in business.	72.4
3	Intuition contributes to harmonious interpersonal relationships.	66.0
4	Intuition is a characteristic associated more with women than with men.	46.2
5	Few managers who use Intuition would openly admit to the same.	61.6
6	The more Intuitive a person is, the more successful he or she will be in life.	50.5
7	Intuition cannot be blocked.	55.6

	Statement	*Index*
8	Intuition has a role to play in almost every facet of life.	71.9
9	Intuition can be cultivated/enhanced.	60.4
10	It is not safe to rely on Intuition in business/management.	48.3

Thus, there is a good measure of agreement* that:

- many managers use Intuition (1);
- Intuition contributes to success in business (2);
- Intuition contributes to harmonious interpersonal relationships (3);
- Intuition has a role to play in almost every facet of life (8).

It will be noted that the suggestion that Intuition contributes to success in life (6) does not meet with the same degree of acceptance as the more restrictive proposition that Intuition contributes to success in business (2). Thus, while the managers seem to believe that Intuition is more relevant to professional life, recalling the discussion in the previous section, the managers' claims indicate that they use Intuition to a larger extent in their personal life than in their professional life. This apparent contradiction probably has something to do with the way the propositions have been formulated: statement 6 is admittedly worded more sharply than statement 2.

Views on Certain Aspects

Views on certain aspects of Intuition were sought by ascertaining agreement with the following propositions, the figures alongside showing the proportions of managers in agreement:

Proposition	%
Dependence of Intuition on external environment	39.2
Possibility of inducing Intuition in others	40.1
Possibility of Intuition being a group process	33.0
Possibility of enhancing Intuition through specific types of practice/training	55.3

The relatively high proportion concerning the efficacy of training is in tune

*An index value of 65 or more has been taken to connote a 'good' measure of agreement.

with the response to statement 9 discussed earlier, which touches on the scope for cultivating/enhancing Intuition.

Proportions of managers who think that Intuition should form part of the curriculum at different levels of instruction are as follows:

Level	%
Primary school	35·9
Secondary school	42.8
College/University	60.8
Management institute	67·5

The proportion of managers supporting inclusion of Intuition in the curriculum thus rises progressively with the grade of institution, reaching a high of 67.5 per cent in respect of study at the management institute level.

Interest in Further Participation

Proportions of managers indicating their willingness to participate further in this research through different means are as follows:

Means	%
Personal interviews	49·3
Experiential workshops	35·8
Seminars/Conferences	35·8

Considering the demands participation in research of this type makes on one's time, the above proportions may be taken to be indicative of a good degree of interest in the subject among the Dutch managers.

Appendix 5 Report for Sweden

Profile of Managers

The sample for Sweden comprises 456 managers representing an estimated 24 500 managers in the country conforming to the Survey specifications. A profile of the Swedish managers, as drawn up by the Survey, is given in table A5.1.

Table A5.1 Profile of the Swedish managers in the Survey population

Category	Sample count	Estimated population (000s)	%	% corrected for NR*
Sex				
Male	412	22.1	90.2	92.5
Female	34	1.8	7.3	7.5
NR*	10	0.6	2.4	
Age				
Below 35	28	1.5	6.1	6.2
35–44	174	9.3	38.0	38.8
45–59	223	11.9	48.6	49.6
Over 59	22	1.3	5.3	5.4
NR*	9	0.5	2.0	
Organization type				
Industry	225	9.3	38.0	38.0
Services	231	15.2	62.0	62.0
Functional area				
General management	87	4.6	18.8	18.8
Finance	81	4.4	18.0	18.0
Marketing	65	3.5	14.3	14.3
Production/Operations	76	4.1	16.7	16.7
Human resources development	75	4.0	16.3	16.3
Other	72	3.9	15.9	15.9
Total	456	24.5	100.0	100.0

*NR = Not reported.

It will be seen that (correcting the proportions for NR):

- 7.5 per cent of the managers are females;
- the majority (55.0 per cent) of the managers are relatively advanced in age, being 45 years old or more.

Data on designation/level of managers could not be obtained in the case of Sweden, hence the omission of the senior/top categorization.

Intuition Ratings

Objective Rating

Paired alternatives

Responses to the query regarding choice between ten given pairs of alternatives (where one of the terms is taken to indicate orientation towards Intuition and the other towards Logic/Reasoning) yield the distribution shown in table A5.2.

Table A5.2 Choice between paired alternatives

Intuition-oriented		Logic/Reasoning-oriented		Extent of non-expression of preference (%)
Description	Extent of preference (%)	Description	Extent of preference (%)	
1 Invent	38.5	Build	49.9*	11.6
2 Vision	28.2	Common sense	62.9*	9.0
3 Abstract	9.0	Concrete	79.7*	11.3
4 Innovative	71.9*	Conventional	17.2	10.9
5 Creative	60.6*	Analytical	30.8	8.6
6 Ideas	59.8*	Facts	29.6	10.7
7 Imaginative	23.0	Realistic	69.0*	8.0
8 Ingenious	39.4	Practical	50.2*	10.5
9 Fascinating	36.2	Sensible	52.9*	10.9
10 Spontaneous	42.4	Systematic	48.3	9.2

*The observed preference is statistically significant (at the 5 per cent level).
The two alternatives in each pair were presented to the respondent in a predetermined random sequence (see question 2 of the questionnaire in appendix 11).

Of the ten observed differences in the proportions, as many as nine turned out to be significant, thanks to the fairly large sample available for this country. In only three out of the nine cases where the differences are significant was the term associated with Intuition preferred over its counterpart associated with Logic/Reasoning, while it is the other way about in the remaining six cases. This indicates *prima facie* that the Intuition orientation of the Swedish managers may not be of a high order. A more comprehensive rating of the managers on this dimension is attempted later in this section.

Overall Intuition score

By assigning 1 to the choice indicating orientation towards Intuition and 0 to the one towards Logic/Reasoning, an overall score has been computed for each responding manager. Where there was no indication of preference for one term over the other in a given pair (evidenced by the respondent ticking both the alternatives or leaving the section blank), a score of ½ has been awarded; however, where no clear preference was indicated in respect of even one of the ten given pairs, it has been treated as a case of 'Not reported' (NR). It is clear that the overall score ranges from 0 to 10 in steps of ½.

Classification

Based on the overall Intuition score, a three-way classification of managers has been devised as follows:

Score	*Category*
0.0–3.5	L: Low orientation
4.0–6.0	M: Medium orientation
6.5–10.0	H: High orientation

It will be noted that this classification has been used as one of the standard backgrounds in tabulation of the Survey responses. This is referred to as 'objective rating' as distinct from the 'self-rating' carried out by the respondents, which is discussed later.

Distribution

The above classification has led to the distribution shown in table A5.3.

It will be seen that the proportion of managers rated high works out to just 18.8 per cent (corrected for NR), which is the lowest among the Survey countries, thus corroborating the inference drawn earlier on the basis of choice between paired alternatives.

Further, the proportion of managers rated high in the age below 35 category is significantly high at 38.5 per cent as compared to 16.5 per cent for the older managers (weighted average for the three older age groups, corrected for NR). This indicates a negative association between age and Intuition orientation, which is somewhat contrary to the trends witnessed in other Survey countries.

Table A5.3 Distribution based on objective rating on Intuition

Category	Low (%)	Medium (%)	High (%)	NR (%)
Sex*				
Male	30.8	49.2	16.9	3.1
Female	30.3	40.3	25.8	3.6
Age*				
Below 35	25.8	35.7	38.5	–
35–44	28.4	50.1	19.8	1.6
45–59	31.7	49.8	13.4	5.0
Over 59	48.0	40.1	11.9	–
Organization type				
Industry	30.2	47.1	19.6	3.1
Services	30.7	48.5	17.3	3.5
Total	30.5	48.0	18.2	3.3
(% corrected for NR)	(31.6)	(49.6)	(18.8)	

*NR (= Not reported) omitted from classification.

Self-Rating

Self-rating by the managers regarding Intuition on a given five-point scale (ranging from very high to very low) has yielded the distribution shown in table A5.4.

Table A5.4 Distribution based on self-rating on Intuition

Category	Very high (%)	High (%)	Average (%)	Low (%)	Very low (%)	NR (%)
Sex*						
Male	8.1	49.8	34.6	6.4	0.6	0.6
Female	16.3	50.7	30.8	2.3	–	–
Age*						
Below 35	4.4	59.9	23.1	8.3	4.4	–
35–44	9.5	47.7	37.1	5.8	–	–
45–59	8.8	50.0	34.0	5.5	0.6	1.1
Over 59	3.3	50.0	30.9	15.8	–	–
Organization type						
Industry	8.9	51.6	32.4	7.1	–	–
Services	8.2	48.5	35.5	6.1	0.9	0.9
Intuition rating†*						
Low	5.4	48.4	36.4	8.9	0.9	–
Medium	6.6	50.4	36.0	5.4	0.6	1.1
High	16.3	51.9	28.0	3.9	–	–
Total	8.5	49.7	34.3	6.5	0.5	0.5
(% corrected for NR)	(8.5)	(49.9)	(34.5)	(6.5)	(0.5)	

*NR (= Not reported) omitted from classification.
†Relates to objective rating presented in table A5.3.

It will be seen that the majority (58.4 per cent, using the corrected proportion) of the managers rated themselves very high/high on Intuition, suggesting that Intuition is generally viewed by the Swedish managers as a positive attribute.

The proportion of managers rating themselves very high/high on Intuition works out to 68.2 per cent in the high group, which is significantly larger than the corresponding proportion of 56.1 per cent for the low and medium groups taken together (weighted average, corrected for NR). This indicates a positive association between the two rating systems. Other observed differences are not statistically significant.

Association Between Ratings

The association between the two rating systems can be tested statistically by forming the contingency table shown as table A5.5.

Table A5.5 Objective rating v. self-rating

	Self-rating			
Classification based on objective rating	Average or lower (number)	High (number)	Very high (number)	Total (number)
Low	64	68	7	139
Medium	91	110	15	216
High	26	44	14	84
Total	181	222	36	439

Seventeen managers whose classification could not be determined in terms of either of the two ratings have been excluded from the above cross-tabulation.

It can be seen that the χ^2 (which will have 4 degrees of freedom) for table A5.5 works out to 12.56, which is significant at the 5 per cent level, confirming the positive association between the two rating systems.

The contingency coefficient, C, works out to 0.17 as follows:

$$C = \sqrt{\frac{\chi^2}{\chi^2 + N}}$$

$$= \sqrt{\frac{451.56}{12.56 + 439}}$$

$$= 0.17$$

This low value of C shows that while there is a positive association between the two rating systems, it is not a strong one.

What is Intuition?

Descriptions Given of Intuition

The questionnaire used for the Survey (see appendix 11) starts with an invitation to the respondent to describe Intuition as understood by him or her so as to get the top-of-the-mind opinion; that is, a response uninfluenced by the sequence of questions that follows in the questionnaire. This has led to diverse descriptions of Intuition, of which the following are the more important:

Description	%
Inherent perception; inexplicable comprehension; a feeling that comes from within	39.4
Integration of previous experience; processing of accumulated information	20.0
Foresight; clairvoyance	13.2
Decision/solution to problem, without complete data/facts	9.8
Decision/perception without recourse to logical/rational methods	9.0
Spontaneous perception/vision	5.8

Thus, the most prominent description is that Intuition is inherent perception/inexplicable comprehension, while other responses include foresight/clairvoyance.

Graphic Expression

The proportion of managers giving graphic expression to their concept of Intuition is rather low at 44.7 per cent, which is in fact the lowest among the Survey countries. This works out as follows for different categories of managers:

Category	%
Male	45.5
Female	25.8
Industry	46.2
Services	43.7
Low	40.3
Medium	46.8
High	46.3

The proportion of 45.5 per cent corresponding to male managers is significantly higher than that for female managers, but the other differences are not statistically significant.

Agreement with Specific Descriptions

The extent of agreement with three given descriptions of Intuition (obtained as three independent assessments and not as choice among three alternatives) can be seen from the distribution shown in table A5.6.

Table A5.6 Extent of agreement with three specific descriptions of Intuition

	Extent of agreement with		
Category	a (%)	b (%)	c (%)
Sex*			
Male	85.9	45.0	23.9
Female	71.5	38.5	30.3
Organization type			
Industry	85.8	43.6	24.4
Services	84.0	45.5	24.7
Intuition rating*			
Low	88.5	43.2	20.0
Medium	84.4	41.5	24.3
High	79.8	54.4	31.7
Total	84.7	44.7	24.6

*NR (= Not reported) omitted from classification.
(a) Spontaneous insight based on prior experience/expertise.
(b) Flash from 'subconscious levels'.
(c) Tuning into 'higher levels of consciousness'.

The observed differences between the extents of agreement with the different descriptions at the aggregate level are statistically significant, resulting in an unambiguous order of acceptance of these descriptions as follows:

(a) > (b) > (c)

> Denotes 'preferred over'.

What is more, this pattern remains invariant whichever way the managers are classified, as may be seen from table A5.6. There is one difference, however, which merits notice: while description (b) and description (c) find greater favour with the high group than with the low and medium groups, it is the other way about for description (a). Considering that integration of previous experience came out as the second most prominent response to the open-ended question on the respondent's concept of Intuition, it is perhaps not surprising that description (a) should find the maximum acceptance with the respondents. However, no such support is available to the other two descriptions.

Perceived Relevance of Intuition

In Business/Management

The perceived relevance of different functional areas of business/management to the application of Intuition can be seen from the following proportions relating to different areas:

	Area	%
1	Corporate strategy and planning	67.9
2	Investment/Diversification	28.9
3	Corporate acquisitions/mergers/alliances	63.3
4	Finance	13.1
5	Marketing	71.9
6	Public relations	56.1
7	Choice of technology/plant and equipment	16.2
8	Production/Operations	11.0
9	Materials management	6.6
10	Human resources development	79.9
11	Research and development	56.6

Thus, the following are perceived as the major areas of application for Intuition in the field of business/management (no order of importance intended):

- corporate strategy and planning;
- corporate acquisitions/mergers/alliances;
- marketing;
- human resources development (HRD).

Sweden is one of the few Survey countries where corporate acquisitions turned out to be one of the major areas of perceived relevance.

There are two other areas at the next tier:

- public relations;
- research and development (R&D).

It will be noted that finance and production/operations are two major functional areas which figure among the least important in terms of perceived relevance.

In Other Fields

As regards fields other than business/management, the following are perceived to be the more important in terms of their relevance to application of Intuition:

Field	%
Human/interpersonal relations	10.7
Sports	9.5
Politics, public life	7.6
Specific disciplines (engineering, medicine, psychology, etc.)	6.9
Love, marriage	5.9

Considering the prominent place Sweden occupies in areas like tennis, it is not surprising that sports should figure high in the above list. However, the fact remains that the Swedish managers turned out to be the least articulate in this context as compared to their counterparts in other Survey countries.

How Does One Identify Intuition?

Stated Means of Identification

The query as to how Intuition could be identified elicited diverse responses, of which the following are the more important:

Response	%
Inability to explain conclusion on the basis of available facts	23.9
Strong inner feeling, emotion	9.0
Deviation of decision from logical reasoning	6.3

The first and third of these responses are in tune with the descriptions given of Intuition in reply to the open-ended question on its meaning (see 'Descriptions Given of Intuition').

Associated Phenomena

The extent to which experience of Intuition is perceived to be accompanied by different phenomena can be seen from table A5.7.

Table A5.7 Associated phenomena

Category	(a) Sensory (%)	(b) Physical (%)	(c) Mental (%)	(d) Emotional (%)
Sex*				
Male	10.2	10.3	17.7	43.7
Female	14.5	14.0	24.9	42.5
Organization type				
Industry	9.3	8.9	16.4	44.9
Services	10.8	12.1	19.0	43.3
Intuition rating*				
Low	11.0	11.6	15.5	41.5
Medium	8.9	8.4	17.3	41.6
High	12.6	15.0	24.2	52.4
Total	10.3	10.9	18.1	43.9

*NR (= Not reported) omitted from classification.

Experience of Intuition is thus most perceived to be accompanied by changes in the emotional aspects, and this accords with the fact that emotion has indeed been mentioned as an important identifying characteristic (see discussion in the preceding subsection).

Use of Intuition

In Professional Life

The proportion of managers who stated that they use more of Intuition in their professional life works out to 8.9 per cent, as against the much larger proportion of 44.6 per cent relating to managers reportedly using more of Logic/Reasoning, the balance of 46.5 per cent stating that they use both in almost equal measure, as may be seen from table A5.8.

It will be noted that the proportion of managers using more of Intuition in their professional life increases from 7.2 per cent in the low group and 7.9 per cent in the medium group to 15.4 per cent in the high group. This rise is not statistically significant, but, looking at the other side of the coin, the proportion of managers using more of Logic/Reasoning drops from 51.4 per cent in the low group and 46.2 per cent in the medium group to a significantly lower level of 26.3 per cent in the high group. This suggests a positive association between the level of Intuition orientation and the extent of use of Intuition in professional life.

Table A5.8 Extent of use of Intuition in professional life

Category	More of Logic/Reasoning (%)	Both in almost equal measure (%)	More of Intuition (%)
Sex*			
Male	46.1	45.2	8.7
Female	30.8	62.4	6.8
Organization type			
Industry	43.1	47.6	9.3
Services	45.5	45.9	8.7
Intuition rating*			
Low	51.4	41.4	7.2
Medium	46.2	45.9	7.9
High	26.3	58.3	15.4
Total	44.6	46.5	8.9

*NR (= Not reported) omitted from classification.

In Personal Life

A majority (55.2 per cent) of the Swedish managers stated that they use Intuition and Logic/Reasoning in almost equal measure in their personal life. The proportion of managers using more of Intuition is significantly high at 28.2 per cent, as compared to the corresponding proportion of 8.9 per cent in respect of use in professional life (see table A5.9).

Table A5.9 Extent of use of Intuition in personal life

Category	More of Logic/Reasoning (%)	Both in almost equal measure (%)	More of Intuition (%)
Sex*			
Male	17.5	57.0	25.5
Female	5.9	39.3	54.8
Organization type			
Industry	15.6	56.9	27.6
Services	17.3	54.1	28.6
Intuition rating*			
Low	18.6	60.3	21.0
Medium	18.5	50.7	30.8
High	9.1	57.8	33.2
Total	16.6	55.2	28.2

*NR (= Not reported) omitted from classification.

It will be noted that the proportion of managers using more of Logic/ Reasoning decreases significantly from 44.6 per cent in the case of professional life to 16.6 per cent in the case of personal life.

Further, the proportion of female managers using more of Intuition in personal life, at 54.8 per cent, is significantly higher than the corresponding proportion of 25.5 per cent for male managers.

The proportion of managers using more of Intuition also rises significantly from 21.0 per cent in the low group to 30.8 per cent in the medium group and 33.2 per cent in the high group. This shows that, just as in the case of professional life, managers with better Intuition orientation reportedly use Intuition in their personal life to a larger extent than those with a low orientation.

It will also be seen that there is hardly any difference in the distribution between the Industry and Services sectors.

Actual Instances

The proportion of managers who could cite specific instances where they had actually used Intuition in their professional/personal life, at 51.8 per cent, is not too low by itself, but it turns out to be one of the lowest among the Survey countries. This proportion rises significantly from 49.5 per cent in the low group and 47.6 in the medium group to 63.7 per cent in the high group. This reinforces the inference drawn earlier on the association between Intuition orientation and the extent of its use in professional/personal life.

Opinions on Certain Notions

The respondents were asked to indicate to what extent they agree or disagree with each of ten given statements and the responses were obtained on a five-point scale, ranging from 'strongly agree' to 'strongly disagree'. Based on these responses, a composite index with range 0 to 100 was worked out by assigning values to different responses as follows:

Strongly agree	100
Agree	75
Can't say	50
Disagree	25
Strongly disagree	0

By choosing appropriate weighting factors, the index can be worked out for a given category as well as for the aggregate.

Aggregate indices worked out for different statements are as follows:

	Statement	*Index*
1	Many senior managers use Intuition in making decisions, at least to some extent.	73.4
2	Higher Intuitive capabilities would contribute to greater success in business.	80.4
3	Intuition contributes to harmonious interpersonal relationships.	71.6
4	Intuition is a characteristic associated more with women than with men.	49.1
5	Few managers who use Intuition would openly admit to the same.	51.1
6	The more Intuitive a person is, the more successful he or she will be in life.	59.4
7	Intuition cannot be blocked.	47.1
8	Intuition has a role to play in almost every facet of life.	76.1
9	Intuition can be cultivated/enhanced.	62.0
10	It is not safe to rely on Intuition in business/management.	85.1

Thus, there is a good measure of agreement* that:

- many managers use Intuition (1);
- Intuition contributes to success in business (2);
- Intuition contributes to harmonious interpersonal relationships (3);
- Intuition has a role to play in almost every facet of life (8);
- It is not safe to rely on Intuition in business/management (10).

Sweden is the only Survey country where the suggestion that it is not safe to rely on Intuition in business/management meets with unequivocal acceptance. This is perhaps not surprising, considering that the Swedish managers have turned out to be the least Intuitive among the Survey countries, as judged by yardsticks like the proportion of managers rated high in terms of the objective rating on Intuition.

Further, the suggestion that Intuition contributes to success in life (6) does not meet with the same degree of acceptance as the more restrictive proposition that Intuition contributes to success in business (2) – but this is a pattern common to all Survey countries. Thus, while the managers seem to believe that Intuition is more relevant to professional life, recalling the discussion in the previous section, the managers' claims indicate that they use Intuition to a larger extent in their personal life than in their professional life. This apparent contradiction probably has something to do with the way the

*An index value of 65 or more has been taken to connote a 'good' measure of agreement.

propositions have been formulated: statement 6 is admittedly worded more sharply than statement 2.

Views on Certain Aspects

Views on certain aspects of Intuition were sought by ascertaining agreement with the following propositions, the figures alongside showing the proportions of managers in agreement:

Proposition	%
Dependence of Intuition on external environment	37.4
Possibility of inducing Intuition in others	30.5
Possibility of Intuition being a group process	26.0
Possibility of enhancing Intuition through specific types of practice/ training	31.5

Though somewhat low in comparison with certain other Survey countries, the above proportions are not without significance.

Proportions of managers who think that Intuition should form part of the curriculum at different levels of instruction are as follows:

Level	%
Primary school	11.5
Secondary school	25.2
College/University	48.8
Management institute	66.4

The proportion of managers supporting inclusion of Intuition in the curriculum thus rises progressively with the grade of institutions, reaching a reasonably good level of 66.4 per cent in respect of study at the management institute stage.

Interest in Further Participation

The translated version of the questionnaire administered in Sweden does not include the question that seeks to ascertain the respondent's interest in participating further in this research. Hence no assessment is possible in this regard.

Appendix 6 Report for the UK

Profile of Managers

The sample for the UK comprises 52 managers representing an estimated 145 400 managers in the country conforming to the Survey specifications. A profile of the UK managers, as drawn up by the Survey, is given in table A6.1.

Table A6.1 Profile of the UK managers in the Survey population

Category	Sample count	Estimated population (000s)	%	% corrected for NR*
Sex				
Male	48	133.8	92.0	92.0
Female	4	11.6	8.0	8.0
Age				
Below 35	2	5.8	4.0	4.0
35–44	16	45.6	31.4	31.4
45–59	31	85.7	58.9	58.9
Over 59	3	8.3	5.7	5.7
Organization type				
Industry	19	62.0	42.6	42.6
Services	33	83.4	57.4	57.4
Functional area				
General management	28	79.6	54.7	57.0
Finance	1	2.5	1.7	1.8
Marketing	2	5.8	4.0	4.2
Production/Operations	11	28.6	19.7	20.5
Human resources development	4	12.3	8.5	8.8
Other	4	10.8	7.4	7.7
NR*	2	5.8	4.0	
Management level				
Senior	20	54.2	37.3	38.8
Top	30	85.4	58.7	61.2
NR*	2	5.8	4.0	
Total	52	145.4	100.0	100.0

NR = Not reported.

It will be seen that (correcting the proportions for NR):

- 8.0 per cent of the managers are females;
- nearly two-thirds of the managers are relatively advanced in age, being 45 years old or more.

Also, a majority (61.2 per cent) belong to the top level according to the Survey estimates, but this is highly unlikely. The sample seems to include quite a few owners/chief executives of small service organizations and, to that extent, may not be quite representative of the Survey population in the UK. The findings reported in the subsequent sections should therefore be regarded as subject to this caveat.

Intuition Ratings

Objective Rating

Paired alternatives

Responses to the query regarding choice between ten given pairs of alternatives (where one of the terms is taken to indicate orientation towards Intuition and the other towards Logic/Reasoning) yield the distribution shown in table A6.2.

Table A6.2 Choice between paired alternatives

Intuition-oriented		Logic/Reasoning-oriented		Extent of non-expression of preference (%)
Description	Extent of preference (%)	Description	Extent of preference (%)	
1 Invent	47.8	Build	50.0	2.2
2 Vision	63.2*	Common sense	34.5	2.2
3 Abstract	29.8	Concrete	67.9*	2.2
4 Innovative	92.5*	Conventional	5.2	2.2
5 Creative	69.7*	Analytical	28.1	2.2
6 Ideas	74.7*	Facts	19.6	5.7
7 Imaginative	54.2	Realistic	43.5	2.2
8 Ingenious	52.0	Practical	45.8	2.2
9 Fascinating	59.4	Sensible	38.3	2.2
10 Spontaneous	48.0	Systematic	49.7	2.2

*The observed preference is statistically significant (at the 5 per cent level).
The two alternatives in each pair were presented to the respondent in a predetermined random sequence (see question 2 of the questionnaire in appendix 11).

It will be seen that of the five cases where the observed differences are statistically significant, in as many as four cases the term associated with Intuition has been preferred over its counterpart associated with Logic/

Reasoning, while it is the other way about in the other case. This indicates *prima facie* a reasonably good orientation towards Intuition among the British managers. A more comprehensive rating of the managers on this dimension is attempted later in this section.

Overall Intuition score

By assigning 1 to the choice indicating orientation towards Intuition and 0 to the one towards Logic/Reasoning, an overall score has been computed for each responding manager. Where there was no indication of preference for one term over the other in a given pair (evidenced by the respondent ticking both the alternatives or leaving the section blank), a score of 1/2 has been awarded; however, where no clear preference was indicated in respect of even one of the ten given pairs, it has been treated as a case of 'Not reported' (NR). It is clear that the overall score ranges from 0 to 10 in steps of 1/2.

Classification

Based on the overall Intuition score, a three-way classification of managers has been devised as follows:

Score	*Category*
0.0–3.5	L: Low orientation
4.0–6.0	M: Medium orientation
6.5–10.0	H: High orientation

It will be noted that this classification has been used as one of the standard backgrounds in tabulation of the Survey responses. This is referred to as 'objective rating' as distinct from the 'self-rating' carried out by the respondents, which is discussed later.

Distribution

The above classification has led to the distribution shown in table A6.3.

The (corrected) proportion of 41.5 per cent relating to managers with high orientation is relatively large, corroborating the preliminary inference based on choice between paired alternatives, which has been discussed earlier.

It will be noted that 46.3 per cent (corrected for NR) of the top managers belong to the high category as against only 34.0 per cent of the senior managers, though the difference is statistically not significant.

Self-Rating

Self-rating by the managers regarding Intuition on a given five-point scale (ranging from very high to very low) has yielded the distribution shown in table A6.4.

Table A6.3 Distribution based on objective rating on Intuition

Category	Low (%)	Medium (%)	High (%)	NR (%)
Sex				
Male	15.1	45.2	39.7	–
Female	–	21.8	50.0	28.2
Age				
Below 35	–	100.0	–	–
35–44	5.5	50.8	36.5	7.2
45–59	17.7	36.7	45.6	–
Over 59	30.4	30.4	39.2	–
Organization type				
Industry	–	52.6	42.1	5.3
Services	24.2	36.4	39.4	–
Management level*				
Senior	14.0	52.0	34.0	–
Top	14.8	36.9	44.5	3.8
Total	13.9	43.3	40.6	2.2
(% corrected for NR)	(14.2)	(44.3)	(44.3)	(41.5)

*NR (= Not reported) omitted from classification.

Table A6.4 Distribution based on self-rating on Intuition

Category	Very high (%)	High (%)	Average (%)	Low (%)	Very low (%)	NR (%)
Sex						
Male	8.7	57.0	22.4	9.4	–	2.4
Female	43.6	28.2	28.2	–	–	–
Age						
Below 35	56.4	43.6	–	–	–	–
35–44	11.1	63.5	19.9	5.5	–	–
45–59	6.8	49.4	28.3	11.8	–	3.8
Over 59	30.4	69.6	–	–	–	–
Organization type						
Industry	10.5	63.2	21.1	–	–	5.3
Services	12.1	48.5	24.2	15.2	–	–
Management level*						
Senior	14.0	52.0	14.0	14.0	–	6.0
Top	10.6	53.4	30.1	5.9	–	–
Intuition rating*†						
Low	12.5	12.5	37.5	37.5	–	–
Medium	9.2	50.0	27.6	8.0	–	5.2
High	14.1	77.3	8.6	–	–	–
Total	11.4	54.7	22.9	8.7	–	2.2
(% corrected for NR)	(11.7)	(55.9)	(23.4)	(8.9)	–	

*NR (= Not reported) omitted from classification.
†Relates to objective rating presented in table A6.3

It will be seen that, on an overall basis, two-thirds of the managers rated themselves very high/high on Intuition, suggesting that it is generally viewed as a positive attribute by the managers.

The proportion of managers rating themselves very high/high rises significantly from 25.0 per cent in the low group to 62.4 per cent (as corrected for NR) in the medium group and further to 91.4 per cent in the high group, suggesting a strong positive association between the two rating systems.

Association Between Ratings

The association between the two rating systems can be tested statistically by forming the contingency table shown as table A6.5.

Table A6.5 Objective rating v. self-rating

	Self-rating		
Classification based on objective rating	Average or lower (number)	Very high/ high (number)	Total (number)
Low	6	2	8
Medium	8	13	21
High	2	19	21
Total	16	34	50

Managers whose classification is indeterminate in terms of either rating have been left out of the cross-tabulation.

It can be seen that the χ^2 for table A6.5 works out to 12.03, which is significant even at the 1 per cent level.

The contingency coefficient, C, works out to 0.44 as follows:

$$C = \sqrt{\frac{\chi^2}{\chi^2 + N}}$$

$$= \sqrt{\frac{12.03}{12.03 + 50}}$$

$$= 0.44$$

This is indicative of a reasonably good association between the two rating systems, more or less in line with the inference drawn from the analysis in the preceding subsection.

What is Intuition?

Descriptions Given of Intuition

The questionnaire used for the Survey (see appendix 11) starts with an invitation to the respondent to describe Intuition as understood by him or her so as to get the top-of-the-mind opinion; that is, a response uninfluenced by the sequence of questions that follows in the questionnaire. This has led to diverse descriptions of Intuition, of which the following are the more important:

Description	%
Decision/perception without recourse to logical/rational methods	23.4
Integration of previous experience; processing of accumulated information	18.9
Gut feeling	18.4
Inherent perception; inexplicable comprehension; a feeling that comes from within	18.4
Instinct	18.2
Insight	9.7
Decision/solution to problem, without complete data/facts	7.5
Spontaneous perception/vision	7.5
(Powerful) inner voice; impulse	5.7

The dominant view appears to be that Intuition is some kind of an antithesis to Logic/Reasoning, though it should be noted that integration of previous experience does claim the second spot in the responses. Further, gut feeling and instinct also figure prominently.

It will be noted that the UK managers were quite articulate in their description of Intuition.

Graphic Expression

The proportion of managers giving graphic expression to their concept of Intuition is quite high at 70.2 per cent, pointing to the keen interest evinced in the subject by the managers. This proportion is significantly higher at 73.8

per cent among male managers than at 28.2 per cent among female managers:

Category	%
Male	73.8
Female	28.2
Senior	61.2
Top	73.7
Low	62.5
Medium	61.5
High	85.9

Observed differences in the second and third classifications are not statistically significant but may perhaps be taken to be indicative of a broad pattern.

Agreement with Specific Descriptions

The extent of agreement with three given descriptions of Intuition (obtained as three independent assessments and not as choice among three alternatives) can be seen from the distribution shown in table A6.6.

Table A6.6 Extent of agreement with three specific descriptions of Intuition

	Extent of agreement with		
Category	a (%)	b (%)	c (%)
Sex			
Male	87.6	75.1	44.6
Female	50.0	71.8	56.4
Organization type			
Industry	84.2	73.7	57.9
Services	84.8	75.8	36.4
Management level*			
Senior	84.7	75.3	32.0
Top	83.5	72.9	54.3
Intuition rating*			
Low	100.0	37.5	37.5
Medium	81.6	75.3	38.0
High	87.1	85.9	53.4
Total	84.6	74.9	45.5

*NR (= Not reported) omitted from classification.
(a) Spontaneous insight based on prior experience/expertise.
(b) Flash from 'subconscious levels'.
(c) Tuning into 'higher levels of consciousness'.

Broadly, the order of agreement with the three descriptions is as follows:

(a) & (b) > (c)

> Denotes 'preferred over'.

Considering that 'spontaneous', 'insight' and 'previous experience' all figure prominently in the responses to the open-ended question on the respondent's concept of Intuition, it is perhaps no surprise that description (a) is one of the two preferred. It is significant, however, that these three terms are perceived to form a harmonious and mutually compatible combination (which is not the case in certain other countries).

It will be noted that neither 'flash' nor 'subconscious' figures among the major responses to the open-ended question referred to above, but description (b), which comprises these two key terms, none the less finds as much acceptance as description (a) with the managers.

It will be noticed that description (c) finds greater acceptance with the top managers and in the high group.

Perceived Relevance of Intuition

In Business/Management

The perceived relevance of different functional areas of business/management to the application of Intuition can be seen from the following proportions relating to different areas:

	Area	%
1	Corporate strategy and planning	83.3
2	Investment/Diversification	63.4
3	Corporate acquisitions/mergers/alliances	71.9
4	Finance	40.6
5	Marketing	92.5
6	Public relations	85.6
7	Choice of technology/plant and equipment	34.8
8	Production/Operations	38.8
9	Materials management	33.1
10	Human resources development	93.0
11	Research and development	80.9

The UK managers were quite articulate in this context, compared to those in other countries, resulting in relatively high proportions for different functional areas. Thus, the following are perceived as the major areas of application for Intuition in the field of business/management (no order of importance intended):

- corporate strategy and planning;
- marketing;
- public relations;
- human resources development (HRD);
- research and development (R&D).

These are followed by two others in the next bracket:

- investment/diversification;
- corporate acquisitions/mergers/alliances.

The UK is one of the few among the Survey countries where corporate acquisitions/mergers/alliances figures as an important area of perceived relevance. In most cases, this has failed to attract attention, possibly because it has been taken to form part of corporate strategy and planning.

It will be noted that finance and production/operations are major functional areas which rank among the least important in terms of perceived relevance.

In Other Fields

As regards fields other than business/management, the following are perceived to be the more important in terms of their relevance to application of Intuition:

Field	%
Specific disciplines (engineering, medicine, psychology, etc.)	31.4
Art, drama, literature, music, etc.	26.8
Sports	23.4
Human relations	20.6
Family (relations)	15.4
Politics, public life	15.4
Love, marriage	13.7
Religion, spiritual quest	10.9
Education, teaching	9.2
Research, inventions	6.2

It will be noted that, in the perceptions of the UK managers, specific disciplines, fine arts and sports take precedence over human/family relations. The fact that the list also includes areas like politics, religion and education shows that the reach of Intuition is viewed as quite extensive by these managers.

How Does One Identify Intuition?

Stated Means of Identification

The query as to how Intuition could be identified elicited diverse responses of which the following are the more important:

Response	%
Strong inner feeling, emotion	22.9
Deviation of decision from logical reasoning	18.9
Inability to explain conclusion on the basis of available facts	14.9
Spontaneous perception/vision	5.7

It will be noted that the emotional aspect is seen to be a stronger indicator of Intuition than deviation from Logic/Reasoning.

Associated Phenomena

The extent to which experience of Intuition is perceived to be accompanied by different phenomena can be seen from table A6.7.

Table A6.7 Associated phenomena

Category	(a) Sensory (%)	(b) Physical (%)	(c) Mental (%)	(d) Emotional (%)
Sex				
Male	31.0	20.5	53.3	78.1
Female	–	–	78.2	78.2
Organization type				
Industry	26.3	15.8	68.4	89.5
Services	30.3	21.2	45.5	69.7
Management level*				
Senior	24.7	14.0	50.7	76.7
Top	30.1	23.3	61.9	81.4
Intuition rating*				
Low	25.0	25.0	50.0	75.0
Medium	19.6	9.2	51.2	65.5
High	41.1	28.2	58.9	91.4
Total	28.6	18.9	55.2	78.1

*NR (= Not reported) omitted from classification.

True to the pattern of responses on means of identification discussed earlier, experience of Intuition is most perceived to be accompanied by changes in emotional aspects.

It will be seen that the various phenomena are perceived to be associated with experience of Intuition to a larger extent by the top managers and those in the high group, though the concerned differences are not statistically significant.

Use of Intuition

In Professional Life

Nearly three out of five managers stated that they use Intuition and Logic/Reasoning in almost equal measure in their professional life. However, only 7.5 per cent of the managers use more of Intuition, as against 33.3 per cent using more of Logic/Reasoning, as may be seen from table A6.8.

Table A6.8 Extent of use of Intuition in professional life

Category	More of Logic/Reasoning (%)	Both in almost equal measure (%)	More of Intuition (%)
Sex			
Male	34.3	57.6	8.1
Female	21.8	78.2	–
Organization type			
Industry	21.1	73.7	5.3
Services	42.4	48.5	9.1
Management level*			
Senior	38.6	52.0	9.3
Top	32.2	61.0	6.8
Intuition rating*			
Low	62.5	37.5	–
Medium	43.6	56.4	–
High	14.1	67.5	18.4
Total	33.3	59.2	7.5

*NR (= Not reported) omitted from classification.

It will be noticed that all the managers using more of Intuition in their professional life are concentrated in the high group. Further, the proportion of managers relying more on Logic/Reasoning drops sharply from 62.5 per cent in the low group to 43.6 per cent in the medium group and again to 14.1 per cent in the high group, underlining the positive association between Intuition orientation and the professed extent of use in the managers' professional life.

In Personal Life

Almost half the UK managers stated that they use more of Intuition in their personal life, while the corresponding proportion for use in professional life is a mere 7.5 per cent, as seen in the previous subsection. The proportion of managers using more of Logic/Reasoning declines concomitantly from 33.3 per cent in the case of professional life to 14.4 per cent in the case of personal life. The professed extent of use of Intuition is significantly larger in respect of personal life whichever way the managers are classified (see table A6.9).

Table A6.9 Extent of use of Intuition in personal life

Category	More of Logic/Reasoning (%)	Both in almost equal measure (%)	More of Intuition (%)
Sex			
Male	15.7	34.9	49.5
Female	–	50.0	50.0
Organization type			
Industry	5.3	31.6	63.2
Services	21.2	39.4	39.4
Management level*			
Senior	15.3	40.0	44.7
Top	14.8	33.0	52.2
Intuition rating*			
Low	50.0	37.5	12.5
Medium	13.2	43.6	43.1
High	4.3	23.9	71.8
Total	14.4	36.1	49.5

*NR (= Not reported) omitted from classification.

It may be noted that the proportion of managers using more of Intuition rises significantly from 12.5 per cent in the low group to 43.1 per cent in the medium group and further to 71.8 per cent in the high group, pointing to the strong association between Intuition orientation and the use of Intuition in personal life.

Actual Instances

The proportion of managers who could cite specific instances where they had actually used Intuition in their professional/personal life is fairly high at 65.7 per cent. The significance of this becomes apparent when it is noted that the managers in question did not merely state that they had used Intuition in practice but gave details of the specific applications.

The above proportion rises significantly from 62.5 per cent in the low group and 46.0 per cent in the medium group to 85.9 per cent in the high group (the difference between the low and medium groups is statistically not significant), further reinforcing the inference drawn earlier regarding the positive association between Intuition orientation and the actual use of Intuition in professional/personal life.

Opinions on Certain Notions

The respondents were asked to indicate to what extent they agree or disagree with each of ten given statements and the responses were obtained on a five-point scale, ranging from 'strongly agree' to 'strongly disagree'. Based on these responses, a composite index with range 0 to 100 was worked out by assigning values to different responses as follows:

Strongly agree	100
Agree	75
Can't say	50
Disagree	25
Strongly disagree	0

By choosing appropriate weighting factors, the index can be worked out for a given category as well as for the aggregate.

Aggregate indices worked out for different statements are as follows:

	Statement	*Index*
1	Many senior managers use Intuition in making decisions, at least to some extent.	83.5
2	Higher Intuitive capabilities would contribute to greater success in business.	78.9
3	Intuition contributes to harmonious inter-personal relationships.	78.1
4	Intuition is a characteristic associated more with women than with men.	58.8
5	Few managers who use Intuition would openly admit to the same.	49.6
6	The more Intuitive a person is, the more successful he or she will be in life.	56.2
7	Intuition cannot be blocked.	41.9
8	Intuition has a role to play in almost every facet of life.	78.9
9	Intuition can be cultivated/enhanced.	68.7
10	It is not safe to rely on Intuition in business/management.	51.4

Thus, there is a good measure of agreement* that:

- many managers use Intuition (1);
- Intuition contributes to success in business (2);
- Intuition contributes to harmonious interpersonal relationships (3);
- Intuition has a role to play in almost every facet of life (8);
- Intuition can be cultivated/enhanced (9).

It will be noted that the extent of agreement is lowest (41.9 per cent) with the suggestion that Intuition cannot be blocked, which is consistent with the fairly high extent of agreement with the proposition that Intuition can be cultivated/enhanced (which is, in a way, the other side of the coin). In other words, the general view appears to be that it is as much possible to cultivate/enhance Intuition as to block it.

The managers appear to be undecided on whether those who use Intuition openly admit to the same and whether it is safe to rely on Intuition in business/management.

It will also be noted that the suggestion that Intuition contributes to success in life (6) does not meet with the same degree of acceptance as the more restrictive proposition that Intuition contributes to success in business (2). Thus, while the managers seem to believe that Intuition is more relevant to professional life, recalling the discussion in the previous section, the managers' claims indicate that they use Intuition to a larger extent in their personal life than in their professional life. This apparent contradiction probably has something to do with the way the propositions have been formulated: statement 6 is admittedly worded more sharply than statement 2.

Views on Certain Aspects

Views on certain aspects of Intuition were sought by ascertaining agreement with the following propositions, the figures alongside showing the proportions of managers in agreement:

Proposition	%
Dependence of Intuition on external environment	23.4
Possibility of inducing Intuition in others	42.3
Possibility of Intuition being a group process	40.6
Possibility of enhancing Intuition through specific types of practice/training	50.3

*An index value of 65 or more has been taken to connote a 'good' measure of agreement.

In line with the pattern observed in other countries, the proportion is highest for the possibility of enhancing Intuition through specific types of practice/training. This is consistent with the responses to the statements discussed earlier. The proportions relating to the possibility of inducing Intuition in others and the possibility of Intuition being a group process are also reasonably large.

Proportions of managers who think that Intuition should form part of the curriculum at different levels of instruction are as follows:

Level	%
Primary school	29.8
Secondary school	33.3
College/University	55.0
Management institute	70.4

While there is strong agreement that Intuition is a fit subject for study at the management institute level, and study at the college/university level is also supported by the majority of the managers, the proportions concerning the suitability of the subject at the primary and secondary school levels are not too low either. Thus, on the whole, the view that Intuition should form part of formal instruction at different levels finds wide acceptance among the UK managers.

Interest in Further Participation

Proportions of managers indicating their willingness to participate further in this research through different means are as follows:

Means	%
Personal interviews	49.7
Experiential workshops	34.8
Seminars/Conferences	37.1

Considering that almost half the managers are agreeable even to personal interviews – the most direct and demanding form of participation – the above proportions may be taken to indicate adequate interest in the subject.

Appendix 7 Report for the USA

Profile of Managers

The sample for the USA comprises 143 managers representing an estimated 638 700 managers in the country conforming to the Survey specifications. A profile of the American managers, as drawn up by the Survey, is given in table A7.1.

Table A7.1 Profile of the American managers in the Survey population

Category	Sample count	Estimated population (000s)	%	% corrected for NR*
Sex				
Male	123	535.6	83.9	83.9
Female	20	103.1	16.1	16.1
Age				
Below 35	7	33.4	5.2	5.2
35–44	44	194.9	30.5	30.5
45–59	76	333.2	52.2	52.2
Over 59	16	77.2	12.1	12.1
Organization type				
Industry	90	224.5	35.1	35.1
Services	53	414.2	64.9	64.9
Functional area				
General management	50	279.0	43.7	44.2
Finance	9	43.7	6.8	6.9
Marketing	9	33.1	5.2	5.2
Production/Operations	14	72.2	11.3	11.4
Human resources development	28	112.4	17.6	17.8
Other	30	90.8	14.2	14.4
NR*	3	7.5	1.2	
Management level				
Senior	97	406.9	63.7	64.5
Top	43	224.3	35.1	35.5
NR*	3	7.5	1.2	
Total	143	638.7	100.0	100.0

*NR = Not reported.

It will be seen that:

- 16.1 per cent of the managers are females;
- the majority (64.3 per cent) of the managers are relatively advanced in age, being 45 years old or more;
- 35.5 per cent of the managers belong to the top level (proportion corrected for NR).

Intuition Ratings

Objective Rating

Paired alternatives

Responses to the query regarding choice between ten given pairs of alternatives (where one of the terms is taken to indicate orientation towards Intuition and the other towards Logic/Reasoning) yield the distribution shown in table A7.2.

Table A7.2 Choice between paired alternatives

Intuition-oriented		Logic/Reasoning-oriented		Extent of non-expression of preference (%)
Description	Extent of preference (%)	Description	Extent of preference (%)	
1 Invent	48.6	Build	49.8	1.6
2 Vision	54.6	Common sense	42.6	2.8
3 Abstract	38.1	Concrete	59.0*	2.8
4 Innovative	82.7*	Conventional	14.4	2.8
5 Creative	62.2*	Analytical	35.8	2.0
6 Ideas	75.5*	Facts	22.9	1.6
7 Imaginative	59.4*	Realistic	38.6	2.0
8 Ingenious	58.2*	Practical	40.1	1.6
9 Fascinating	47.0	Sensible	51.4	1.6
10 Spontaneous	48.2	Systematic	48.9	2.8

*The observed preference is statistically significant (at the 5 per cent level).
The two alternatives in each pair were presented to the respondent in a predetermined random sequence (see question 2 of the questionnaire in appendix 11).

It will be seen that of the six cases where the observed differences are statistically significant, in as many as five cases the term associated with Intuition has been preferred over its counterpart associated with Logic/Reasoning, while it is the other way about in the other case. This indicates *prima facie* a good orientation towards Intuition among the American managers. A more comprehensive rating of the managers on this dimension is attempted later in this section.

Overall Intuition score

By assigning 1 to the choice indicating orientation towards Intuition and 0 to the one towards Logic/Reasoning, an overall score has been computed for each responding manager. Where there was no indication of preference for one term over the other in a given pair (evidenced by the respondent ticking both the alternatives or leaving the section blank), a score of ½ has been awarded; however, where no clear preference was indicated in respect of even one of the ten given pairs, it has been treated as a case of 'Not reported' (NR). It is clear that the overall score ranges from 0 to 10 in steps of ½.

Classification

Based on the overall Intuition score, a three-way classification of managers has been devised as follows:

Score	*Category*
0.0–3.5	L: Low orientation
4.0–6.0	M: Medium orientation
6.5–10.0	H: High orientation

It will be noted that this classification has been used as one of the standard backgrounds in tabulation of the Survey responses. This is referred to as 'objective rating' as distinct from the 'self-rating' carried out by the respondents, which is discussed later.

Distribution

The above classification has led to the distribution shown in table A7.3.

It will be seen that, on an overall basis, a good 43.0 per cent of the managers merited a rating above average (namely, high), corroborating the preliminary inference drawn earlier on the basis of choice between paired alternatives.

The observed differences between groups are not statistically significant.

Self-Rating

Self-rating by the managers regarding Intuition on a given five-point scale (ranging from very high to very low) has yielded the distribution shown in table A7.4.

The proportion of managers who rated themselves very high/high on Intuition is as large as 78.7 per cent, suggesting that Intuition is viewed by the American managers as a highly positive attribute.

Table A7.3 Distribution based on objective rating on Intuition

Category	Low (%)	Medium (%)	High (%)
Sex			
Male	21.5	37.3	41.2
Female	17.6	30.0	52.4
Age			
Below 35	30.8	14.9	54.2
35–44	22.4	40.9	36.7
45–59	16.9	35.3	47.8
Over 59	30.0	36.4	33.6
Organization type			
Industry	21.1	40.0	38.9
Services	20.8	34.0	45.3
Management level*			
Senior	15.7	35.9	48.4
Top	29.9	35.4	34.7
Total	20.9	36.1	43.0

*NR (= Not reported) omitted from classification.

Table A7.4 Distribution based on self-rating on Intuition

Category	Very high (%)	High (%)	Average (%)	Low (%)	Very low (%)
Sex					
Male	16.7	60.8	20.1	2.4	–
Female	17.6	67.3	15.2	–	–
Age					
Below 35	–	92.5	7.5	–	–
35–44	9.3	59.0	30.5	1.3	–
45–59	19.2	63.1	14.6	3.1	–
Over 59	33.2	50.2	16.6	–	–
Organization type					
Industry	16.7	64.4	16.7	2.2	–
Services	17.0	60.4	20.8	1.9	
Management level*					
Senior	15.1	64.1	18.3	2.5	
Top	20.6	59.7	19.6	–	–
Intuition rating†					
Low	3.7	55.7	30.9	9.6	–
Medium	17.7	49.9	32.4	–	–
High	22.5	74.8	2.7	–	–
Total	16.9	61.8	19.3	2.0	–

*NR (= Not reported) omitted from classification.
†Relates to objective rating presented in table A7.3.

The proportion of high group managers rating themselves very high/high on Intuition is as large as 97.3 per cent, which is significantly higher than the corresponding proportions of 59.4 per cent for the low group and 67.6 per cent for the medium group, indicating a positive association between the two rating systems. The other observed differences between different groups are not statistically significant.

Association Between Ratings

The association between the two rating systems can be tested statistically by forming the contingency table shown as table A7.5.

Table A7.5 Objective rating v. self-rating

Classification based on objective rating	Self-rating: Average or lower (number)	Self-rating: Very high/ high (number)	Total (number)
Low	12	18	30
Medium	16	38	54
High	1	58	59
Total	29	114	143

It can be seen that the χ^2 (which will have 2 degrees of freedom) for table A7.5 works out to 22.67, which is significant even at the 1 per cent level, confirming that there is a good positive association between the two rating systems.

The contingency coefficient, C, works out to 0.37 as follows:

$$C = \sqrt{\frac{\chi^2}{\chi^2 + N}}$$

$$= \sqrt{\frac{22.67}{22.67 + 143}}$$

$$= 0.37$$

This value of C may be taken as a measure of the association between the two ratings.

What is Intuition?

Descriptions Given of Intuition

The questionnaire used for the Survey (see appendix 11) starts with an invitation to the respondent to describe Intuition as understood by him or her so as to get the top-of-the-mind opinion; that is, a response uninfluenced by the sequence of questions that follows in the questionnaire. This has led to diverse descriptions of Intuition, of which the following are the more important:

Description	%
Decision/perception without recourse to logical/rational methods	24.0
Inherent perception; inexplicable comprehension; a feeling that comes from within	23.8
Gut feeling	20.1
Integration of previous experience; processing of accumulated information	15.9
Decision/solution to problem, without complete data/facts	13.3
Insight	9.2
Sixth sense	8.9
Instinct	5.2

Thus, there are three prominent concepts of Intuition among the American managers: (1) something of an antithesis to Logic/Reasoning; (2) inherent perception/inexplicable comprehension; and (3) gut feeling.

It will be noted that the list also includes 'sixth sense', besides 'instinct' and 'insight'.

Graphic Expression

The proportion of managers giving graphic expression to their concept of Intuition is quite high at 82.0 per cent, signifying the keen interest evinced in the subject by the American managers. This proportion is fairly constant among different categories of managers:

Category	%
Male	81.9
Female	82.4
Industry	80.0

Services	83.0
Senior	81.1
Top	84.0
Low	77.1
Medium	83.5
High	83.1

Agreement with Specific Descriptions

The extent of agreement with three given descriptions of Intuition (obtained as three independent assessments and not as choice among three alternatives) can be seen from the distribution shown in table A7.6.

Table A7.6 Extent of agreement with three specific descriptions of Intuition

	Extent of agreement with		
Category	a (%)	b (%)	c (%)
Sex			
Male	88.0	71.4	44.1
Female	74.8	97.6	82.4
Organization type			
Industry	91.1	68.9	45.6
Services	83.0	79.2	52.8
Management level*			
Senior	87.3	79.4	50.3
Top	83.8	68.0	51.8
Intuition rating			
Low	76.8	57.4	40.3
Medium	78.7	76.8	45.7
High	96.2	83.4	59.0
Total	85.9	75.6	50.3

*NR (= Not reported) omitted from classification.
(a) Spontaneous insight based on prior experience/expertise.
(b) Flash from 'subconscious levels'.
(c) Tuning into 'higher levels of consciousness'.

The observed differences between the extents of agreement with the different descriptions are statistically significant, the order of acceptance being as follows:

$$(a) > (b) > (c)$$

> Denotes 'preferred over'.

It will be recalled that integration of previous experience and insight, which may be viewed as two components of description (a), figured in the major responses to the open-ended question on the respondent's concept of

Intuition (though not as prominently as some others). The other descriptions do not derive any such support from these responses.

It will be noted that description (a) meets with a significantly higher extent of acceptance among high group managers than among those in the other two groups, while description (b) and description (c) find greater favour with female managers than with male managers to a significant extent.

Perceived Relevance of Intuition

In Business/Management

The perceived relevance of different functional areas of business/management to the application of Intuition can be seen from the following proportions relating to different areas:

	Area	%
1	Corporate strategy and planning	92.0
2	Investment/Diversification	64.3
3	Corporate acquisitions/ mergers/alliances	64.6
4	Finance	45.1
5	Marketing	88.7
6	Public relations	76.3
7	Choice of technology/plant and equipment	51.4
8	Production/Operations	37.8
9	Materials management	34.2
10	Human resources development	88.0
11	Research and development	83.1

Thus, the following are perceived as the major areas of application for Intuition in the field of business/management (no order of importance intended):

- corporate strategy and planning;
- marketing;
- human resources development (HRD);
- research and development (R&D).

There are three other areas which come in the next tier (again, no order of importance intended):

- investment/diversification;
- corporate acquisitions/mergers/alliances;
- public relations.

The USA is one of the few Survey countries where corporate acquisitions has been clearly identified as an important area of relevance to application of Intuition.

It will be noted that finance and production/operations are two major functional areas which rank among the least important in terms of perceived relevance.

In Other Fields

As regards fields other than business/management, the following are perceived to be the more important in terms of their relevance to application of Intuition:

Field	%
Education, teaching	27.7
Specific disciplines (engineering, medicine, psychology, etc.)	26.9
Art, drama, music, literature, etc.	18.6
Sports	14.4
All fields	11.7
Family (relations)	8.5
Politics, public life	8.1
Military/police affairs	8.1
Recreation, entertainment etc.	6.8
Love, marriage	6.4
Government	6.4
Religion, spiritual quest	6.0
Human/interpersonal relations	6.0
Children (bringing up children, children's education, etc.)	5.2

It is significant that education/teaching and study of specific disciplines top the list, which is a major deviation from the pattern observed in other countries. Fine arts and sports are important among the other fields perceived to be relevant to the application of Intuition.

How Does One Identify Intuition?

Stated Means of Identification

The query as to how Intuition could be identified elicited diverse responses, of which the following are the more important:

Response	%
Strong inner feeling, emotion	22.2
Inability to explain conclusion on the basis of available facts	20.5
Deviation of decision from logical reasoning	12.5
Spontaneous perception/vision	5.6

Thus, emotional feeling and deviation of decision/conclusion from available facts/logical reasoning are perceived to be the chief identifying characteristics of Intuition.

Associated Phenomena

The extent to which experience of Intuition is perceived to be accompanied by different phenomena can be seen from table A7.7.

Table A7.7 Associated phenomena

Category	(a) Sensory (%)	(b) Physical (%)	(c) Mental (%)	(d) Emotional (%)
Sex				
Male	29.7	35.5	70.4	66.5
Female	40.3	30.0	55.2	54.8
Organization type				
Industry	23.3	28.9	64.4	65.6
Services	35.8	37.7	69.8	64.2
Management level*				
Senior	33.5	33.4	71.1	70.5
Top	28.8	36.9	61.0	53.9
Intuition rating				
Low	19.5	31.2	69.3	59.7
Medium	25.6	41.2	63.4	65.4
High	42.2	30.8	71.0	66.4
Total	31.4	34.6	67.9	64.6

*NR (= Not reported) omitted from classification.

Consistently with the pattern of responses to the question on means of identification discussed earlier, experience of Intuition is most perceived to be accompanied by changes in the mental and emotional aspects.

Use of Intuition

In Professional Life

Nearly half the managers stated that they use Intuition and Logic/Reasoning in almost equal measure in their professional life. As for the others, the proportion of managers reportedly using more of Intuition is only 8.9 per cent, as against 42.6 per cent using more of Logic/Reasoning, as may be seen from table A7.8.

Table A7.8 Extent of use of Intuition in professional life

Category	More of Logic/Reasoning (%)	Both in almost equal measure (%)	More of Intuition (%)
Sex			
Male	46.0	45.4	8.6
Female	24.8	65.2	10.0
Organization type			
Industry	41.1	51.1	7.8
Services	43.4	47.2	9.4
Management level*			
Senior	39.0	51.6	9.4
Top	47.2	44.7	8.1
Intuition rating			
Low	67.5	26.7	5.9
Medium	51.2	47.7	1.1
High	23.3	59.9	16.8
Total	42.6	48.6	8.9

*NR (= Not reported) omitted from classification.

It will be noted that as against 5.9 per cent in the low group and 1.1 per cent in the medium group, the percentage of managers using more of Intuition is 16.8 per cent in the high group. The association between Intuition orientation and the stated extent of use in professional life comes out more clearly when it is noted that the proportion of managers using more of Logic/Reasoning drops from 67.5 per cent in the low group and 51.2 per cent in the medium group to a significantly lower level of 23.3 per cent in the high group.

Female managers also can be credited with greater use of Intuition in professional life, as only 24.8 per cent of them use more of Logic/Reasoning as against a significantly higher proportion of 46.0 per cent in respect of male managers.

Other observed differences are not statistically significant.

In Personal Life

A majority (55.8 per cent) of the American managers stated that they use Intuition and Logic/Reasoning in almost equal measure in their personal life. The proportion of managers using more of Intuition is significantly high at 24.5 per cent, as compared to the corresponding percentage of 8.9 per cent in respect of use in professional life. There is a concomitant drop in the proportion of managers using more of Logic/Reasoning from 42.6 per cent in the case of professional life to 19.7 per cent in the case of personal life. This pattern is in evidence whichever way the managers are classified (see table A7.9).

Table A7.9 Extent of use of Intuition in personal life

Category	More of Logic/Reasoning (%)	Both in almost equal measure (%)	More of Intuition (%)
Sex			
Male	20.1	58.4	21.5
Female	17.6	42.4	40.0
Organization type			
Industry	21.1	54.4	24.4
Services	18.9	56.6	24.5
Management level*			
Senior	20.7	59.8	19.5
Top	17.3	48.3	34.4
Intuition rating			
Low	29.1	57.6	13.3
Medium	23.3	60.2	16.5
High	12.0	51.4	36.6
Total	19.7	55.8	24.5

*NR (= Not reported) omitted from classification.

The proportion of managers using more of Intuition is significantly large at 36.6 per cent in the high group as compared to 13.3 per cent in the low group and 16.5 per cent in the medium group. This shows that, just as in the case of professional life, managers with better Intuition orientation reportedly use Intuition in their personal life to a larger extent than those with a low orientation.

The above distribution also indicates that the extent of use of Intuition in personal life is greater among female managers than among male managers, and among top managers than among senior managers, but the concerned differences are not statistically significant.

Actual Instances

The proportion of managers who could cite specific instances where they had actually used Intuition in their professional/personal life is quite high at 76.3 per cent – a majority (53.1 per cent) of them in fact cited two instances each. This proportion is particularly high among the female managers (87.6 per cent) and in the high group (85.1 per cent).

Opinions on Certain Notions

The respondents were asked to indicate to what extent they agree or disagree with each of ten given statements and the responses were obtained on a five-point scale, ranging from 'strongly agree' to 'strongly disagree'. Based on these responses, a composite index with range 0 to 100 was worked out by assigning values to different responses as follows:

Strongly agree	100
Agree	75
Can't say	50
Disagree	25
Strongly disagree	0

By choosing appropriate weighting factors, the index can be worked out for a given category as well as for the aggregate.

Aggregate indices worked out for different statements are as follows:

	Statement	*Index*
1	Many senior managers use Intuition in making decisions, at least to some extent.	82.6
2	Higher Intuitive capabilities would contribute to greater success in business.	78.5
3	Intuition contributes to harmonious interpersonal relationships.	74.6
4	Intuition is a characteristic associated more with women than with men.	52.2
5	Few managers who use Intuition would openly admit to the same.	56.2

	Statement	*Index*
6	The more Intuitive a person is, the more successful he or she will be in life.	60.4
7	Intuition cannot be blocked.	39.7
8	Intuition has a role to play in almost every facet of life.	81.4
9	Intuition can be cultivated/ enhanced.	72.2
10	It is not safe to rely on Intuition in business/management.	29.1

Thus, there is a good measure of agreement* that:

- many managers use Intuition (1);
- Intuition contributes to success in business (2);
- Intuition contributes to harmonious interpersonal relationships (3);
- Intuition has a role to play in almost every facet of life (8);
- Intuition can be cultivated/enhanced (9).

It will be noted that the suggestion that Intuition contributes to success in life (6) does not meet with the same degree of acceptance as the more restrictive proposition that Intuition contributes to success in business (2). Thus, while the managers seem to believe that Intuition is more relevant to professional life, recalling the discussion in the previous section, the managers' claims indicate that they use Intuition to a larger extent in their personal life than in their professional life. This apparent contradiction probably has something to do with the way the propositions have been formulated: statement 6 is admittedly worded more sharply than statement 2.

It will also be seen that the negative suggestion that it is not safe to rely on Intuition in business/management (10) has been firmly rejected, reinforcing the inference on the perceived relevance of Intuition in this domain.

Views on Certain Aspects

Views on certain aspects of Intuition were sought by ascertaining agreement with the following propositions, the figures alongside showing the proportions

*An index value of 65 or more has been taken to connote a 'good' measure of agreement.

of managers in agreement:

Proposition	%
Dependence of Intuition on external environment	38.6
Possibility of inducing Intuition in others	31.4
Possibility of Intuition being a group process	49.8
Possibility of enhancing Intuition through specific types of practice/training	63.6

The relatively high proportion concerning the efficacy of training is quite in tune with the response to statement 9 discussed earlier, which touches on the scope for cultivating/enhancing Intuition.

Proportions of managers who think that Intuition should form part of the curriculum at different levels of instruction are as follows:

Level	%
Primary school	44.4
Secondary school	54.9
College/University	67.3
Management institute	80.9

The proportion of managers supporting inclusion of Intuition in the curriculum thus rises progressively with the grade of institutions, reaching a level as high as 80.9 per cent in respect of study at the management institute stage.

Interest in Further Participation

Proportions of managers indicating their willingness to participate further in this research through different means are as follows:

Means	%
Personal interviews	48.3
Experiential workshops	37.1
Seminars/Conferences	41.1

Considering the demands participation in research of this type makes on one's time, the above proportions may be taken to be indicative of a good degree of interest in the subject among the American managers.

Appendix 8 Report for Japan

Profile of Managers

The sample for Japan comprises 56 managers representing an estimated 298 400 managers in the country conforming to the Survey specifications. A profile of the Japanese managers, as drawn up by the Survey, is given in table A8.1.

Table A8.1 Profile of the Japanese managers in the Survey population

Category	Sample count	Estimated population (000s)	%	% corrected for NR*
Sex				
Male	47	252.8	84.7	87.9
Female	7	34.9	11.7	12.1
NR*	2	10.7	3.6	
Age				
Below 35	6	21.6	7.2	7.5
35–44	20	106.0	35.5	36.8
45–59	25	149.3	50.0	51.9
Over 59	3	10.8	3.6	3.8
NR*	2	10.7	3.6	
Organization type				
Industry	29	104.2	34.9	41.6
Services	18	146.2	49.0	58.4
NR*	9	48.0	16.1	
Functional area				
General management	19	123.4	41.4	51.5
Finance	–	–	–	–
Marketing	8	37.8	12.7	15.8
Production/Operations	8	42.3	14.2	17.7
Human resources development	–	–	–	–
Other	10	35.9	12.0	15.0
NR*	11	59.0	19.8	
Management level				
Senior	31	152.8	51.2	65.8
Top	12	79.4	26.6	34.2
NR*	13	66.2	22.2	
Total	56	298.4	100.0	100.0

*NR = Not reported.

It will be seen that (correcting the proportions for NR):

- 12.1 per cent of the managers are females;
- over half the managers are relatively advanced in age, being 45 years old or more;
- about a third of the managers belong to the top level.

It may be noted here that the proportion of non-response is unusually high in respect of organization type, functional area and management level. This is reflected, inter alia, in the absence of any identifiable representation in the sample from the functional areas of finance and human resources development (HRD).

Intuition Ratings

Objective Rating

Paired alternatives

Responses to the query regarding choice between ten given pairs of alternatives (where one of the terms is taken to indicate orientation towards Intuition and the other towards Logic/Reasoning) yield the distribution shown in table A8.2.

Table A8.2 Choice between paired alternatives

Intuition-oriented		Logic/Reasoning-oriented		Extent of non-expression of preference (%)
Description	Extent of preference (%)	Description	Extent of preference (%)	
1 Invent	35.2	Build	62.1*	2.7
2 Vision	84.0*	Common sense	13.3	2.7
3 Abstract	33.8	Concrete	63.5*	2.7
4 Innovative	63.8*	Conventional	33.5	2.7
5 Creative	86.4*	Analytical	10.8	2.7
6 Ideas	71.6*	Facts	25.7	2.7
7 Imaginative	60.6	Realistic	36.7	2.7
8 Ingenious	43.4	Practical	53.9	2.7
9 Fascinating	72.8*	Sensible	24.4	2.7
10 Spontaneous	63.3*	Systematic	34.0	2.7

*The observed difference is statistically significant (at the 5 per cent level).
The two alternatives in each pair were presented to the respondent in a predetermined random sequence (see question 2 of the questionnaire in appendix 11).

It will be seen that of the eight cases where the observed differences are statistically significant, in as many as six cases the term associated with Intuition has been preferred over its counterpart associated with Logic/Reasoning, while it is the other way about in the other two cases. This indicates *prima facie* a good orientation towards Intuition among the Japanese managers. A more comprehensive rating of the managers on this dimension is attempted later in this section.

Overall Intuition score

By assigning 1 to the choice indicating orientation towards Intuition and 0 to the one towards Logic/Reasoning, an overall score has been computed for each responding managers. Where there was no indication of preference for one term over the other in a given pair (evidenced by the respondent ticking both the alternatives or leaving the section blank), a score of ½ has been awarded; however, where no clear preference was indicated in respect of even one of the ten given pairs, it has been treated as a case of 'Not reported' (NR). It is clear that the overall score ranges from 0 to 10 in steps of ½.

Classification

Based on the overall Intuition score, a three-way classification of managers has been devised as follows:

Score	*Category*
0.0–3.5	L: Low orientation
4.0–6.0	M: Medium orientation
6.5–10.0	H: High orientation

It will be noted that this classification has been used as one of the standard backgrounds in tabulation of the Survey responses. This is referred to as 'objective rating' as distinct from the 'self-rating' carried out by the respondents, which is discussed later.

Distribution

The above classification has led to the distribution shown in table A8.3.

The (corrected) proportion of 45.8 per cent relating to managers with high Intuition orientation is relatively large, corroborating the preliminary inference based on choice between paired alternatives, which has been discussed earlier.

The observed differences between different categories are not statistically significant.

Table A8.3 Distribution based on objective rating on Intuition

Category*	Low (%)	Medium (%)	High (%)	NR (%)
Sex				
Male	12.1	41.2	43.4	3.2
Female	–	48.8	51.2	–
Age				
Below 35	–	50.0	50.0	–
35–44	14.4	33.9	44.0	7.7
45–59	10.2	47.5	42.2	–
Over 59	–	33.3	66.7	–
Organization type				
Industry	13.8	41.4	44.8	–
Services	11.1	38.9	44.4	5.6
Management level				
Senior	14.7	42.3	43.0	–
Top	10.2	39.8	39.8	10.2
Total	10.3	42.4	44.6	2.7
(% corrected for NR)	(10.6)	(43.6)	(45.8)	

*NR (= Not reported) omitted from all categories.

Self-Rating

Self-rating by the managers regarding Intuition on a given five-point scale (ranging from very high to very low) has yielded the distribution shown in table A8.4.

It will be seen that, on an overall basis, a majority (52.4 per cent) of the managers rated themselves very high/high on Intuition, suggesting that it is generally viewed as a positive attribute by the managers.

The proportion of female managers rating themselves very high/high is significantly higher at 89.7 per cent than the corresponding proportion of 47.3 per cent for male managers. Likewise, the observed difference in this proportion between top managers (80.7 per cent) and senior managers (34.0 per cent) is also significant. Further, the proportion of managers rating themselves to this extent (very high/high) rises significantly from 11.7 per cent in the low group to 42.6 per cent in the medium group and again to 68.1 per cent in the high group, suggesting a good degree of association between the two rating systems.

Association Between Ratings

The association between the two rating systems can be tested statistically by forming the contingency table shown as table A8.5.

Table A8.4 Distribution based on self-rating on Intuition

Category*	Very high (%)	High (%)	Average (%)	Low (%)	Very low (%)
Sex					
Male	12.8	34.5	45.2	7.5	–
Female	10.3	79.4	10.3	–	–
Age					
Below 35	16.7	–	83.3	–	–
35–44	5.0	50.0	30.5	14.4	–
45–59	15.7	41.5	40.4	2.4	–
Over 59	33.3	–	66.7	–	–
Organization type					
Industry	13.8	27.6	48.3	10.3	–
Services	11.1	44.4	38.9	5.6	–
Management level					
Senior	10.0	24.0	55.9	10.0	–
Top	14.8	65.9	14.8	4.5	–
Intuition rating†					
Low	–	11.7	38.3	50.0	–
Medium	5.7	36.9	54.6	2.8	–
High	25.6	42.5	31.8	–	–
Total	13.8	38.6	41.3	6.3	–

*NR (= Not reported) omitted from all categories.
†Relates to objective rating presented in table A8.3.

Table A8.5 Objective rating v. self-rating

	Self-rating		
Classification based on objective rating	Average or lower (number)	Very high/high (number)	Total (number)
Low and medium	19	11	30
High	8	17	25
Total	27	28	55

The low and medium categories have been combined together as, otherwise, the expected frequencies fall below 5 in 2 out of 6 cells, which is not permissible for application of the χ^2 test.

Using the special method of computation appropriate for 2 × 2 contingency tables (that is, incorporating a correction for continuity), it can be seen that the χ^2 value in the present case works out to 4.18, which is significant at the 5 per cent level (with 1 degree of freedom), confirming the positive association between the two ratings.

The contingency coefficient, C, works out to 0.26 as follows:

$$C = \sqrt{\frac{\chi^2}{\chi^2 + N}}$$

$$= \sqrt{\frac{4.18}{4.18 + 55}}$$

$$= 0.26$$

Even considering that the maximum value that can be attained by C for a 2×2 contingency table is only $\sqrt{\frac{1}{2}}$ or 0.71, the observed value of C should be considered rather low. This shows that while there is a significant association between the two ratings, it is not as strong as suggested by the simple comparison attempted earlier.

What is Intuition?

Descriptions Given of Intuition

The questionnaire used for the Survey (see appendix 11) starts with an invitation to the respondent to describe Intuition as understood by him or her so as to get the top-of-the-mind opinion; that is, a response uninfluenced by the sequence of questions that follows in the questionnaire. This has led to diverse descriptions of Intuition, of which the following are the more important:

Description	%
Integration of previous experience; processing of accumulated information	23.8
Spark; flash	16.3
Decision/perception without recourse to logical/rational methods	12.7
Subconscious process	12.0
Sixth sense	11.7
Spontaneous perception/vision	10.8
Initial reaction	7.5
(Powerful) inner voice; impulse	6.6

It is interesting to note that the perception that Intuition stems from accumulated information claims the largest proportion of proponents, though the next two places go respectively to 'Spark; flash' and the view that it is some kind of an antithesis to logic.

Graphic Expression

The proportion of managers giving graphic expression to their concept of Intuition is quite high at 75·3 per cent, pointing to the keen interest evinced in the subject by the Japanese managers. This proportion is higher for female managers than for male managers and in the industry sector than in the services sector:

Category	%
Male	70.8
Female	100.0
Industry	86.2
Services	66.7
Low	100.0
Medium	74·4
High	68.9

The proportion for the low group is significantly higher than those for the medium and high groups, implying a negative association between propensity to graphic expression and Intuition orientation, which is contrary to the pattern observed in other countries.

Agreement with Specific Descriptions

The extent of agreement with three given descriptions of Intuition (obtained as three independent assessments and not as choice among three alternatives) can be seen from the distribution shown in table A8.6.

Broadly, the order of agreement with the three descriptions is as follows:

(b) > (a) & (c)

> Denotes 'preferred over'.

With the solitary exception of the top managers, the unequivocal preference for description (b) is evident in all categories. Further, the proportion of managers in agreement with description (c) is distinctly high among top managers and in the high group.

It is interesting to compare the extent of agreement with these different

Table A8.6 Extent of agreement with three specific descriptions of Intuition

Category*	Extent of agreement with a (%)	b (%)	c (%)
Sex			
Male	67.2	85.0	63.0
Female	35.9	100.0	69.4
Organization type			
Industry	69.0	79.3	62.1
Services	61.1	88.9	66.7
Management level			
Senior	76.5	95.3	53.0
Top	50.0	76.2	80.7
Intuition rating			
Low	100.0	100.0	64.8
Medium	58.0	81.5	51.1
High	60.9	89.2	72.3
Total	64.7	87.3	63.3

*NR (= Not reported) omitted from all categories.
(a) Spontaneous insight based on prior experience/expertise.
(b) Flash from 'subconscious levels'.
(c) Tuning into 'higher levels of consciousness'.

descriptions with the pattern of responses to the open-ended question on the respondent's concept of Intuition at the beginning of the investigation. Description (b) comprises two components, 'flash' and 'subconscious', which figure in the first half of the top-of-the-mind descriptions of Intuition. Judging from the fact that integration of previous experience claims the top spot in the responses to the open-ended question and that spontaneous perception does figure as one of the major responses, one would have expected description (a) to have met with the maximum extent of agreement, which is not the case. It seems reasonable to infer, therefore, that the Japanese managers do not view the combination of spontaneous insight and prior experience (comprised in description (a)) as quite compatible.

Perceived Relevance of Intuition

In Business/Management

The perceived relevance of different functional areas of business/management to the application of Intuition can be seen from the following proportions relating to different areas:

	Area	%
1	Corporate strategy and planning	56.9
2	Investment/Diversification	45.5
3	Corporate acquisitions/ mergers/alliances	26.0
4	Finance	5.4
5	Marketing	44.0
6	Public relations	38.5
7	Choice of technology/plant and equipment	12.6
8	Production/Operations	9.1
9	Materials management	5.1
10	Human resources development	51.2
11	Research and development	49.7

It may be noted that the above proportions are rather low in comparison with other countries. None the less, going by the relative order of magnitudes witnessed here, the following are perceived as the major areas of application for Intuition in the field of business/management (no order of importance intended):

- corporate strategy and planning;
- human resources development (HRD);
- research and development (R&D);
- investment/diversification;
- marketing.

It will be observed that R&D ranks fairly high in terms of perceived relevance.

One might have expected an area like corporate acquisitions/mergers/alliances to figure in the major areas of perceived importance, but this may have been taken to form part of corporate strategy and planning.

It will be noted that finance and production/operations are two major functional areas which rank among the least important in terms of perceived relevance.

In Other Fields

As regards fields other than business/management, the following are perceived to be the more important in terms of their relevance to application of

Intuition:

Field	%
Sports	24.1
Art, drama, literature, music, etc.	16.2
Human/interpersonal relations	15.0
Love, marriage	13.0
Specific disciplines (engineering, medicine, psychology, etc.)	7.5

Thus, sports is perceived to be the most relevant field outside the domain of business/management as regards application of Intuition. This is significant considering that Japan occupies a pre-eminent position in the field of sports in the Asian region.

How Does One Identify Intuition?

Stated Means of Identification

The query as to how Intuition could be identified elicited diverse responses, of which the following are the more important:

Response	%
Deviation of decision from logical reasoning	5.1
Spontaneous perception/vision	5.1
Strong inner feeling, emotion	3.9
Rapidity with which a decision is taken	3.6

One reason for the low articulation on this issue could be that the question was not understood properly by the Japanese managers.

Associated Phenomena

The extent to which experience of Intuition is perceived to be accompanied by different phenomena can be seen from table A8.7.

On an overall basis, experience of Intuition is thought to be accompanied by changes in sensory and mental aspects to a greater extent than by changes of physical and emotional aspects. The low percentage relating to emotional aspects is at variance with the trends observed in the case of other countries.

Table A8.7 Associated phenomena

Category*	(a) Sensory (%)	(b) Physical (%)	(c) Mental (%)	(d) Emotional (%)
Sex				
Male	40.5	23.1	50.6	31.7
Female	84.7	35.9	61.4	61.4
Organization type				
Industry	51.7	34.5	44.8	37.9
Services	38.9	16.7	55.6	27.8
Management level				
Senior	49.4	17.6	52.4	42.3
Top	29.5	25.0	50.0	19.3
Intuition rating				
Low	50.0	23.5	76.5	50.0
Medium	44.7	28.4	41.9	23.3
High	49.3	14.8	52.7	36.4
Total	46.1	23.8	51.8	34.0

*NR (= Not reported) omitted from all categories.

It will be noted that sensory and emotional aspects are mentioned by female managers to a significantly higher extent than by male managers.

Use of Intuition

In Professional Life

Nearly two-thirds of the managers stated that they use Intuition and Logic/Reasoning in almost equal measure in their professional life. However, only 7.5 per cent of the managers use more of Intuition, as compared to 28.3 per cent using more of Logic/Reasoning, as may be seen from table A8.8.

It will be seen that the senior and top managers evince two distinctly different patterns. It is not merely that 14.8 per cent of the top managers stated that they use more of Intuition, as against none among the senior managers: nearly half (47.0 per cent) of the senior managers rely, according to their own admission, more on Logic/Reasoning in their professional life, while the corresponding proportion for top managers is a mere 4.5 per cent.

Further, there seems to be a positive association between Intuition orientation and the extent of its use in professional life, judging from the fact that the proportion of managers with high orientation using more of Intuition (14.1 per cent) is significantly higher than the corresponding proportions for the low and medium groups.

Table A8.8 Extent of use of Intuition in professional life

Category*	More of Logic/Reasoning (%)	Both in almost equal measure (%)	More of Intuition (%)
Sex			
Male	27.7	65.5	6.7
Female	40.9	59.1	–
Organization type			
Industry	34.5	62.1	3.4
Services	22.2	72.2	5.6
Management level			
Senior	47.0	53.0	–
Top	4.5	80.7	14.8
Intuition rating			
Low	11.7	88.3	–
Medium	35.4	61.7	2.8
High	27.0	58.8	14.1
Total	28.3	64.2	7.5

*NR (= Not reported) omitted from all categories.

In Personal Life

Over half (57.6 per cent) of the managers stated that they use Intuition and Logic/Reasoning in almost equal measure in their personal life. This proportion compares with the one of 64.2 per cent corresponding to professional life, discussed in the preceding subsection. However, the proportion of managers using more of Intuition, at 38.5 per cent, is significantly larger than the corresponding proportion of 7.5 per cent witnessed in the case of professional life. Another way of looking at it is that whereas 28.3 per cent of the managers stated that they use more of Logic/Reasoning in their professional life, the corresponding proportion is a mere 3.9 per cent in the case of personal life. In other words, hardly any of the Japanese managers relies on Logic/Reasoning so far as his or her personal life is concerned (see table A8.9).

The proportion of female managers relying more on Intuition is significantly higher at 76.7 per cent than the corresponding proportion of 32.8 per cent for male managers. Likewise, the extent of reliance on Intuition is significantly higher among top managers (50.0 per cent) than among senior managers (22.9 per cent), just as in the case of professional life.

Table A8.9 Extent of use of Intuition in personal life

Category*	More of Logic/Reasoning (%)	Both in almost equal measure (%)	More of Intuition (%)
Sex			
Male	4.6	62.6	32.8
Female	–	23.3	76.7
Organization type			
Industry	3.4	58.6	37.9
Services	5.6	61.1	33.3
Management level			
Senior	7.7	69.4	22.9
Top	–	50.0	50.0
Intuition rating			
Low	–	61.7	38.3
Medium	9.3	55.9	34.8
High	–	55.5	44.5
Total	3.9	57.6	38.5

*NR (= Not reported) omitted from all categories.

Actual Instances

The proportion of managers who could cite specific instances where they had actually used Intuition in their professional/personal life is limited to 31.9 per cent. This does not square with the comparatively high degree of Intuition orientation witnessed among the Japanese managers and represents a deviation from the pattern observed in other countries.

Opinions on Certain Notions

The respondents were asked to indicate to what extent they agree or disagree with each of ten given statements and the responses were obtained on a five-point scale, ranging from 'strongly agree' to 'strongly disagree'. Based on these responses, a composite index with range 0 to 100 has been worked out by assigning values to different responses as follows:

Strongly agree	100
Agree	75
Can't say	50
Disagree	25
Strongly disagree	0

By choosing appropriate weighting factors, the index can be worked out for a given category as well as for the aggregate.

Aggregate indices worked out for different statements are as follows:

	Statement	*Index*
1	Many senior managers use Intuition in making decisions, at least to some extent.	72.6
2	Higher Intuitive capabilities would contribute to greater success in business.	80.4
3	Intuition contributes to harmonious interpersonal relationships.	61.2
4	Intuition is a characteristic associated more with women than with men.	57.2
5	Few managers who use Intuition would openly admit to the same.	38.1
6	The more Intuitive a person is, the more successful he or she will be in life.	57.2
7	Intuition cannot be blocked.	60.5
8	Intuition has a role to play in almost every facet of life.	80.5
9	Intuition can be cultivated/ enhanced.	30.1
10	It is not safe to rely on Intuition in business/management.	53.9

Thus, there is a good measure of agreement* that:

- many managers use Intuition (1);
- Intuition contributes to success in business (2);
- Intuition has a role to play in almost every facet of life (8).

The suggestion that managers generally do not admit to use of Intuition has been virtually rejected. So has the suggestion that Intuition can be enhanced/cultivated, and this is a significant deviation from the pattern observed in other countries.

*An index value of 65 or more has been taken to connote a 'good' measure of agreement.

Views on Certain Aspects

Views on certain aspects of Intuition were sought by ascertaining agreement with the following propositions, the figures alongside showing the proportions of managers in agreement:

Proposition	%
Dependence of Intuition on external environment	21.1
Possibility of inducing Intuition in others	23.8
Possibility of Intuition being a group process	24.4
Possibility of enhancing Intuition through specific types of practice/training	59.6

The proportions are generally low excepting the last one. There is some inconsistency here in that responses to a given set of statements show, as pointed out earlier, that the suggestion that Intuition can be cultivated/enhanced has been virtually rejected.

Proportions of managers who think that Intuition should form part of the curriculum at different levels of instruction are as follows:

Level	%
Primary school	46.7
Secondary school	38.2
College/University	30.1
Management institute	41.2

Thus, the general view seems to be that the study of Intuition could well start at the primary school level.

Interest in Further Participation

Proportions of managers indicating their willingness to participate further in this research through different means are as follows:

Means	%
Personal interviews	20.5
Experiential workshops	28.3
Seminars/Conferences	33.8

Having regard to the composition of the target group and considering the amount of time that participation in research of this type entails, the above propositions may be considered reasonable.

Appendix 9 Report for Brazil

Profile of Managers

The sample for Brazil comprises 204 managers representing an estimated 80 400 managers in the country conforming to the Survey specifications. A profile of the Brazilian managers, as drawn up by the Survey, is given in table A9.1.

Table A9.1 Profile of the Brazilian managers in the Survey population

Category	Sample count	Estimated population (000s)	%	% corrected for NR*
Sex				
Male	197	77.7	96.6	97.1
Female	6	2.3	2.9	2.9
NR*	1	0.4	0.5	
Age				
Below 35	23	9.1	11.3	11.7
35–44	95	37.3	46.4	47.8
45–59	70	27.8	34.6	35.6
Over 59	10	3.8	4.7	4.9
NR*	6	2.3	2.9	
Organization type				
Industry	88	36.3	45.1	45.1
Services	116	44.1	54.9	54.9
Functional area				
General management	65	25.6	31.8	32.0
Finance	32	12.5	15.5	15.6
Marketing	35	13.9	17.3	17.4
Production/Operations	19	7.7	9.6	9.6
Human resources development	18	7.1	8.8	8.9
Other	34	13.2	16.4	16.5
NR*	1	0.4	0.5	
Management level				
Senior	142	55.9	69.5	69.5
Top	62	24.5	30.5	30.5
Total	204	80.4	100.0	100.0

*NR = Not reported.

It will be seen that:

- 2.9 per cent of the managers are females;
- the majority (59.5 per cent, using the corrected proportion) of the managers are relatively young, being less than 45 years old;
- 30.5 per cent of the managers belong to the top level.

Intuition Ratings

Objective Rating

Paired alternatives

Responses to the query regarding choice between ten given pairs of alternatives (where one of the terms is taken to indicate orientation towards Intuition and the other towards Logic/Reasoning) yield the distribution shown in table A9.2.

Table A9.2 Choice between paired alternatives

Intuition-oriented		Logic/Reasoning-oriented		Extent of non-expression of preference (%)
Description	Extent of preference (%)	Description	Extent of preference (%)	
1 Invent	39.2	Build	59.4	1.5
2 Vision	73.4	Common sense	24.1	2.5
3 Abstract	22.4	Concrete	75.2	2.4
4 Innovative	85.3	Conventional	12.3	2.5
5 Creative	84.9	Analytical	13.2	1.9
6 Ideas	63.3	Facts	35.3	1.5
7 Imaginative	41.1	Realistic	57.5	1.4
8 Ingenious	31.9	Practical	66.2	1.9
8 Fascinating	27.9	Sensible	70.2	2.0
10 Spontaneous	72.9	Systematic	25.2	1.9

All the observed differences in the above table are statistically significant (at the 5 per cent level).
The two alternatives in each pair were presented to the respondent in a predetermined random sequence (see question 2 of the questionnaire in appendix 11).

It will be seen that in five out of ten cases, the term associated with Intuition was preferred, while in the other five cases, the term associated with Logic/Reasoning was preferred, indicating even division between the two on an overall basis. This indicates *prima facie* that the Intuition orientation of the Brazilian managers may not be of a high order. A more comprehensive rating of the managers on this dimension is attempted later in this section.

Overall Intuition score

By assigning 1 to the choice indicating orientation towards Intuition and 0 to the one towards Logic/Reasoning, an overall score has been computed for each responding manager. Where there was no indication of preference for one term over the other in a given pair (evidenced by the respondent ticking both the alternatives or leaving the section blank), a score of ½ has been awarded; however, where no clear preference was indicated in respect of even one of the ten given pairs, it has been treated as a case of 'Not reported' (NR). It is clear that the overall score ranges from 0 to 10 in steps of ½.

Classification

Based on the overall Intuition score, a three-way classification of managers has been devised as follows:

Score	*Category*
0.0–3.5	L: Low orientation
4.0–6.0	M: Medium orientation
6.5–10.0	H: High orientation

It will be noted that this classification has been used as one of the standard backgrounds in tabulation of the Survey responses. This is referred to as 'objective rating' as distinct from the 'self-rating' carried out by the respondents, which is discussed later.

Distribution

The above classification has led to the distribution shown in table A9.3.

Table A9.3 Distribution based on objective rating on Intuition

Category	Low (%)	Medium (%)	High (%)	NR (%)
Sex*				
Male	20.4	46.3	32.9	0.5
Female	17.6	33.8	32.4	16.2
Age*				
Below 35	13.2	56.1	30.7	–
35–44	18.0	43.3	37.7	1.0
45–59	25.8	45.9	26.9	1.4
Over 59	19.8	49.6	30.6	–
Organization type				
Industry	22.7	48.9	28.4	–
Services	18.1	43.1	37.1	1.7
Management level				
Senior	19.9	48.6	30.9	0.7
Top	20.8	39.2	38.4	1.6
Total	20.2	45.7	33.2	0.9
(% corrected for NR)	(20.4)	(46.1)	(33.5)	

*NR (= Not reported) omitted from classification.

It will be seen that about a third of the managers have merited a rating above average, confirming the preliminary inference drawn earlier on the basis of choice between paired alternatives.

The observed differences between different groupings are not statistically significant, but there is a broad indication that managers in the services sector have a better orientation towards Intuition than their counterparts in the industry sector. Likewise, top managers seem to score over senior managers in this respect.

Self-Rating

Self-rating by the managers regarding Intuition on a given five-point scale (ranging from very high to very low) has yielded the distribution shown in table A9.4.

Table A9.4 Distribution based on self-rating on Intuition

Category	Very high (%)	High (%)	Average (%)	Low (%)	Very low (%)	NR (%)
Sex*						
Male	3.6	45.7	43.5	5.6	1.0	0.5
Female	–	100.7	–	–	–	–
Age*						
Below 35	–	39.0	43.6	8.7	4.2	4.5
35–44	2.2	49.5	43.0	5.3	–	–
45–59	5.8	47.0	41.3	4.5	1.4	–
Over 59	–	60.3	39.7	–	–	–
Organization type						
Industry	5.7	47.7	38.6	6.8	–	1.1
Services	1.7	47.4	44.8	4.3	1.7	–
Management level						
Senior	1.5	48.0	42.0	7.1	0.7	0.7
Top	8.2	46.4	42.2	1.7	1.6	–
Intuition rating*†						
Low	2.3	41.8	43.7	7.4	4.7	–
Medium	3.4	40.0	49.2	7.5	–	–
High	4.5	60.0	32.3	1.5	–	1.5
Total	3.5	47.6	42.0	5.4	0.9	0.5
(% corrected for NR)	(3.5)	(47.8)	(42.2)	(5.5)	(1.0)	

*NR (= Not reported) omitted from classification.
†Relates to objective rating presented in table A9.3.

It will be seen that a little over half the managers consider themselves above average (very high/high) on Intuition.

The proportion of managers rating themselves very high/high on Intuition rises progressively from 40.8 per cent (corrected proportion) in the age below

35 group to 60.3 per cent in the over 59 group, suggesting that the older managers probably regard themselves as more Intuitive than the younger ones.

Association Between Ratings

The association between the two rating systems can be tested statistically by forming the contingency table shown as table A9.5.

Table A9.5 Objective rating v. self-rating

Classification based on objective rating	Self-rating: Average or lower (number)	Self-rating: Very high/ high (number)	Total (number)
Low	23	18	41
Medium	53	40	93
High	23	44	67
Total	99	102	201

Three managers whose classification is indeterminate in terms of either of the rating systems have been omitted from the above cross-tabulation.

It can be seen that the χ^2 (which will have 2 degrees of freedom) for table A9.5 works out to 9.10, which is significant at the 5 per cent level, showing that there is a positive association between the two ratings.

The contingency coefficient, *C*, works out to 0.21 as follows:

$$C = \sqrt{\frac{\chi^2}{\chi^2 + N}}$$

$$= \sqrt{\frac{9.10}{9.10 + 201}}$$

$$= 0.21$$

The low value of *C* shows that while there is association between the two rating systems, it is not strong.

What is Intuition?

Descriptions Given of Intuition

The questionnaire used for the Survey (see appendix 11) starts with an invitation to the respondent to describe Intuition as understood by him or her so as to get the top-of-the-mind opinion; that is, a response uninfluenced by the sequence of questions that follows in the questionnaire. This has led to diverse descriptions of Intuition, of which the following are the more important:

Description	%
Decision/perception without recourse to logical/rational methods	29.4
Foresight	23.3
Inherent perception; inexplicable comprehension; a feeling that comes from within	18.3
Integration of previous experience; processing of accumulated information	15.1
Spontaneous perception/vision	9.3
Subconscious process	8.8
Sixth sense	7.5
Premonition	6.4
Decision/solution to problem, without complete data/facts	6.0

The Brazilian managers were quite articulate on this issue. It will be seen that the top slot in the responses goes to the perception that Intuition is something of an antithesis to Logic/Reasoning, while foresight and inherent perception claim the second and third positions. The proportions corresponding to sixth sense and premonition are rather low.

Graphic Expression

The proportion of managers giving graphic expression to their concept of Intuition is quite high at 84.3 per cent, pointing to the keen interest evinced in the subject by the Brazilian managers. This proportion is significantly higher among the managers with medium/high rating on Intuition than among the low group, indicating a positive association between Intuition orientation and the propensity to express oneself graphically on Intuition:

Rating	%
Low	68.2
Medium	87.2
High	89.8

Agreement with Specific Descriptions

The extent of agreement with three given descriptions of Intuition (obtained as three independent assessments and not as choice among three alternatives) can be seen from the distribution shown in table A9.6.

Table A9.6 Extent of agreement with three specific descriptions of Intuition

	Extent of agreement with		
Category	a (%)	b (%)	c (%)
Organization type			
Industry	77.3	73.9	56.8
Services	81.0	70.7	56.0
Management level			
Senior	80.3	74.0	55.0
Top	77.2	67.9	59.6
Intuition rating*			
Low	82.8	68.2	55.9
Medium	77.1	71.2	50.6
High	81.1	76.5	64.9
Total	79.3	72.1	56.4

In this and the subsequent tables, the sex classification has been omitted in view of the low sample count corresponding to the female managers.
*NR (= Not reported) omitted from classification.
(a) Spontaneous insight based on prior experience/expertise
(b) Flash from 'subconscious levels'.
(c) Tuning into 'higher levels of consciousness'.

On an overall basis, the order of acceptance of the three descriptions is as follows:

(a) & (b) > (c)

> Denotes 'preferred over'.

Considering that spontaneous perception/vision and integration of previous experience do figure in the major responses to the open-ended question on the respondents' concept of Intuition (though not right at the top), it is perhaps no surprise that description (a) should have met with the highest degree of acceptance. However, the almost equally good acceptance claimed by description (b) does not quite square with the fact that subconscious process figures far down the list and flash finds no mention at all in the major responses to the open-ended question.

It may be noted that description (c) meets with a relatively high degree of acceptance among top managers as well as in the high group.

Perceived Relevance of Intuition

In Business/Management

The perceived relevance of different functional areas of business/management to the application of Intuition can be seen from the following proportions relating to different areas:

	Area	%
1	Corporate strategy and planning	81.8
2	Investment/Diversification	69.8
3	Corporate acquisitions/ mergers/alliances	55.6
4	Finance	43.3
5	Marketing	76.7
6	Public relations	46.6
7	Choice of technology/plant and equipment	33.6
8	Production/Operations	25.0
9	Materials management	25.3
10	Human resources development	70.7
11	Research and development	64.6

Thus, the following are perceived as the major areas of application for Intuition in the field of business/management (no order of importance intended):

- corporate strategy and planning;
- investment/diversification;
- marketing;
- human resources development (HRD);
- research and development (R&D).

One might have expected an area like corporate acquisitions/mergers/ alliances to figure in the major areas of perceived importance, but this may have been taken to form part of corporate strategy and planning.

It will be noted that finance and production/operations are two major functional areas which rank among the least important in terms of perceived relevance.

In Other Fields

As regards fields other than business/management, the following are perceived to be the more important in terms of their relevance to application of

Intuition:

Field	%
Family (relations)	19.1
Specific disciplines (engineering, medicine, psychology, etc.)	18.1
Sports	16.7
Human/interpersonal relations	15.6
Education, teaching	11.5
Politics, public life	10.8
Personal life	6.9
Art, drama, music, literature, etc.	6.4

It will be seen that while the top slot goes to family (relations), human/interpersonal relations also figures prominently in the responses, underlining the importance attached by the Brazilian managers to the role of Intuition in interpersonal dealings. Specific disciplines, taken together with education/teaching, is seen to be nearly as important. That sports should rank third accords with the important position held by Brazil in certain areas like soccer.

How Does One Identify Intuition?

Stated Means of Identification

The query as to how Intuition could be identified elicited diverse responses of which the following are the more important:

Response	%
Deviation of decision from logical reasoning	15.4
Spontaneous perception/vision	14.6
Strong inner feeling, emotion	13.2
Strong urge/impulse to take a particular decision	11.7
Inability to explain conclusion on the basis of available facts	7.8
(Strong) feeling of certitude, reassurance	5.9

It will be seen that, apart from deviation of decision from logical reasoning, spontaneity, emotion and strong urge are all taken as important identifying characteristics of Intuition.

Associated Phenomena

The extent to which experience of Intuition is perceived to be accompanied by different phenomena can be seen from table A9.7.

Table A9.7 Associated phenomena

Category	(a) Sensory (%)	(b) Physical (%)	(c) Mental (%)	(d) Emotional (%)
Organization type				
Industry	22.7	18.2	37.5	59.1
Services	23.3	16.4	44.0	50.0
Management level				
Senior	24.0	17.0	38.6	51.7
Top	20.8	17.6	46.6	59.5
Intuition rating*				
Low	19.5	17.0	41.2	46.9
Medium	20.4	10.9	34.2	53.8
High	29.4	25.1	48.8	59.1
Total	23.0	17.2	41.0	54.1

*NR (= Not reported) omitted from classification.

Experience of Intuition is thus perceived to be accompanied mostly by changes in emotional aspects, and this accords broadly with the pattern of responses to the query on means of identification discussed earlier.

It may be noted that the extent of association of different phenomena is relatively large in the high group as compared to the low and medium groups, though the observed differences are not statistically significant.

Use of Intuition

In Professional Life

The majority (53.5 per cent) of the managers stated that they use more of Logic/Reasoning in their professional life, the proportion using more of Intuition being almost negligible at 4.4 per cent, as may be seen from table A9.8.

Unlike their counterparts in certain other countries, a majority of the Brazilian managers stated in clear terms whether they use more of Intuition or Logic/Reasoning in their professional life.

It will be noted that the proportion of managers using more of Intuition rises moderately from the low to the high group. Looking at it the other way, the proportion of managers using more of Logic/Reasoning drops from 68.0 per cent in the low group and 58.2 per cent in the medium group to a significantly

Table A9.8 Extent of use of Intuition in professional life

Category	More of Logic/Reasoning (%)	Both in almost equal measure (%)	More of Intuition (%)
Organization type			
Industry	55.7	39.8	4.5
Services	51.7	44.0	4.3
Management level			
Senior	54.8	41.6	3.6
Top	50.5	43.2	6.3
Intuition rating*			
Low	68.0	32.0	–
Medium	58.2	37.5	4.3
Top	38.4	54.2	7.4
Total	53.5	42.1	4.4

*NR (= Not reported) omitted from classification.

lower level of 38.4 per cent in the high group. This indicates a positive association between Intuition orientation and the professed extent of its use in the field of business/management.

In Personal Life

A majority (57.9 per cent) of the Brazilian managers stated that they use Intuition and Logic/Reasoning in almost equal proportions in their personal life. Managers using more of Intuition constitute 16.2 per cent of the total, a proportion significantly larger than the corresponding one of 4.4 per cent for use in professional life. There is a concomitant group in the proportion of managers using more of Logic/Reasoning from 53.5 per cent in the case of professional life to 25.9 per cent in the case of personal life. This pattern is evident whichever way the managers are classified (see table A9.9).

The proportion of managers using more of Intuition in their personal life rises progressively from the low group to the high group, but the observed differences are not statistically significant. The drop in the proportion of managers using more of Logic/Reasoning from 31.4 per cent in the low group to 17.7 per cent in the high group is more pronounced, indicating a broad association between Intuition orientation and the stated extent of its use in personal life.

Actual Instances

The proportion of managers who could cite specific instances where they had actually used Intuition in their professional/personal life is fairly high at 61.6

Table A9.9 Extent of use of Intuition in personal life

Category	More of Logic/Reasoning (%)	Both in almost equal measure (%)	More of Intuition (%)
Organization type			
Industry	23.9	59.1	17.0
Services	27.6	56.9	15.5
Management level			
Senior	26.7	59.1	14.2
Top	24.1	55.1	20.8
Intuition rating*			
Low	31.4	56.1	12.5
Medium	28.9	57.0	14.1
High	17.7	61.8	20.4
Total	25.9	57.9	16.2

*NR (= Not reported) omitted from classification.

per cent. This proportion is higher in the services sector (65.5 per cent) than in the industry sector (56.8 per cent) and among top managers (67.5 per cent) than among senior managers (59.0 per cent), though the observed differences are not statistically significant.

Opinions on Certain Notions

The respondents were asked to indicate to what extent they agree or disagree with each of ten given statements and the responses were obtained on a five-point scale, ranging from 'strongly agree' to 'strongly disagree'. Based on these responses, a composite index with range 0 to 100 was worked out by assigning values to different responses as follows:

Strongly agree	100
Agree	75
Can't say	50
Disagree	25
Strongly disagree	0

By choosing appropriate weighting factors, the index can be worked out for a given category as well as for the aggregate.

Aggregate indices worked out for different statements are as follows:

	Statement	*Index*
1	Many senior managers use Intuition in making decisions, at least to some extent.	71.9
2	Higher Intuitive capabilities would contribute to greater success in business.	76.7
3	Intuition contributes to harmonious interpersonal relationships.	70.5
4	Intuition is a characteristic associated more with women than with men.	42.5
5	Few managers who use Intuition would openly admit to the same.	60.1
6	The more Intuitive a person is, the more successful he or she will be in life.	52.8
7	Intuition cannot be blocked.	64.9
8	Intuition has a role to play in almost every facet of life.	75.0
9	Intuition can be cultivated/enhanced.	61.8
10	It is not safe to rely on Intuition in business/management.	42.8

Thus, there is a good measure of agreement* that:

- many managers use Intuition (1);
- Intuition contributes to success in business (2);
- Intuition contributes to harmonious interpersonal relationships (3);
- Intuition has a role to play in almost every facet of life (8).

It will be noted that the suggestion that Intuition contributes to success in life (6) does not meet with much agreement, while the more restrictive proposition that Intuition contributes to success in business (2) is readily accepted. Thus, while the managers seem to believe that Intuition is more relevant to professional life, recalling the discussion in the previous section, the managers' claims indicate that they use Intuition to a larger extent in their personal life than in their professional life. This apparent contradiction

*An index value of 65 or more has been taken to connote a 'good' measure of agreement.

probably has something to do with the way the propositions have been formulated: statement 6 is admittedly worded more sharply than statement 2.

It will also be noted that the negative suggestion that it is not safe to rely on Intuition in business/management (10) has been virtually rejected, offering additional evidence of the perceived relevance of Intuition in this domain.

Views on Certain Aspects

Views on certain aspects of Intuition were sought by ascertaining agreement with the following propositions, the figures alongside showing the proportions of managers in agreement:

Proposition	%
Dependence of Intuition on external environment	36.4
Possibility of inducing Intuition in others	31.2
Possibility of Intuition being a group process	27.0
Possibility of enhancing Intuition through specific types of practice/ training	49.1

Agreement with the first three proportions is rather low, but agreement with the last one (49.1 per cent) offers reasonable evidence of the managers' belief in the efficacy of training in the enhancement of Intuition.

Proportions of managers who think that Intuition should form part of the curriculum at different levels of instruction are as follows:

Level	%
Primary school	23.1
Secondary school	29.5
College/University	54.6
Management institute	54.5

There is thus good agreement that Intuition should form part of the curriculum at the college and management institute levels, though not at the school level.

Interest in Further Participation

Proportions of managers indicating willingness to participate further in this research through different means are as follows:

Means	%
Personal interviews	52.4
Experiential workshops	48.0
Seminars/Conferences	69.9

Considering the demands that participation in research of this type makes on a respondent's time, the above proportions may be taken to testify the keen interest generated by this investigation among the Brazilian managers.

Appendix 10 Report for India

Profile of Managers

The sample for India comprises 80 managers representing an estimated 120 800 managers in the country conforming to the Survey specification. A profile of the Indian managers in the population, as drawn up by the Survey, is given in table A10.1.

Table A10.1 Profile of the Indian managers in the Survey population

Category	Sample count	Estimated population (000s)	%	% corrected for NR*
Sex				
Male	77	114.8	95.0	95.0
Female	3	6.0	5.0	5.0
Age				
Below 35	15	21.8	18.0	18.2
35–44	30	45.3	37.5	37.9
45–59	29	44.9	37.2	37.5
Over 59	5	7.6	6.3	6.4
NR*	1	1.2	1.0	
Organization type				
Industry	48	56.6	46.9	46.9
Services	32	64.2	53.1	53.1
Functional area				
General management	36	54.8	45.4	45.4
Finance	3	6.0	5.0	5.0
Marketing	15	20.2	16.7	16.7
Production/Operations	12	18.3	15.1	15.1
Human resources development	4	6.4	5.3	5.3
Other	10	15.1	12.5	12.5
Management level				
Senior	49	73.5	60.8	60.8
Top	31	47.3	39.2	39.2
Total	80	120.8	100.0	100.0

*NR = Not reported.

It will be seen that:

- 5 per cent of the managers are females;
- the majority (56.1 per cent) are relatively young, being less than 45 years old;
- 39.2 per cent of the managers belong to the top level.

Intuition Ratings

Objective Rating

Paired alternatives

Responses to the query regarding choice between ten given pairs of alternatives (where one of the terms is taken to indicate orientation towards Intuition and the other towards Logic/Reasoning) yield the distribution shown in table A10.2.

Table A10.2 Choice between paired alternatives

Intuition-oriented		Logic/Reasoning-oriented		Extent of non-expression of preference (%)
Description	Extent of preference (%)	Description	Extent of preference (%)	
1 Invent	56.0	Build	44.0	–
2 Vision	54.6	Common sense	42.1	3.3
3 Abstract	20.8	Concrete	77.5*	1.7
4 Innovative	86.1*	Conventional	12.9	1.0
5 Creative	60.8*	Analytical	37.5	1.7
6 Ideas	63.6*	Facts	34.8	1.7
7 Imaginative	35.8	Realistic	62.5*	1.7
8 Ingenious	39.5	Practical	58.9*	1.7
9 Fascinating	36.2	Sensible	63.8*	–
10 Spontaneous	46.8	Systematic	51.6	1.7

*The observed preference is statistically significant (at the 5 per cent level).
The two alternatives in each pair were presented to the respondent in a predetermined random sequence (see question 2 of the questionnaire in appendix 11).

It will be seen that of the seven cases where the observed differences are statistically significant, in three instances the term associated with Intuition was preferred to its counterpart associated with Logic/Reasoning, while it is the other way about in the other four cases. This indicates *prima facie* that the Intuition orientation of the Indian managers is not of a high order. A more comprehensive rating of the managers on this dimension is attempted later in this section.

Overall Intuition score

By assigning 1 to the choice indicating orientation towards Intuition and 0 to the one towards Logic/Reasoning, an overall score has been computed for each responding manager. Where there was no indication of preference for one term over the other in a given pair (evidenced by the respondent ticking both the alternatives or leaving the section blank), a score of ½ has been awarded; however, where no clear preference was indicated in respect of even one of the ten given pairs, it has been treated as a case of 'Not reported' (NR). It is clear that the overall score ranges from 0 to 10 in steps of ½.

Classification

Based on the overall Intuition score, a three-way classification of managers has been devised as follows:

Score	*Category*
0.0–3.5	L: Low orientation
4.0–6.0	M: Medium orientation
6.5–10.0	H: High orientation

It will be noted that this classification has been used as one of the standard backgrounds in tabulation of the Survey responses. This is referred to as 'objective rating' as distinct from the 'self-rating' carried out by the respondents, which is discussed later.

Distribution

The above classification has led to the distribution shown in table A10.3.

Table A10.3 Distribution based on objective rating on Intuition

Category	Low (%)	Medium (%)	High (%)	NR* (%)
Sex				
Male	33.9	39.1	27.0	–
Female	33.3	–	66.7	–
Age*				
Below 35	21.6	54.6	23.8	–
35–44	30.7	22.6	46.6	–
45–59	42.5	38.1	19.4	–
Over 59	42.2	57.8	–	–
Organization type				
Industry	33.3	43.8	22.9	–
Services	34.4	31.3	34.4	–
Management level				
Senior	35.2	36.1	28.7	–
Top	31.9	38.7	29.4	–
Total	33.9	37.1	29.0	–

*NR (= Not reported) omitted from classification.

The proportion of 29.0 per cent relating to managers with high orientation is relatively low, corroborating the preliminary inference based on choice between paired alternatives, which has been discussed earlier.

It will also be noted that the proportion of managers with high orientation is highest in the age group 35–44 years.

Self-Rating

Self-rating by the managers regarding Intuition on a given five-point scale (ranging from very high to very low) has yielded the distribution shown in table A10.4.

Table A10.4 Distribution based on self-rating on Intuition

Category	Very high (%)	High (%)	Average (%)	Low (%)	Very low (%)	NR (%)
Sex						
Male	6.6	53.3	36.3	2.8	–	1.0
Female	33.3	33.3	33.3	–	–	–
Age*						
Below 35	–	30.8	69.2	–	–	–
35–44	8.9	57.0	31.5	2.6	–	–
45–59	12.3	54.1	29.1	4.5	–	–
Over 59	–	68.8	15.6	–	–	15.6
Organization type						
Industry	6.3	47.9	41.7	2.1	–	2.1
Services	9.4	56.3	31.3	3.1	–	–
Management level						
Senior	4.3	48.6	42.7	4.3	–	–
Top	13.5	58.1	25.9	–	–	2.5
Intuition rating†						
Low	2.9	45.8	48.4	2.9	–	–
Medium	–	61.1	31.8	4.5	–	2.6
High	23.9	48.8	27.3	–	–	–
Total	7.9	52.3	36.1	2.6	–	1.0
(% corrected for NR)	(8.0)	(52.9)	(36.5)	(2.7)	–	

*NR (= Not reported) omitted from classification.
†Relates to objective rating presented in table A10.3.

It will be seen that, on an overall basis, over 60 per cent of the managers have rated themselves very high/high on Intuition, showing that it is generally viewed as a positive attribute.

It will also be noted that the proportion of managers who have rated themselves very high/high rises significantly from 30.8 per cent in the age below 35 category to 66.4 and 68.8 per cent in the older age groups, suggesting that Intuition is not viewed as a positive attribute by the younger managers to the same extent as it is by the older ones. Considering that the younger managers (below 35 years) have in fact been found to be low on Intuition in terms of the objective rating (see distribution in table A10.3), another way of looking at it may be that the younger managers are well aware of their own Intuition orientation.

The proportion of managers rating themselves very high/high on Intuition rises from 52.9 per cent in the senior group to 73.4 per cent in the top group (as corrected for 'Not reported'), though the difference is not statistically significant. Likewise, the observed increase in the proportion from 48.7 per cent in the low group to 62.7 per cent in the medium group (corrected for NR), and further to 72.7 per cent in the high group, can only be taken as a broad indicator of positive association between the two rating systems, as these differences are not statistically significant.

Association Between Ratings

The association between the two rating systems can be tested statistically by forming the contingency table shown as table A10.5.

Table A10.5 Objective rating v. self-rating

	Self-rating		
Classification based on objective rating	Average or lower (number)	Very high/ high (number)	Total (number)
Low	14	13	27
Medium	12	18	30
High	6	16	22
Total	32	47	79

One manager in the medium category whose classification was indeterminate in terms of self-rating has been omitted from the above cross-tabulation.

It can be seen that the χ^2 (which will have 2 degrees of freedom) for table A10.5 works out to 3.1, which falls below the 5 per cent significance level of 5.99.

This analysis thus shows that there is no significant association between the two rating systems, corroborating the inference drawn in the preceding subsection. Broadly speaking, if the objective rating is taken as standard, the Indian managers seem to have a rather exaggerated notion of their own Intuition orientation.

What is Intuition?

Descriptions Given of Intuition

The questionnaire used for the Survey (see appendix 11) starts with an invitation to the respondent to describe Intuition as understood by him or her so as to get the top-of-the-mind opinion; that is, a response uninfluenced by the sequence of questions that follows in the questionnaire. This has led to diverse descriptions of Intuition, of which the following are the more important:

Description	%
Decision/perception without recourse to logical/rational methods	30.9
Integration of previous experience; processing of accumulated information	19.4
Gut feeling	15.7
Subconscious process	11.8
Spontaneous perception/vision	11.8
Insight	11.5
Inherent perception; inexplicable comprehension; a feeling that comes from within	10.5
Decision/solution to problem, without complete data/facts	8.9
(Powerful) inner voice; impulse	8.6
Spark; flash	6.5

The dominant view appears to be that Intuition is some kind of an antithesis to Logic/Reasoning, though integration of previous experience does claim the second spot in the responses. Other responses that figure prominently include gut feeling, subconscious process, spontaneous perception and insight.

It will be noted that the Indian managers were quite articulate in their description of Intuition.

Graphic Expression

The proportion of managers giving graphic expression to their concept of Intuition is quite high at 71.5 per cent, pointing to the keen interest evinced in the subject by the Indian managers. This proportion is significantly higher at 81.3 per cent in the services sector than at 60.4 per cent in the industry sector:

Category	%
Industry	60.4
Services	81.3
Senior	75.8
Top	64.8
Low	69.2
Medium	70.8
High	75.1

The observed differences in the second and third classifications are not statistically significant.

Agreement with Specific Descriptions

The extent of agreement with three given descriptions of Intuition (obtained as three independent assessments and not as choice among three alternatives) can be seen from the distribution shown in table A10.6.

Table A10.6 Extent of agreement with three specific descriptions of Intuition

	Extent of agreement with		
Category	a (%)	b (%)	c (%)
Organization type			
Industry	77.1	83.3	47.9
Services	81.3	78.1	56.3
Management level			
Senior	80.6	77.8	55.7
Top	77.3	84.8	47.1
Intuition rating			
Low	65.1	76.7	52.5
Medium	85.8	76.1	40.8
High	87.5	90.9	67.0
Total	79.3	80.6	52.3

In this and the subsequent tables, the sex classification has been omitted in view of the low sample count corresponding to the female managers.
(a) Spontaneous insight based on prior experience/expertise.
(b) Flash from 'subconscious levels'.
(c) Tuning into 'higher levels of consciousness'.

Broadly, the order of agreement with the three descriptions is as follows:

(a) & (b) > (c)

> Denotes 'preferred over'.

Considering that 'spontaneous', 'insight' and 'previous experience' all figure prominently in the responses to the open-ended question on the respondents' concept of Intuition, it is perhaps no surprise that description (a) comes out as one of the two preferred descriptions. It is significant, however, that these three terms are perceived by the Indian managers to form a harmonious and mutually compatible combination (which is not the case in certain other countries).

It will be seen that while 'subconscious process' figures as a fairly important response to the open-ended question on Intuition, 'spark; flash' is located far down the list; none the less, description (b), which essentially comprises these two terms, is on a par with description (a) in terms of the extent of acceptance by the managers.

It may be noted that description (c) meets with a significantly large extent of agreement (in relative terms) in the high group.

Perceived Relevance of Intuition

In Business/Management

The perceived relevance of different functional areas of business/management to the application of Intuition can be seen from the following proportions relating to different areas:

	Area	%
1	Corporate strategy and planning	74.6
2	Investment/Diversification	74.3
3	Corporate acquisitions/ mergers/alliances	57.8
4	Finance	18.5
5	Marketing	81.9
6	Public relations	57.0
7	Choice of technology/plant and equipment	25.4
8	Production/Operations	24.7
9	Materials management	26.7
10	Human resources development	80.4
11	Research and development	66.2

Thus, the following are perceived as the major areas of application for Intuition in the field of business/management (no order of importance

intended):

- corporate strategy and planning;
- investment/diversification;
- marketing;
- human resources development (HRD);
- research and development (R&D).

One might have expected an area like corporate acquisitions/mergers/alliances to figure in the major areas of perceived importance, but this may have been taken to form part of corporate strategy and planning.

It will be noted that finance and production/operations are two major functional areas which rank among the least important in terms of perceived relevance.

In Other Fields

As regards fields other than business/management, the following are perceived to be the more important in terms of their relevance to application of Intuition:

Field	%
Human/interpersonal relations	19.1
Politics, public life	14.2
Love, marriage	13.9
Art, drama, music, literature, etc.	13.6
Family (relations)	12.2
Speculation (covering stockmarkets, gambling, etc.)	10.5
Children (bringing up children, children's education, etc.)	10.3
Recreation, entertainment, etc.	9.3
Sports	8.6
Specific disciplines (engineering, medicine, psychology, etc.)	7.9
Education, teaching	7.6

It will be seen that while the top spot goes to human/interpersonal relations, politics/public life emerges as the second most important field in terms of perceived relevance, pointing to the high level of political consciousness among the Indian managers. Love/marriage, family (relations) and children figure among the other major responses, indicating that family represents an important domain of concern to these managers. If sports follows far down the list, it should come as no surprise, considering the low standing of India in the world of sports.

On the whole, the Indian managers were highly articulate in their responses to this question.

How Does One Identify Intuition?

Stated Means of Identification

The query as to how Intuition could be identified elicited diverse responses, of which the following are the more important:

Response	%
Deviation of decision from logical reasoning	20.7
Strong inner feeling, emotion	19.8
Inability to explain conclusion on the basis of available facts	16.1
Spontaneous perception/vision	15.7

It will be seen that deviation of decision from logical reasoning and the emotional aspect are seen to be two major characteristics by which Intuition can be identified.

Associated Phenomena

The extent to which experience of Intuition is perceived to be accompanied by different phenomena can be seen from table A10.7.

Table A10.7 Associated phenomena

Category	(a) Sensory (%)	(b) Physical (%)	(c) Mental (%)	(d) Emotional (%)
Organization type				
Industry	35.4	10.4	66.7	64.6
Services	18.8	34.4	59.4	56.3
Management level				
Senior	33.4	25.5	60.5	57.8
Top	16.0	19.5	66.3	63.8
Intuition rating				
Low	24.2	19.6	70.9	60.2
Medium	25.5	16.8	58.4	52.1
High	30.6	35.4	58.9	70.4
Total	26.6	23.1	62.8	60.2

Consistently with the pattern of responses on means of identification discussed earlier, experience of Intuition is most perceived to be accompanied by changes in the mental and emotional aspects.

Use of Intuition

In Professional Life

About half the managers stated that they use Intuition and Logic/Reasoning in almost equal measure in their professional life. However, only 4.6 per cent of the managers use more of Intuition, as against 44.0 per cent using more of Logic/Reasoning, as may be seen from table A10.8.

Table A10.8 Extent of use of Intuition in professional life

Category	More of Logic/Reasoning (%)	Both in almost equal measure (%)	More of Intuition (%)
Organization type			
Industry	47.9	45.8	4.8
Services	40.6	56.3	3.1
Management level			
Senior	45.4	53.0	1.6
Top	41.9	48.9	9.2
Intuition rating			
Low	51.3	48.7	–
Medium	43.4	49.5	7.1
High	36.4	56.9	6.7
Total	44.0	51.4	4.6

It will be noted that the proportion of managers using more of Intuition rises sharply from 1.6 per cent in the senior group to 9.2 per cent in the top group, though the Intuition orientation of these two groups is more or less the same. Further, the proportion of managers using more of Intuition is practically the same (*c.*7 per cent) in the medium and high groups, though it is nil in the low group. Thus, the association, if any, between Intuition orientation and the extent of its use in professional life does not come out strongly from the above distribution.

In Personal Life

An estimated 42.1 per cent of the Indian managers use Intuition and Logic/Reasoning in almost equal measure. However, a sizable 31.6 per cent of the managers stated that they use more of Intuition in their personal life, while the corresponding proportion for use in professional life is a mere 4.6 per cent, as noted above. There is a concomitant decline in the proportion of managers using more of Logic/Reasoning from 44.0 per cent in the case of professional life to 26.3 per cent in the case of personal life. The professed extent of use of Intuition is significantly larger in respect of personal life than in professional life whichever way the managers are classified (see table A10.9).

Table A10.9 Extent of use of Intuition in personal life

Category	More of Logic/Reasoning (%)	Both in almost equal measure (%)	More of Intuition (%)
Organization type			
Industry	31.3	43.8	25.0
Services	21.9	40.6	37.5
Management level			
Senior	22.2	45.9	31.9
Top	32.7	36.2	31.2
Intuition rating			
Low	33.7	40.9	25.4
Medium	28.4	47.6	23.9
High	14.8	36.4	48.8
Total	26.3	42.1	31.6

The proportion of managers using more of Intuition increases from 25.4 per cent in the low group and 23.9 per cent in the medium group to 48.8 per cent in the high group. Looking at it the other way, the proportion of managers using more of Logic/Reasoning declines from 33.7 per cent in the low group to 28.4 per cent in the medium group and further to 14.8 per cent in the high group. However, none of the differences pointed out here is statistically significant in view of the small sample sizes involved. Thus, the same inference as drawn earlier follows from this analysis, namely that any possible association between Intuition orientation and the professed extent of its use does not come out clearly from the distribution presented above.

Actual Instances

The proportion of managers who could cite specific instances where they had actually used Intuition in their professional/personal life is fairly high at 63.9 per cent. It is significant to note that as many as 54.7 per cent of the managers could provide details of application in two instances.

Opinions on Certain Notions

The respondents were asked to indicate to what extent they agree or disagree with each of ten given statements and the responses were obtained on a five-point scale, ranging from 'strongly agree' to 'strongly disagree'. Based on these responses, a composite index with range 0 to 100 has been worked out by assigning values to different responses as follows:

Strongly agree	100
Agree	75
Can't say	50
Disagree	25
Strongly disagree	0

By choosing appropriate weighting factors, the index can be worked out for a given category as well as for the aggregate.

Aggregate indices worked out for different statements are as follows:

	Statement	*Index*
1	Many senior managers use Intuition in making decisions, at least to some extent.	77.9
2	Higher Intuitive capabilities would contribute to greater success in business.	71.2
3	Intuition contributes to harmonious interpersonal relationships.	66.3
4	Intuition is a characteristic associated more with women than with men.	44.5
5	Few managers who use Intuition would openly admit to the same.	55.5
6	The more Intuitive a person is, the more successful he or she will be in life.	54.8
7	Intuition cannot be blocked.	65.6
8	Intuition has a role to play in almost every facet of life.	74.7
9	Intuition can be cultivated/enhanced.	51.2
10	It is not safe to rely on Intuition in business/management.	41.0

Thus, there is a good measure of agreement* that:

- many managers use Intuition (1);
- Intuition contributes to success in business (2);
- Intuition contributes to harmonious interpersonal relationships (3);
- Intuition cannot be blocked (7);
- Intuition has a role to play in almost every facet of life (8).

The ambivalence noted above on whether Intuition can be cultivated/enhanced is consistent with thc fairly good agreement with what is practically a contrary suggestion, namely that Intuition cannot be blocked.

It will be noted that the suggestion that Intuition contributes to success in life (6) does not meet with the same degree of acceptance as the more restrictive proposition that Intuition contributes to success in business (2). Thus, while the managers seem to believe that Intuition is more relevant to professional life, recalling the discussion in the previous section, the managers' claims indicate that they use Intuition to a larger extent in their personal life than in their professional life. This apparent contradiction probably has something to do with the way the propositions have been formulated: statement 6 is admittedly worded more sharply than statement 2.

Views on Certain Aspects

Views on certain aspects of Intuition were sought by ascertaining agreement with the following propositions, the figures alongside showing the proportions of managers in agreement:

Proposition	%
Dependence of Intuition on external environment	38.9
Possibility of inducing Intuition in others	21.1
Possibility of Intuition being a group process	24.4
Possibility of enhancing Intuition through specific types of practice/training	42.2

In line with the pattern observed in other countries, the proportion is highest for the possibility of enhancing Intuition through specific types of practice/training. The perceived efficacy of training, however, is not quite consistent with the ambivalance on this very matter which has been noted in the previous

*An index value of 65 or more has been taken to connote a 'good' measure of agreement.

section. While there is reasonable agreement as regards dependence on external environment, the other two suggestions have met with only limited acceptance.

Proportions of managers who think that Intuition should form part of the curriculum at different levels of instruction are as follows:

Level	%
Primary school	21.2
Secondary school	28.0
College/University	49.0
Management institute	64.1

Thus, Intuition is perceived to be a fit subject for study at the college and management institute levels, but not so much at the school level.

Interest in Further Participation

Proportions of managers indicating their willingness to participate further in this research through different means are as follows:

Means	%
Personal interviews	69.4
Experiential workshops	60.2
Seminars/Conferences	68.1

These proportions are among the highest in the Survey countries, underlining the keen interest evinced in the subject by the Indian managers.

Appendix 11 Survey Questionnaire

Dear Respondent
One of IMD's founding institutions in 1988 initiated one international research project on 'the use of Intuition in Business Vision and Decisions'.

Over the past three decades, an impressive edifice has been built up of systematic knowledge in the field of business management, greatly aided by the advent of the computer and development of diverse disciplines. However, there is growing realization that science and technology are not all: there are several phenomena, at both the macro and micro levels, which defy satisfactory explanation in rigid cause-and-effect terms. In the ensuing search for possible factors lying outside the realm of rational theories/practices, attention is increasingly focused on the role played by Intuition.

It is against this background that IMD is continuing this pioneering research effort, which is multifaceted, involving: contemporary literature review, field surveys, experiential workshops and interaction with specialists through round tables, conferences etc. This is being carried out through the IMD Intuition Network comprising presently six regions: Europe, USA, USSR, Japan, India and Latin America.

As a part of this effort, we have designed a questionnaire for eliciting responses from a carefully selected sample of top/senior professional managers. A copy of this questionnaire is enclosed.

We shall be grateful if you could spare about an hour of your valuable time to fill in the questionnaire. Your cooperation in this effort will mean a significant contribution to the advancement in management thinking and practice. We sincerely hope you will therefore give this questionnaire the importance and urgency that it deserves.

A summary of the research findings will be made available to all the respondents.
With warm regards
Sincerely

Dr Jagdish Parikh
Chairman
IMD Intuition Research Project

QUESTIONNAIRE©

Guidelines

1 Please answer the questions exactly in the same sequence in which they are presented. In other words, keep recording your responses as you move on from one question to another.

2 There are no right or wrong answers. Please feel free, therefore, to record your responses purely on the basis of your own perceptions.

3 In case the space provided in the questionnaire is insufficient anywhere, please use and append additional sheets.

REC 1
SR NO 1–4
COUNTRY 5–6

COL

1.1	'Intuition' is understood in different ways by different people. How would you describe it?	(7–8) (13–14)
1.2	Concepts like Intuition are sometimes better expressed graphically. Could you draw in the space provided below a symbol/picture/diagram to convey your understanding of 'Intuition'.	(15–16) (19–20)

REC 1

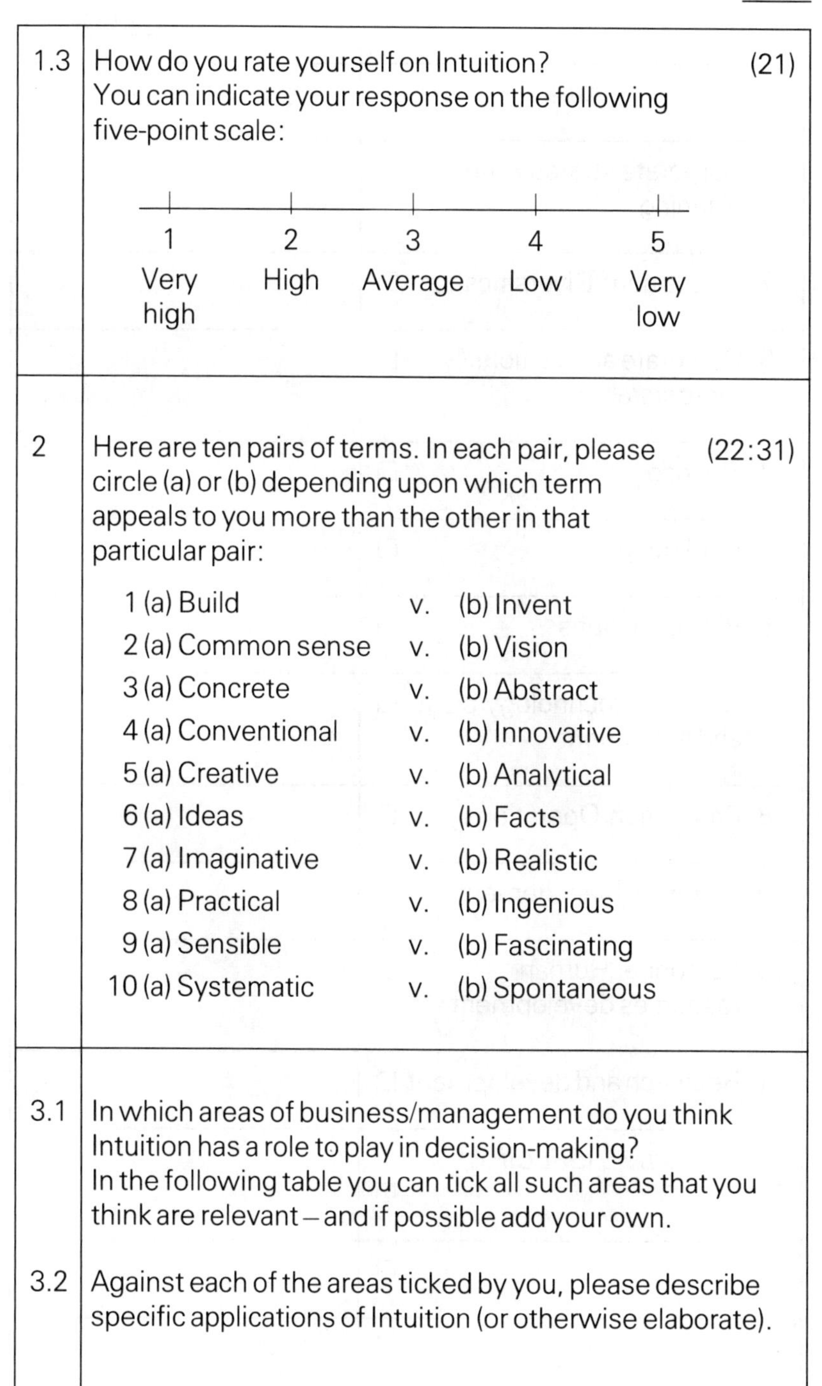

1.3	How do you rate yourself on Intuition? You can indicate your response on the following five-point scale: 1 Very high — 2 High — 3 Average — 4 Low — 5 Very low	(21)
2	Here are ten pairs of terms. In each pair, please circle (a) or (b) depending upon which term appeals to you more than the other in that particular pair: 1 (a) Build v. (b) Invent 2 (a) Common sense v. (b) Vision 3 (a) Concrete v. (b) Abstract 4 (a) Conventional v. (b) Innovative 5 (a) Creative v. (b) Analytical 6 (a) Ideas v. (b) Facts 7 (a) Imaginative v. (b) Realistic 8 (a) Practical v. (b) Ingenious 9 (a) Sensible v. (b) Fascinating 10 (a) Systematic v. (b) Spontaneous	(22:31)
3.1	In which areas of business/management do you think Intuition has a role to play in decision-making? In the following table you can tick all such areas that you think are relevant – and if possible add your own.	
3.2	Against each of the areas ticked by you, please describe specific applications of Intuition (or otherwise elaborate).	

REC 1/COL 32–76; 80 = 1

REC 2/COL 7:31

Area		Applications/Elaboration
1 Corporate strategy and planning	☐	
2 Investment/Diversification	☐	
3 Corporate acquisitions/ mergers/alliances	☐	
4 Finance	☐	
5 Marketing	☐	
6 Public relations	☐	
7 Choice of technology/plant and equipment	☐	
8 Production/Operations	☐	
9 Materials management	☐	
10 Personnel/Human resources development	☐	
11 Research and development	☐	
Others (SPECIFY.) 12	☐	
13	☐	
14	☐	

REC 2

COL

3.3 Could you think of any other fields (that is, apart from business/management) where Intuition has a role to play? Please identify such fields and describe the role/application of Intuition in each one. (32:55)

Field	Role/Application of Intuition
(a)	
(b)	
(c)	
(d)	

4 There is a view that Intuition is used by almost all people and it is only the extent that varies, depending upon the individual and the situation. Would you say that your actions are guided more by Logic/Reasoning or by Intuition in your: (a) professional life; and (b) personal life? (CIRCLE APPROPRIATE CODE.) (56:57)

	More by Logic/Reasoning	By both in almost equal measure	More by Intuition
(a) Professional life	1	2	3
(b) Personal life	1	2	3

5 Please indicate by circling the appropriate code whether you agree or disagree with each of the following definitions/descriptions of Intuition: (58:60)

Definition/Description	Agree	Disagree
(a) Spontaneous insight based on prior experience/expertise.	1	2
(b) Flash from 'subconscious levels'.	1	2
(c) Tuning into 'higher levels of consciousness'.	1	2

REC 2

6 Here is a set of ten statements. In each case, circle the appropriate code depending upon the extent to which you agree/disagree with the given statement. (61:70)

Statement	Strongly agree	Agree	Can't say	Disagree	Strongly disagree
1 Many senior managers use Intuition in making decisions, at least to some extent.	1	2	3	4	5
2 Higher Intuitive capabilities would contribute to greater success in business.	1	2	3	4	5
3 Intuition contributes to harmonious interpersonal relationships.	1	2	3	4	5
4 Intuition is a characteristic associated more with women than with men.	1	2	3	4	5
5 Few managers who use Intuition would openly admit to the same.	1	2	3	4	5
6 The more Intuitive a person is, the more successful he or she will be in life.	1	2	3	4	5
7 Intuition cannot be blocked.	1	2	3	4	5
8 Intuition has a role to play in almost every facet of life.	1	2	3	4	5
9 Intuition can be cultivated/enhanced.	1	2	3	4	5
10 It is not safe to rely on Intuition in business/management.	1	2	3	4	5

COL 80 = 2

REC 3
SR NO 1–4
COUNTRY 5–6

7 As part of this research effort, we are trying to collect as much case study material as possible on actual instances of the application of Intuition. Please recall, if possible, two instances during the past few years, preferably one from the field of business/management and another from other areas, where you have used Intuition (at least to some extent) in making decisions. Please elaborate on the following lines:

Aspect	Instance–1 (COL 7:12)	Instance–2 (COL 22:27)
1 Context/Situation		
2 Nature of decision taken		
3 Whether adequate facts relevant to the situation were available		
4 Whether it was a case of choosing between two or more equally good/bad alternatives		

PLEASE USE ADDITIONAL SHEETS IF REQUIRED.

REC 3

Aspect	Instance–1 (COL 13:21)	Instance–2 (COL 28:36)
5 Whether it was a case of taking or not taking action on the basis of some inner urge/compulsion rather than choosing between alternatives		
6 Whether the decision taken was different from what was warranted by available facts		
7 Any special sensory/physical/ emotional experience while (or just before/after) taking the decision		
8 Whether subsequent events have shown that the decision taken was 'right' or 'wrong' (or it would not have mattered much either way, in retrospect)		
9 Whether you have disclosed the basis of your decision to anyone else – either in the organization or outside		
10 Whether you would act similarly should a similar situation arise again		

PLEASE USE ADDITIONAL SHEETS IF REQUIRED.

REC 3
COL

8	How do you identify the presence/occurrence of Intuition?	(37:46)
9.1 9.2	Do you think that the experience of Intuition is accompanied by any identifiable changes in the following aspects? (PLEASE CIRCLE APPROPRIATE CODE.) (IF 'No' OR 'Can't say', PROCEED TO QUESTION 10.1.) (IF 'Yes':) Please specify.	(47:70)

Aspect	9.1			9.2
	Yes	Can't say	No	Elaboration (47:70)
1 Sensory (images, sounds, etc.)	1	2	3	
2 Physical	1	2	3	
3 Mental/ Intellectual	1	2	3	
4 Emotional	1	2	3	
Others (SPECIFY.) 5	1			
6	1			COL 80 =3

REC 4
SR NO 1–4
COUNTRY 5–6

		COL
10.1	Does the occurrence of Intuition depend upon the external environment? (IF 'Can't say' or 'No', PROCEED TO QUESTION 11.1.) 1 Yes 2 Can't say 3 No	(7)
10.2	(IF 'Yes':) Please mention any specific characteristics of the external enviornment that could facilitate Intuition.	(8:10)
11.1	Do you think that it is possible for one to induce Intuition in another person? (IF 'Can't say' OR 'No', PROCEED TO QUESTION 12.1.) 1 Yes 2 Can't say 3 No	(11)
11.2	(IF 'Yes':) Please elaborate.	(12:14)
12.1	Do you think Intuition can be a group process? (IF 'Can't say' OR 'No', PROCEED TO QUESTION 13.1.) 1 Yes 2 Can't say 3 No	(15)
12.2	(IF 'Yes':) Please elaborate.	(16:18)
13.1	Do you think it is possible to enhance/unblock Intuition through any specific types of practice/training? (IF 'Can't say' OR 'No', PROCEED TO QUESTION 14.) 1 Yes 2 Can't say 3 No	(19)
13.2	(IF 'Yes':) Please elaborate.	(20:22)

COL

14	Should Intuition form part of the curriculum at the level of: (23:25)			
	Level	Yes	Can't say	No
	(a) School (primary)	1	2	3
	(b) School (secondary)	1	2	3
	(c) College (University)	1	2	3
	(d) Management institute	1	2	3

15 Would you be interested in participating in the subsequent phases of this research? (26:28)

	Yes	*No*
(a) Personal interviews	1	2
(b) Experiential workshops	1	2
(c) Seminars/Conferences	1	2

16 Could you give any information on any individuals/ institutions/organizations who are involved or might be interested in research on or applications of Intuition? (29:32)

Name	Address

17 We shall value any additional comments you may have on the subject of Intuition and/or the research project. (33:36)

REC 4

COL

18	Please provide the following particulars for classification purpose:	
	(a) Name (OPTIONAL)	(37:56)
	(b) Sex	1 Male 2 Female (57)
	(c) Age	1 34 years or below 2 35–44 years 3 45–59 years 4 60 years or more (58)
	(d) Educational qualifications	(59:62)
	(e) Name and address of the organization	(63:66)
	(f) Department/ Functional area	(67:69)
	(g) Designation (Title)	(70–71)
	(h) Brief description of responsibilities	(72:76)
THANKS FOR YOUR COOPERATION		

COL 80 = 4

Index